**Tom Fairey** is largely unimpressive. He grew up on the Isle of Wight and did unimpressive things. Then three years ago he went from being broke and unemployed to building a world-leading business in a sector he'd never worked in and hosting one of the UK's largest entrepreneurship shows. Tom now lives in Kent and dreams of one day owning a rugby club that he can brag about to his friends.

# HOW NOT TO F*CK UP YOUR STARTUP

## LESSONS ON BUILDING SOMETHING AMAZING

TOM FAIREY

ROBINSON

ROBINSON

First published in Great Britain in 2023 by Robinson

10 9 8 7 6 5 4 3 2 1



A CIP catalogue record for this book is available from the British Library.

ISBN: 978-1-47214-752-3

Typeset in Perpetua and Univers
by Mousemat Design Limited
Printed and bound in Great Britain by Clays Ltd, Elcograf S.p.A.

Papers used by Robinson are from well-managed forests and other responsible sources.

Robinson
An imprint of
Little, Brown Book Group
Carmelite House
50 Victoria Embankment
London EC4Y 0DZ

An Hachette UK Company
www.hachette.co.uk

www.littlebrown.co.uk

How To Books are published by Robinson, an imprint of Little, Brown Book Group. We welcome proposals from authors who have first-hand experience of their subjects. Please set out the aims of your book, its target market and its suggested contents in an email to howto@littlebrown.co.uk.

For my girls

# CONTENTS


Introduction 1
Acknowledgements 4
1. Don't Fuck Up Your Life 5
2. Ideation: The Mother of All Startups 16
3. Who Gives a Fuck About Your New Product? 37
4. What the Fuck Am I Gonna Do With My Idea Now? 58
5. Who the Fuck Am I Gonna Work With? 72
6. What the Fuck Am I Gonna Build? 83
7. How Much Money Am I Gonna Need? 94
8. Learning the Hard Way 106
9. The Game-Changer 110
10. Don't Fuck Up Your Pitch Deck 116
11. Don't Fuck Up Your Personal Profile 127
12. Don't Fuck Up Your Email 135
13. Don't Fuck Up Your Pitch Meeting 141
14. Who the Fuck Should I Hire? (And Why the Fuck Should They Work With Me?) 149
15. How the Fuck Am I Gonna Reach My Market? 167
16. The Rise of the Nouveau Town Criers 190
17. How Not to Fuck Up Your Brand 201
18. What the Fuck is Product Marketing? 221
19. How Not to Fuck Up Your Business Development 232
20. Don't Fuck Up by Being Complacent 254
21. You Haven't Made It 267
Epilogue 271
Index 272

# INTRODUCTION

## January 2019

I was unemployed, and I had the same career prospects as a member of a nineties boyband that nobody can remember the name of. The company I had been working for was great, but I hated what I had been doing for the last decade, and the thought of continuing for even another week filled me with misery.

Despite the state of my situation, I felt fricken awesome. I had made this choice and left my job because I had the most sensational idea for a business. Everything was going to be fine, because I was going to build a startup and become something magical: a tech entrepreneur.

The game was on. I was going to wear T-shirts to work every day, do conference calls in edgy coffee shops and have a slide in my office. I was going to be the new Steve Jobs. Zuckerberg would be inviting me to join him for jiu-jitsu sessions and Jessica Alba would be calling me for advice on very complex entrepreneurial things. I was already planning which rugby club I was going to buy when I sold the business in three years for eleven squillion pounds.

Ambition, or lack of it, had never been my issue.

The problem was, as great as the idea was, if I was going to succeed I would need to work in an industry I had never worked in before. I came from a data background and I was moving into gaming. I was a sales guy and I needed to code. I knew compliance people at banks and I needed to know video game influencers. Looking at it conventionally, I was destined for failure. And to make things worse, I was effectively broke, and this was going to cost a lot of money. People told me I was making a mistake and this was going to be a massive fuckup.

Society is pretty good at telling people they can't do things. 'You need this qualification.' 'You need this expertise.' And there are undeniably situations where these statements are true. As great as I am at Googling medical procedures and watching TikTok instructional videos, it is reassuring to know that the surgeon opening me up has some relevant letters after their name. But in general, you don't need a PhD or 10,000 hours to do what you want to do. Usain Bolt was told he was too tall to be a sprinter. Bill Gates was told he was an idiot for dropping out of Harvard. I took confidence from this and thought, *Screw these haters; I'm doing this!*

I produced a simple strategy: I wrote down what I'm good at and made a list of all the skills and knowledge I would need but didn't have. Pretty basic. From there, I consumed all the startup and entrepreneurship material I could find – podcasts, books, articles, events, videos . . . So. Much. Content. And on top of that, I found people who had the skills I needed, sold them the dream of what I was doing and asked if they wanted to come along for the ride.

As I charged through this montage-style journey of education, networking and self-discovery, three things occurred to me:

Business books, on the whole, were painfully inauthentic and far removed from the specific problems I was facing. They were written by people who experienced the problem ten years earlier and had become so successful they couldn't remember the pain. Nothing's changed, and I still believe that is the case today. As much as I love Reed Hastings and admire what he's achieved at Netflix, when I'm choosing between a $6- or $5-per-month software package, it's hard for me as a one-man show to relate to his billion-dollar problems.

Secondly, the business books I had read were a waste of three hundred pages. Typically, the main lessons would be covered in the opening chapter, and everything else was written to justify the concept, so they could say they'd authored a book rather than a tweet.

The third thing that occurred to me was that if I was experiencing these issues as a budding entrepreneur, surely everyone else in the same boat must have been too. And that's how this book was born. There are so many lessons out there and solutions to problems you will face on the journey that I wanted to lay them down in one place, so other founders like you and me could hopefully avoid fucking up their startups.

The advice that I've presented in this book comes from people who are living the problem at the time of writing or have just been through it. This is stuff you can put into practice. I've tested every single piece of it on my own startup, and anything that didn't work didn't make the cut.

It's been three years since my moment of startup epiphany. I don't have an exit, but I do have a slide in my office. My company is the biggest in the world at what it does, it employs people I love working with and I get to wear T-shirts to work.

It's not been easy, I have cried a lot and it will continue to be great one day and heartbreaking the next; but all of that is worth it, because nothing will bring more sense of reward than doing something that takes you beyond what you and others thought you could. It could all collapse tomorrow, but nothing can take away the lessons I've learned, the experiences I've had and the positive impact on people's careers. You win, or you learn.

If there are only three things you take away from this book, I hope they are these:

1. You are a winner. The fact that you have taken a single step on the path towards building something that is truly yours and have taken the risk to do something that could fail in a million ways means that you are a world changer.

   In truth, founders shape the world. All our daily practices – from the way we consume food, the way we communicate, the clothes we wear and the bed we sleep in – started with a founder having an idea and striving to make it happen. You're in that club now. Salute yourself.
2. Every problem you are facing has been faced by someone else before you. Some of them are covered in this book, but if they aren't, ask for help. You will be astonished by how much people are willing to support you if you ask. And most of the time, they'll do it out of the goodness of their hearts.
3. Never ever (ever) let anyone tell you that you can't do something. Everyone started from zero at some point.

Let's smash this!

# ACKNOWLEDGEMENTS

In truth, I am not a writer. Or rather, I was never meant to be. Deep down, I'm just a competitor who fell into entrepreneurship. So, for this book to be taken off the shelf and be in your hands right now, it needed the support, wisdom and encouragement of lots and lots of people. So many in fact that I will likely forget someone; if you are that person, please feel free to troll me on whichever social channel you choose and send me a guilt-inducing message. I deserve it, and I'm sorry.

Firstly, I would like to thank Jason, my agent and the sexiest man in publishing. You took a risk on me and dealt with my incessant messaging with effortless poise. Along those same lines, to my editor Tom A, for working faster than any editor in history and having a high threshold for profanities, and Martin for being tier-one from day one.

As the meat of this book is the guests of the *Back Yourself Show*, I want to thank all of you for sharing your wisdom and trying to make other people successful. A special mention here to Max K, Molly and JBish, whom I met through the show and who have become dear friends and supported me on this journey.

On the subject of friends, I don't keep many, but those I do have been architectural in getting me to this point. Thank you, Ross, for never letting the dream die and Emma for being an inspiration and guiding force.

I literally wouldn't be here without my mum and dad, so thanks for making me. Brother, thanks for being smarter than me so I have to make up the deficit with hard work.

Matilda and Hermione, you are the reason for everything. I am truly blessed to have two wonderful daughters, and watching you grow is the greatest honour. Nancy, thank you for always being the answer, no matter the question.

And finally, Amanda, without your support and motivation I'd never have been here. Thank you for raising such beautiful girls.

1.

# DON'T FUCK UP YOUR LIFE

I could easily have called this chapter 'Why Do You Want to Start a Business?', but if you're not cut out for the role of founder, you're better off putting this book down now and looking for a full-time job that suits your temperament. There's nothing easy about launching and nurturing a startup. The only short cut is doing it right and putting more effort into it than an Irish dancer on Haribo gummies, and when things go belly up, which they can and will, it will feel as though you have completely fucked up your life. That's a risk worth taking if that's the path you're meant to choose, but a hell of a lot of unnecessary pain and aggravation if it's not; so, if it's not for you, figure that out now, use this book as a doorstop, and don't fuck up your life.

> 'The single biggest thing that will make a better world will be if every single person becomes more self-aware, understanding who they are, how they react to things, start architecting more of the life they want; it will stop people from being angry, emotional, frustrated, depressed.'
>
> *Alex Dunsdon – Partner at Saatchinvest*

## How Do You Know If You're an Entrepreneur?

What kind of person gives up the perceived security of a monthly paycheque to go on the roller-coaster ride that is launching a startup? In my case, it was the only option because I was becoming increasingly unemployable. The more time I spent in any job, the more I would start pulling things apart and looking for ways to make them better. That's not because I'm special or smarter than the next person, but because I questioned everything. Most managers don't want people like that on their teams because their answer to a lot of questions will be,

**'That's how we've always done it.'**

*Unknown . . . but quoted by unimaginative business execs all around the globe!*

I was in sales, and if you know anything about that role, you will know that it's all about recognising the pain points that your customers care about and offering solutions that take those pains away. Salespeople are naturally curious. They are problem solvers through and through, and are driven by the belief that they can offer improvement, just like entrepreneurs. I wanted to work for an organisation where I could do what the fuck I wanted, and I could create rather than being told what to create. That company didn't exist. If you're not happy with the way someone else is running the company you work for, and you think you could do a better job, why not start one of your own?

According to Alex Dunsdon, a partner at early-stage tech fund Saatchinvest and a bit of a philosopher, entrepreneurs can't do anything else but become founders. They can't not be entrepreneurs. The pull becomes so strong that they will have to do it. He sees people as 'pre-baked' from birth but distracted from their inner mission because of conditioning from their parents, their peers and wider society.

Alex did ten years in advertising before diving into the world of venture capitalism, and he describes that period as a decade of working hard, feeling like an imposter, and being terrified of failure. It wasn't where he was supposed to be, and the voice of doubt grew steadily louder until he had to take the leap of faith into the unknown.

Self-knowledge is the key to freedom, so take the time to reflect and know who you are and what you want, and dare to control your destiny instead of trying to meet other people's expectations. That's Alex's message to the world, and it's a mindset that a lot of entrepreneurs share. Take Emma Davidson, for example.

**'So, what does your success look like? Not what everybody else thinks. What do you want? What does your eighty-year-old self look back on and is proud of?'**

*Emma Davidson – Director at Staude Capital*

After a whirlwind career in investment banking, which saw her smashing through every obstacle and becoming the stuff of legend in the process, she went on to found Affinity Capital, her own successful London-based investment boutique, specialising in structured investments and derivatives.

Her main motivation for leaving her steady corporate job was because she'd come to realise that she couldn't stand having to follow other people's rules and 'was not the easiest person to control as an employee'. She was also sick of corporate politics and a culture that allowed mediocre people to gain promotion not because they were gifted or qualified but because of tenure. Success should be earned, not inherited. Remember what I said about thinking you can run a better company than your boss?

## Go Where Your Heart Takes You

Having put all the hard work in to create a company that was thriving and bringing in an excellent income, Emma gave it up to support her husband's company, Staude Capital, even though it wasn't making as much money as Affinity. Ironically, her husband, Miles, had set up Staude because he was inspired by Emma's business.

Although both companies were successful, the twelve-hour days were taking their toll on Emma and her husband. They used to imagine themselves as octogenarians looking back at their younger selves and reflecting on their lives, and they concluded that something needed to change. Miles needed Emma's help to run his business, and he needed money to grow it. Emma was keen to start a family and wanted a better work–life balance, and she could see Staude's potential, so she jumped aboard.

If you're thinking about launching a business, ask yourself why, and understand what success will look like for you. What will the older, balder, toothless version of yourself think about you when they're sitting on the commode and complaining about their haemorrhoids?

## Who's That? Is He a Doctor, an Accountant or a Lawyer?

He's Chris Smith, the managing director of Playfair Capital, an early-stage fund that's on a mission to commit to companies early and with conviction; however, he spent the first ten years of his professional life as a lawyer. What made him leave such a lucrative career after giving so much of his energy to the legal industry?

'When I was working as a lawyer, I felt like I was a persona. I was a fake version of myself!'

*Chris Smith – Managing Director of Playfair Capital*

At the traditional school where he was educated, Chris's teachers identified that he was smart and hard-working and encouraged him to work towards becoming either a lawyer, an accountant or a doctor. He hated the sight of blood and didn't have a passion for numbers, so he opted for the legal profession.

Once he was enrolled at university as a law school undergraduate, law firms began reaching out to him on campus, where they were holding regular events two to three times a week and talking up how wonderful their firms were. He was invited to spend the summer working for them following his first year of study, and with that came the chance to walk straight into a job with a starting salary of £40,000 upon graduation.

To a young man of eighteen, this all sounded incredibly exciting, and he was easily seduced. Have you seen what a typical big-name law office looks like? When you think of lawyers, what do you see? Sharp suits, flash cars, champagne wallets and early retirement! Then he started working for a firm, and reality bit.

He was spending most of his time photocopying, proofreading and filing, and there were no opportunities for creative thinking. Worse still, he looked upstream to those who had been working there for decades and guess what he saw: a bunch of very miserable human beings who were usually overweight, divorced and bored out of their minds. A dollop of turd rolled in glitter is still a dollop of turd, and if those people were what his future looked like, he was doing something wrong because that life was a turd rolled in glitter.

Initially, Chris thought he could change the situation by hopping over to another firm but soon discovered he'd gone from watching red paint dry on one wall to watching green paint dry on another. Either way, it was soul-destroying, and he felt no passion for what he was doing.

Lawyers must look and act a certain way, and Chris felt as though he couldn't bring his authentic self to work. It was as though he was putting a mask on every day, standing tall and straightening his tie as he entered the building, and he'd have to maintain this pretence when talking to clients. No matter how rough it gets, lawyers have to remain deferential to clients, incredibly responsive, and never appear to be flustered or concerned about anything. It was stifling, and he knew he had to get out.

When he finally quit the profession, some of his colleagues were stunned because he was so close to becoming a partner, the holy grail for legal eagles, but that just goes to show how desperate he was to get out and breathe again. We can only shine when we play to our strengths and indulge in our passion, and Chris has found his, as the managing partner of a venture capitalist (VC).

## Fancy a Kick in the Teeth?

Warwick Hill has always worn many hats but one of his main ones is being the general partner at Supercapital Partners LLP, which provides investment services to tech startups. He is also the chief executive officer (CEO) of Electricboxx.com, which provides businesses with innovative solutions to move to sustainable mobility. His CV reads like a novella. He's worked in business development, was the CEO of an Indian and Middle Eastern wholesale carrier company, spent nearly three years in Hong Kong as the CEO of 3rd Space Services Ltd, worked as an advisor to NHS England, was a board advisor to Fineqia in Canada, led startups at Microsoft, and has served as a non-executive board member, non-executive director, chairman of the board and ambassador for a long list of dynamic, state-of-the-art London-based businesses. Am I launching the Warwick Hill Appreciation Society? Is this book going to be all about Warwick? Nope, but I wanted you to know that when it comes to startups, this guy knows his onions; and besides, he's a Kiwi, with a terrific accent. What's not to love?

> **'Being the CEO of an emerging company is like being kicked in the face daily.'**
>
> *Warwick Hill – General Partner at Supercapital Partners LLP*

As a founder, I can attest to this, but the taste of winning is like the finest honey that you've ever had the pleasure of experiencing, and that's what makes it worthwhile. Founding a company and doing everything you can to watch it grow is as near as it gets to giving birth and raising a child without giving birth and raising a child. When you hear people referring to their startup as their baby, they mean it, and that feeling gets stronger the more time, money and energy they invest into it.

## Are You a Quitter?

Let's look at the statistics because they will tell you all you need to know about what you're up against. Around 80 per cent of startups fail for reasons ranging from running out of money to building products that have a poor product fit or that don't work as well as they should. But do you know what the real reason for failure is? Giving up. Founders give up.

If you've spent tens of thousands of pounds developing a pair of trousers that sings Rick Astley's 'Never Gonna Give You Up' every time the wearer breaks wind, only to discover that no one's buying them, I hate to break this to you, but that's probably not going to change no matter how much money you throw at it. Give up. For the love of God, give it up. There's a difference between having the resilience and determination to keep going and self-delusion.

For those of you who have given a little more thought to the market and created a product that people want, it's worth turning over every stone to find a solution before throwing in the towel. Even if you've fucked up, and no one's buying your heated beanie that you're flogging for the bargain price of £78.50, you may just need to make a few tweaks to turn things around.

Whatever happens, don't let you be the reason that your business fails, and that's why you need to know why you're getting into this right from the beginning and know that you're going to be getting kicked in the teeth daily, as Warwick puts it.

## Don't Be a Control Freak

When I interviewed Warwick for the *Back Yourself Show* and asked him what he thought his biggest mistake was, it was thinking that he could do everything himself. Running a startup is an intensely emotional roller-coaster ride. He advises founders to look for someone they trust to mentor them and help them discover if they are ready for the journey.

You are better off joining forces with other co-founders anyway, because no one can be the best at everything. Perhaps you are a superb developer or a marketing wizard. More than likely, you fancy yourself as a conceptualist, an idea person, and you think you've discovered the golden fleece – you won't be the first to have come up with that idea, by the way, but more on that in the next chapter. Working with others, who are better at the things you are not as good at and whom you trust to challenge your thinking, will make your company stronger; and according to Max Kelly, managing director of the UK branch of Techstars, the world's biggest startup accelerator, sole founders are far less likely to attract investors at every stage.

## Take Care of Your Money Maker

Your brain, that is! Yes, even if someone chooses to shake their arse to make money, and I'm not here to judge, it's the brain that calls the shots. Dan Murray, a co-founder of Heights, a company that produces a range of food supplements designed to improve brain health, turned his attention to nutrition and how it affects the brain while on a quest to resolve his mental health issues. He had started having trouble sleeping for no obvious reason, and it wasn't long before his sleepless nights began to impact him in other ways, making him feel anxious and depressed. Dan's doctor referred him to a dietician.

The dietician diagnosed the cause of Dan's mental health problems within minutes and prescribed a course of nutritional supplements. They worked so well and so quickly that Dan couldn't wait to thank the dietician for facilitating what amounted to a miraculous recovery. She was having none of it, however, because she had known it would work from the moment she had diagnosed him and couldn't understand why others don't see what is so clear to her: brains need to be fed correctly just as other parts of the body do. Looking after our grey matter is a no-brainer, right? It's the thing that's going to make us successful.

> 'Your brain is your money maker. However you look at this, it is the thing that gives you your energy. It gives you your thoughts. It gives you your career.'
>
> *Dan Murray – Co-Founder of Heights*

And it's not just the fuel that we inject into our brains that will affect how they function. We also need to think about how we use the brain. Think of it as a muscle. If you spent all day every day flexing your biceps without taking a rest, it wouldn't take long for those muscles to tear or burn out. Why would we treat the brain any differently?

## . . . And Your Mind!

Even if you're eating the right foods and taking supplements to ensure it's fully fuelled, it's worth investing a little time to find out how best to maintain your brain and the mindset that lives in it.

I know the big buzzword is 'mindfulness' these days, and I'm not knocking that, but rest for the brain comes in many shapes and sizes, from sitting back for five minutes to the sound of baroque classical music or a dose of heavy metal, if that's what floats your boat. It's about disengaging from the intensity of running a business.

Taking care of the body is also part and parcel of taking care of the brain, and that doesn't have to mean doing a Rocky Balboa and sprinting to the top of the nearest set of outdoor steps. They say going for a walk is remarkably good for mental and physical health, and you're not going to injure yourself or burn out in the process. In fact, according to a 2016 study from psychologists at Iowa State University,[1] walking for just twelve minutes, even without traditional happiness-inducing magic such as sunshine, nature, social contact and up-tempo music, turns out to be a powerful mood-lifter.

Let me insert a disclaimer here:

**My name's Tom Fairey, and I'm a founder and investor, not a bloody clinician, so don't take anything I say as medical advice, and don't start legal proceedings against me if you slip on a dog shit while you're taking your morning stroll. It's always best to consult with a professional before embarking on any new diet or exercise campaign.**

All I'm saying is that, if you haven't planned stuff into your daily routine to ensure you're at your best, mentally and physically, get it done before you embark on a startup mission, because you're going to need all the strength you can muster.

---

[1] Miller, J. C. & Krizan, Z., 'Walking facilitates positive affect (even when expecting the opposite)', *Emotion*, 2016 Aug;16 (5):775–85. doi: 10.1037/a0040270. Epub 2016 Apr 21. PMID: 27100368.

## Know How to Keep Going When It's Feeling Fucked Up

The world doesn't like you. We need to accept this. The hard truth is that it's much easier to fail constantly and die than it is to live and succeed. Just give up, then. Stick to commuting to an office job in the city, drinking tall lattes at lunchtimes and admiring each other's Oliver Sweeneys, and stick it out, bouncing from job to job, until you are ready to cash in your retirement package, which may pay for your gas and electric if you're lucky.

Wrong.

You said you want to be an entrepreneur the moment you bought this book! The clue's in the title. Go for it but remember this: you don't have time to feel down, and your ability to perform is the lifeblood of your business, so the burden of being upbeat is heavier than a bacon cheeseburger and fries at Five Guys washed down with three pints of Guinness.

My company Stakester is only four years old and has already had enough issues to make my hair fall out and give me more wrinkles than Mick Jagger. Oh, and my hamstring's killing me. The cost of pushing too hard on a run. What can I say? I'm competitive! I'm also tired, very tired, and that's the timeless thief of motivation. How do I fix this, and how will you fix it when making progress feels like trying to wade through three feet of treacle? When we feel like giving up, how do we rise again like that beautiful orange bird in Dumbledore's office?

I'm not a motivational speaker and don't plan to be, I'm not a psychologist, and I've never met Tony Robbins, but I hate feeling down, negativity and anguish, and I know the importance of getting back on track as quickly as possible. Let's look at a few ways of doing that.

## You're a Winner

I can hear you. You're thinking, *You said you're not a motivational speaker, Tom. I smell bullshit!* Hold on. Before you dismiss what I'm saying, look at the stats. They're not complex. If you're reading this, you have a 100 per cent survival rate. You can't beat that. All the shit you've ever been through, you've survived. Every. Single. Time.

This time is no different. Yes, it might be rough and, yes, you might pick up some scars, but those scars are trophies; trophies you only pick up from being in the competition.

## Action Kills Doubt

Doing nothing changes nothing and will probably make things worse. A muscle that isn't used will waste away. When you're in a rut, and you're not feeling it, ask yourself how you got there, and you'll soon figure out a way to get back on track.

Start with something small, whether that's writing a quick thought piece, building that spreadsheet, or even cooking a lasagne. Do something and get a win under your belt. That said, if your problem's procrastination, you're probably better doing something constructive that helps you progress before finding those other jobs to distract you . . . and the lasagne can wait until dinner time.

## Talk About It

This doesn't come to me easily, as I'm an entertainer by nature and being misery guts isn't a crowd-pleaser, but it helps exponentially. Talking about it doesn't have to mean being the killjoy at parties and sobbing to everyone you meet. It's about making sure you have a confidante in your life, that one person you can share with, who is not going to judge you or say the wrong thing when you're already feeling like a loser. You can do the same for them.

Verbalising your feelings will help you rationalise, and it will take the weight off your shoulders. There's a reason why therapy is a squillion-dollar industry. If you're the sort who likes to dig deeper with a little research, visit MentalHealth.org. They rank talking as the best thing you can do for improving overall mental health, so be ready to pick up the phone, jump on a Zoom, or go for a coffee. It'll make all the difference when you need it to.

So, before you carry on reading this book, reflect on the main takeaways of this chapter. As Alex Dunsdon pointed out, self-awareness is one of the most important life skills you can develop. Whether you have a super-glam, well-paid role, a crap job on the till in the local supermarket, or you are founding a sexy startup that produces a cool product, make sure that the path you take is right for you.

Sometimes, that person who appears to be going nowhere in life, doing the job that would drive you nuts, is as happy as a fly on a dog dollop. If they know in their heart that they haven't got what it takes to run a business or don't want the aggravation, that's a sign of true wisdom.

Likewise, as Chris Smith's story teaches us, having more money in the bank than you know what to do with, a home that a Hollywood star would be glad to live in, and a motor that's so beautiful you look forward to driving in the densest London traffic doesn't guarantee contentment.

Be mindful and brave enough to choose the path that's right for you, so that the old, cantankerous version of you doesn't moan every time they reflect on what they did with their lives. And whatever you do, make sure you look after your mind and your body. It's not about having the body of Adonis. It's about feeling energised enough to live your best life. It sounds corny, but your health is your wealth.

Are you ready to start a business without fucking up your life?

You're going to need an idea . . .

# 2.
# IDEATION: THE MOTHER OF ALL STARTUPS

The fact that you're still here after I said everything I could to put you off the journey speaks volumes. You know what you're up against, you're ready for it, and you're fully invested in the journey. Good. I wouldn't have it any other way, and that's why I launched the *Back Yourself Show* – to encourage others to back themselves. Everyone has what it takes to control their destiny, so I want everyone to know how they can back themselves and take charge of their lives.

## It's Time to Back Yourself

The *Back Yourself Show* is for the dreamers, the creators, the builders, the inventors and the founders, so they can tap into the mindsets, experience, knowledge and wisdom of the entrepreneurs who have already succeeded (and failed many times, believe me) and hear how investment decisions are made, directly from the mouths of angels, VCs and other funders.

And now, you, my friends, will get to benefit from all that gold dust without having to listen to a single minute of a podcast, read a single line of any of my *Medium* articles, or enrol on a 'How to Succeed In Business' course, because it's all condensed here in this book. That said, the people I've interviewed for the podcast are all remarkable and have shared far too many wonderful anecdotes for me to cram into a single volume, so they're still well worth a listen when you get the chance.

## Lightbulb Moments

I am also guessing the other reason you're still here is that you've had an idea. Who hasn't, right? People get them all the time, but what makes you, me and the other seemingly crazy people like us different is that we act upon those ideas and strive to make something of them.

Where did it all start for me? When was my lightbulb moment, when I was struck with a concept so simple but so useful that I had to jump into the abyss to make it happen? It started in a local jiu-jitsu club and because of a chance meeting with a huge Russian guy called . . .

## Meet Sergei

The first time I saw Sergei, he was rolling with someone on the mat in a jiu-jitsu gym. *Rolling*, I hear some of you thinking, *What's rolling? Were you making dough?* 'Rolling' is the term we use for ground fighting or wrestling because participants often end up looking like a tangled web of arms and legs rolling around on the floor.

Sergei was a big guy; taller, heavier, more conspicuously muscled than me, and he had that no-effort haircut that some Russian guys sport when they want to draw attention to their biceps rather than their head or what may lie within it. He was wearing a vest, always a slightly dodgy choice, so when he rolled over and slowly looked my lightweight frame up and down, I wasn't sure what to expect.

'I recognise you,' he said. 'You win competition.'

'Yeah, I did win a competition,' I replied with a slightly surprised tone, and it was true; I had recently won a local Muay Thai tournament – a completely different discipline to jiu-jitsu. I appreciated the acknowledgement, and it was good while it lasted because what followed was not as complimentary.

'But you look so weak,' he continued as a puzzled expression took shape across his brow. Then his eyes lit up, and it was obvious that he'd had a thought. 'Do you want a match?'

'Sure,' I said, without hesitation. I'm competitive; I always have been, always will be, and I can't help it, even if the odds don't look great, which in this case they didn't. It's fair to say that I don't think Sergei rated my chances very highly and, looking at the size of his biceps, I couldn't blame him. Any opportunity to beat up the little guy!

'Shall we do it for money?' he asked. By this point, a couple of my gym buddies had tuned in to the conversation, and I sensed them willing me to take the bet.

'Name your stake!' I said, picking up the gauntlet.

'Okay . . . ' For a second or two, Sergei looked away and his face took on the demeanour of someone in a pawn shop pricing up an old necklace. 'Maybe ten pounds, yes?'

'Let's do it!'

It was game on. Confidence, competitiveness, arrogance . . . that's me.

## A Short Bout

We shook hands and made our way to the nearest bit of mat space, where I had no time to contemplate my fate before we were grasping each other's tops and vying for dominance. For a moment, I was aware of the tension in his frame, the strength in his arms, and his single-minded will to win. Then, in just a matter of seconds, it was over; a whirl of limbs, my body dropping down, my leg flying up, the impact of my back on the mat . . . and there was Sergei, safely pinned and helpless in a triangle lock between my legs. Well, I wouldn't be telling you this story if I had lost, would I?

At this point, I should confess that the move I pulled, a triangle choke from guard, is the classic beginner's play. I'm not very good at jiu-jitsu, but fortunately for me, my opponent just happened to be a lot worse. Confidence, competitiveness and arrogance are not always the smartest combination of personality traits to possess, but on this occasion they had served me well, and now Sergei owed me ten pounds.

## Winning and Getting Paid Are Two Separate Things

Winning the bet had been easy. Collecting, on the other hand, was another matter.

'No cash. Maybe next time?' Sergei announced without even a hint of embarrassment.

'Can you PayPal me?' I asked, feeling slightly miffed.

'Sorry. No PayPal,' he shrugged.

Would a more open question save the day?

'So . . . how can you pay me?' I asked with as much gusto and confidence as I could muster. I wanted to believe he was going to pay, but his answer said it all:

'Maybe next time.'

Who says 'maybe' in a situation like that? There wasn't any 'maybe' about it. It was Sergei's idea to bet on the contest, he had lost, and he owed me a tenner. That was when I realised that what I needed, at that exact moment, was an app that would let me set up a wager with someone, knowing that whoever won would be paid; an app version of the person who holds the stake until the bet is over.

## The Napkin Moment

Here was a pain point, and I had thought of the solution. Then, I looked past Sergei's maybe-next-time bullshit and recognised that it wasn't just me. If I needed it, so did other people, and such an app would work just as well for people playing Tekken, FIFA, streetball or chess. That was the 'napkin moment', the instant I had a great idea, and Stakester was born.

Everybody's different, but if there's one thing that most people have in common, it's that they can't predict when they're going to get an idea. It could happen during a morning stroll, while jogging, in the shower, or even while taking a dump.

When the sparks start flying in your brain unexpectedly, and you know you're onto something precious, what do you do? You have to make a note of it somewhere, and that's why some of the greatest ideas have started life on a napkin.

These days, with modern technology, there shouldn't be any excuse for not capturing an idea – you can record it as a voice note, type it into a cloud-based notebook, or even WhatsApp it to your mum, but try to get it off your chest as quickly as you can. If it ever happens during an intimate moment, never – seriously, never – pause proceedings to write it down. Sometimes, you just have to let things go, and your partner's highly unlikely to appreciate your genius if you show that your mind was on other things.

## Creativity Comes in Many Shapes and Sizes

Creativity is a broad term that can include anything from producing art by putting random shapes together, to solving a riddle by thinking differently. What counts for us, as entrepreneurs, is how effective we are at coming up with fresh ideas that we can use, and when it comes to that skill, everybody's different. Is there anything we can do to increase our CQ, our creativity quota? If you hear anyone else using the term 'CQ', tell them I got there first.

Apart from feeding our brains with the right nutrients, exposing them to as many ideas as possible, and putting them through their paces with regular mental exercises, we probably can't improve our base level of creativity, but there is plenty we can do to make the most of our quota.

I've spent my life asking two questions – wouldn't it be cool if and wouldn't it be better if – and that's how Stakester came about. Having discovered I was screwed because I had no way to claim my winnings from Sergei, I asked whether it wouldn't be cool to have an app that would solve that problem.

> **'If you're a creative, your education doesn't matter. It's your passion that makes you stand out.'**
>
> *Mae Yip – Co-Founder of ERIC Festival*

## Find a Different Way to Achieve the Same Goal

There are other questions that you can ask to prompt the brain to do its magic. When I came up with Stakester, I took an idea that wasn't new – having a stakeholder to mind the stakes until the bet's over – and created an app to do the same job. That simple change made all the difference because it meant two or more people could engage in a fair bet without the need of a human stakeholder.

## Take a Product and Make it Better

Co-founder of Snag Tights, Brie Read, looked at an idea that had already been developed into a product but was determined to find a way to make the product better. This kind of questioning still falls under the umbrella of 'Wouldn't it be better if . . . ', but instead of asking whether it would be better if we replace a human with an app, as I had done, she asked whether the product she was wearing could be made to perform its job more effectively.

### From a Tight Situation to Tights That Stay Up

Brie's problem began when the tights she was wearing kept slipping down her legs as she was trying to walk down a street in Edinburgh.

In the end, being a practical person, she stopped in her tracks, took her shoes off, and promptly removed her tights where she was standing. *All's good in the hood*, you may be thinking. *It's a free country, and if she wants to strip in the street, good on her.* Well, this wasn't any old street. This was George Street, which Brie describes as being quite 'judgy', where everyone is dressed to the nines and checking each other out. Think of it as the Knightsbridge of Edinburgh.

Brie was so wrapped up with sorting her tights out, that she completely forgot about her environment. Her Levi 501 stunt almost brought the street to a complete standstill, and once she'd finished with the tights, Brie noticed she was being stared at by around a hundred gobsmacked people. Was she overcome with embarrassment? Oh, hold on . . . some of you are still wondering what I meant by the 'Levi 501 stunt', aren't you?

Lev Strauss and Co. pulled off a stroke of genius in the mid-eighties when they hired a young, well-toned, fiendishly handsome male model, in the shape of Nick Kamen, to strip down to his socks and boxer shorts in the middle of a busy 1950s launderette and load his Levi 501 jeans in the washing machine for an award-winning commercial. The beautifully produced video was accompanied by the smooth tones of a Marvin Gaye soundalike singing Gaye's 1967 hit *I Heard It on The Grapevine.*

Essex-born Kamen, who died in May 2021, aged fifty-nine, became an overnight sensation, with almost every young person in the land either wanting to be him or get with him; the soundtrack became a chart-topping success for the first time since its release in the 1960s; and sales of Levi's 501 jeans went up by a whopping 800 per cent! RIP Nick. You breathed new life into the Levi brand, sold tons of jeans and records, and all with just one fifty-second commercial.

So, after being caught stripping off her tights in the middle of Edinburgh's most fashionable street, was Brie left red-faced and almost fainting with embarrassment? Not really. She did what any self-respecting twenty-first-century person would do: she had a laugh about it on social media. That's when she discovered her tights fail had nothing to do with her body shape. Most women had the same problem. The next question naturally followed: were there any tights out there that did fit and would stay up? If so, where could she find them?

> **'Nobody could find tights that fit, and everybody thought it was them, not the tights, that were wrong, so everybody thought they had a weird body, or it was their shape that tights didn't fit, and actually, it was tights that were broken and not the people.'**
>
> *Brie Read – Co-Founder of Snag Tights*

In her quest for knowledge, Brie purchased all the tights she could get her hands on from every retail outlet she could think of, in the high street and online. Apart from not fitting, every pair of tights she bought had one thing in common: while the leg lengths varied, the widths of the waist and the legs were the same across the board. She had identified why none of the tights on the market fitted properly. What followed was some clever detective work to find out why tights were made this way, and that led Brie and her co-founder, Tom Martin, on a two-year adventure to create innovative designs and find a manufacturer to produce them.

I guess you could say the rest is history because by the time I interviewed Brie and Tom for the podcast, their startup, Snag Tights, had gone from scratch to almost £2 million a month in less than two years!

Where Brie and Tom struck gold was in providing a solution to a problem people cared about. They weren't just selling tights. They were selling peace of mind, comfort and the product that their customers had been wanting to buy since the year dot but had been unable to purchase. The best bit? Brie's background had nothing to do with making any garments, let alone tights. All she needed was the idea and the passion to take it forward.

## If It Works There, It Will Work Here

Back in the days when a Tamagotchi counted as a real pet, Dawson was still with Joey and boybands ruled the charts, a young and ambitious Kiwi made the pilgrimage to the UK. Like many an intrepid Antipodean explorer, he spent 90 per cent of his time in the gym and the other 10 per cent working in hospitality.

One evening, as Warwick Hill, whom you met in the last chapter, waited for a cab home from a late shift, he took his first step onto the entrepreneurial ladder. The last tube typically reached its terminus around midnight, and the service wouldn't resume until 5 a.m., so there was a clear opportunity for someone to plug the gap, and Warwick was determined to be that someone. He'd seen the problem before, he knew how to solve it, so all he needed to do was to replicate that solution in London.

## From Auckland to London – The Staff Night Bus

While in Auckland, he had worked in the hotel and leisure industry, a sector that depends on staff working around the clock. All forms of public transport used to close around 11 p.m., and hotels had been racking up taxi bills of thousands of dollars a month to make sure that employees finishing work after that time got home safely. Warwick wondered if anyone was operating a similar service in London.

He began making calls to hotels to see if any of them would be interested in using a late-night bus service for their employees and got four sign-ups within a matter of days. It was a fantastic start, but Warwick was left with a new challenge. He had an excellent proposition and four customers who wanted the service he was offering, but he had no buses, no drivers and no company. Oops!

> **'If somebody offers you an amazing opportunity but you are not sure you can do it, say "yes" – then learn how to do it later!'**
>
> *Richard Branson – Founder of Virgin Group*

There's nothing like the promise of paying customers and the whiff of success to motivate action, and Warwick was confident he had a winner, so he approached the Prince's Youth Business Trust for help, and they gave him the funds he needed to kickstart his business.

One of the most important steps for any startup is finding the right people. The wrong people, especially in those roles that form the fabric of the business, such as customer-facing roles, can destroy even the most promising young company. Warwick chose his drivers carefully and funded their training to obtain their public service vehicle (PSV) operator licences. He took out a £5,000 loan, which he leveraged against a couple of leases of minibuses, and he was ready to make money. The customers were already lined up, so Warwick's newly formed company began bringing in £18,000 per month almost immediately. Instant profit!

Warwick ran that business for five years before successfully exiting. The idea wasn't rocket science because he'd already seen it implemented on the other side of the world. All it took was the will and determination to go for it. No venture is risk-free, but Warwick could march forward more confidently than most because the idea had already been validated in Auckland and by the four hotels that signed up in London.

## No Frills with All the Benefits

It's great when you get that feeling that you're the first to come up with an idea, but you don't have to be original to strike gold. Sometimes, it isn't what you do but how you deliver it.

Samantha Hornsby and Mae Yip are unusual for co-founders because they were best mates before they started a company together – and still are, which is even more surprising. Friends going into business is not usually considered a sensible idea as it invariably means one of them has to be the boss, and conflicts can arise around the issue of who does what. For that reason, funders are sometimes hesitant when it comes to investing in startups founded by friends.

Some people are naturals, and they don't even know it, and that's the case for Samantha and Mae, whose backstories couldn't be further apart but eventually came together because they realised that they needed to solve a problem in the world. They took the highly risky step of giving up successful careers to go it alone, together. Now, they run ERIC, the largest creative careers festival in the UK, and are pivoting to create market-changing tech.

One of the beautiful qualities about Mae and Samantha is that, without even knowing it, every time they play their hand, they land on best practice. These superheroes of entrepreneurship don't wear MBAs and VC money. They wear capes hewn of humility and passion. Let's delve a little into their backgrounds.

### Meet Samantha Hornsby

Samantha was a creative soul and wanted to study for an art degree at Falmouth University but didn't get in, so she chose to study law at the

University of Leeds instead because, you know, art and law are so similar!

> **'Don't do it. It's a terrible idea – even worse than smoking in a space suit!'**
>
> *Tom Fairey – Founder of Stakester*

Her dad knew what Samantha was letting herself in for because he was a lawyer, and he tried his best to convince her that going to law school was the worst idea since Doctor Yoshiro Nakamatsu's Love Spray – you should Google that when you get the chance – and she would hate it, but she was eighteen years old; how many of us listened to our parents or knew what we were doing at that age?

Pops was right, of course, and even before she'd completed the first year, she couldn't wait to leave. Not only did she find the course about as stimulating as a snail race in an empty room, but she wasn't into university culture either. Why make a small error in judgement when you can get it completely wrong?

The University of Leeds has been around the fifth largest in the UK for years, the city has a massive student community, and it is well known for being a buzzing place to be. While that's heaven for many young people, who are determined to 'discover' themselves – i.e., socialising and partying – Samantha wanted a quiet life and had chosen one of the noisiest and busiest places to get one.

Persuaded by her father not to quit without finding work first, she bagged one of the few jobs on Gumtree that didn't involve having to strip off for a photographer, transport strange packages from one county to another, or help an amateur filmmaker with his new and exciting project.

The job she landed was working for a public relations startup, specialising in serving high-end restaurants. While Samantha was not destined to stay there for the long haul, she enjoyed the two years she spent there and gained some insight into the day-to-day running of a startup.

> **'I think everyone is naturally entrepreneurial. I was just so lucky to be exposed to people who were essentially unafraid to make and take risks themselves.'**
>
> *Samantha Hornsby – Co-Founder of ERIC Festival*

She left that company for an exciting opportunity at Decoded, an innovative tech startup that creates software to help people learn to code. Samantha had no interest in tech whatsoever but had joined the company only six months after it had formed, as their second hire. The four founders each had specific roles within the organisation, and they regularly included Samantha and her co-worker in discussions about company strategy.

Her time at Decoded formed the basis of what I call 'the startup degree'. By the time she moved on, she had watched the organisation grow its team from two to fifty and had learnt enough from the experience to know that she wanted to set up something of her own.

Samantha believes everyone is naturally entrepreneurial, but most people don't take the plunge because they are held back by fear. By being around people who were ambitious and prepared to take risks, she adopted the skill through a process of osmosis, so when the time came for her to start something, she didn't feel it was that much of a big deal.

### Meet Mae Yip

Mae's parents, originally from China, worked hard to give her a good life. She loved art just as much as her friend Samantha did, but although her parents were also creative and encouraged her to study art as a hobby, they didn't take the arts seriously as a career route. Mae was expected to train to become a doctor or an accountant. She had a head for figures, so she chose the latter.

As a young, typical teenager, she had no idea what being an accountant entailed, but she knew it was a job that pays good money. Accountants, like law firms, can look glamorous to the outside world – plush new offices, Armani suits, evenings in fashionable cocktail bars and trendy restaurants, and personalised number plates on Bentleys to boot – but the reality is hard graft, hours on end of number-crunching, and the huge responsibility of looking after the financial affairs of multimillion-pound or even multibillion-pound clients.

After completing an accounting degree, Mae strolled into a job at PricewaterhouseCoopers LLC, where the only activity she enjoyed was changing the fonts and colours on the spreadsheets she had to use. Everything else felt as exciting as sitting in a doctor's waiting room for hours on end without the latest copy of *Cosmopolitan* to get stuck into.

## What Was Their First Startup Idea?

As they were already friends and both working in London, Samantha and Mae used to meet for coffee to put the world to rights and complain about their jobs. Both of them were fascinated by creative, interesting people who had managed to succeed on their terms. The biggest issue they had with their jobs was the feeling that their creativity was being stifled, and they wanted more.

They wanted to know how other people had managed to make a living or launch businesses on their terms, as creatives, so they cold-emailed people who they thought were interesting, and Mae would go and meet them for lunch to interview them about their journeys. She started writing about the people she was interviewing in a blog that she and Samantha had launched. They were speaking to everyone and anyone who was winning in the creative industries, from a local graffiti artist to the founders of Hummus Bros, a legendary cafe chain that specialised in homemade hummus products.

### A Magazine for Gen Ys

In a way, what they were doing was market research, even if that hadn't been their original intention. What had begun because of their own need to break free and grow had evolved into a bigger mission: to help young people find a route to the creative industries. The pair were so determined to do this, they quit their jobs to focus on it.

At that time, just about everyone had a blog, so only the most well-established and fandabulous were being noticed, and no one was reading Samantha and Mae's posts. The blog market was saturated, but that didn't stop them, however, from persevering and developing their page into a full-on online magazine targeting young generation Ys.

### What About the Bills?

Meeting so many extraordinary people was fun, and they enjoyed drafting the articles, but while they were trying to inspire young people to dare to do something different, they still had bills to pay, and there was no money coming in. No one can live on dreams alone.

Fortunately, Samantha had been given the chance to try so many things in her previous job, she had some ('very limited', to quote her directly) experience with video production. While blogging had died with the noughties, video had replaced it as the hottest way to share content. Samantha spotted the opportunity and suggested that they set up a video production company. Mae agreed.

They bought a tripod and a camera and immediately started pitching businesses. Unfazed by the fact that, compared to the competition, their combined experience was minimal, they began winning business by offering simple talking-head promotional videos, and you have to admire the sheer audacity of it. They embodied the perfect blend of naivety, the spirit of who dares wins, and a nothing-to-lose attitude.

### We Can Do That, and We're Fucking Cheap!

They succeeded in turning their relative lack of experience and video training into an advantage. Their email pitch was along the lines of 'You don't need a massive production to create a basic talking head or explainer video for what you do as a business. We are a team of two people, and we are fucking cheap. We can do that for you' (not a direct quote, just to be crystal). And they offered a taster video for free. They'd identified a gap in the market. The competition had not adapted to what clients wanted – cheap, cheerful, simple content that they could share on social media. Business owners were biting the pair's hands off in their eagerness to book them.

By stripping video production down to its bare bones, delivering the value proposition without the extra expense of unnecessary trimmings, videographic snobbery and perfectionism, they were giving customers exactly what they wanted at an affordable price. They'd stumbled upon a niche opportunity almost by accident, because they were sticking to what they knew rather than trying to provide the bells and whistles that other more expensive production companies were charging megabucks for. Customers were loving them for it.

They specialised in filming events and making heavy use of B-roll material to produce finished content. 'B-roll' is the industry term for secondary footage and can be anything from a dramatic reconstruction of the story being told to natural, undirected shots of people and activities. By carefully splicing B-roll material with the main footage (a talking-head video, for example), you can take an otherwise amateur video and make it look slick and professional.

## ERIC

While they were making money as a video-production company, they had not lost sight of their mission to help young people break into the creative industries. A key part of their business development strategy, which was highly effective, was trawling Eventbrite for female-focused or female-run events and pitching themselves as a female-focused, female-run video company. They'd usually email prospects, but they also attended events for the chance to network, and this is where serendipity lent its hand beautifully.

At one such event, they got chatting to one of the organisers, a lady they had already emailed. The timing couldn't have been better because she was about to run an event about marketing to millennials, and she asked Samantha and Mae to shoot the video.

> **'Most people in senior roles have forgotten what it's like to be a grad. If you want to attract them, you need to put yourself in their shoes.'**
>
> *Samantha Hornsby – Co-Founder of ERIC Festival*

They showed up for the shoot, and their first impression was that the event was excellent. All the exhibitors had made a massive effort to engage and be interesting, and there was an excellent line-up of speakers. An otherwise boring company had set up an oxygen bar, another cosmetics brand was giving away skincare products, and everywhere they looked there was something quirky going on.

It was an amazing event . . . except that not one millennial was in the room to say what they were into and how they wanted to be engaged. There were plenty of senior-level marketers, who were busy explaining how to market to millennials, but where were all the millennials? Surely, it would be beneficial to hear from them about their perspective. When they looked around the room, they felt it was a cool event that young people would love, but there were no young people there.

And that's when Samantha and Mae experienced their eureka moment. Why not take the same kind of ideas they had seen at this fair, and apply them to a careers event aimed at millennials? And this is where naivety worked wonders for them yet again.

> **'Do you think career fairs are boring? Because we do!'**
>
> *ERIC Festival Marketing Blurb*

They had never run an event, but they were driven by pure enthusiasm, impulsiveness and the belief that no one had done what they wanted to do before. Without even booking a venue, they created an event on Eventbrite and called it the Educational Revolutionary Inspirational Creative (ERIC) festival. The name was another clever ploy to attract the attention of the people they wanted to reach. Even now, young people ask them who 'Eric' is, what the name means and how they came up with it. What did they write in the blurb?

***'Are you 16 to 25? Do you think career fairs are boring?***

***Because we do!***

***Are you bored of recruiters in suits? Are you bored with free pens?***

***Come to a different festival where we will show you how to enter the creative industries, and you will be able to meet creative professionals.'***

It was the perfect pitch because it showed empathy and an understanding of the pain point that they were addressing. They highlighted an issue and solved it. How did they do?

Only TWO THOUSAND sign-ups . . .

With NO MARKETING!

They just uploaded a logo and some blurb to Eventbrite, and the magic happened. Not only did they not have a venue, but they didn't have a date. They had made everything up on the spot because they hadn't expected to get any bookings. Typically with free events there's a 75 per cent dropout rate, but that still left them with five hundred ideal candidates that they could leverage to attract paying exhibitors. It was beautiful.

## You Make Your Own Luck

Their story is a perfect example of how we can make our own luck. Success hadn't happened by itself. They succeeded because they knew their audience, they understood what they needed, and they were impulsive and naive enough to give it a go.

Neither of them paid me to mention them or say so much about them in this book (perhaps I missed a trick), and I supplied refreshments for the interview. The reason I wanted to make a bit of a fuss about them is that their story highlights some excellent approaches to ideation.

They weren't the first people to set up a video production company, and they probably had less experience and training than any of the others out there. And let's face it, it is also unlikely that they were the first female-run organisation to target other female-run organisations.

Where they pulled off a stroke of genius was thinking that they could dive into the market as absolute beginners and offer a bog-standard, back-to-basics, grassroots video production service, compete with the experts, and win. They won because they were cheaper, easy to get on with, and delivered the value that people wanted and needed in an ever-changing digital age.

Then, they did it again with ERIC. They had the audacity and innocence to believe they could run events, something they had never even tried before, better than everyone else. You also have to admire their bravery – giving up well-paid jobs to dive into the unknown with nothing more than passion, charisma and the determination to accomplish a mission. There are so many takeaways from Samantha and Mae's story, but one that sticks in the mind is this: if you think something's naff, and you believe you can do it better, just pretend you can, and give it a go. Sometimes, it pays to be naive.

## Find the Sliver of a Gap in the Market

To illustrate the next method for making money from an idea, let's look at how co-founders Nick Telson and Andrew Webster found the sliver of a gap in the market and built a company that managed to grow from $500,000 angel funding to a $30 million exit.

Nick had a high-flying career in marketing, working for L'Oréal, and they had offered him the chance to go to Paris to be an MD. Andrew was succeeding in a well-paid role at Axentia. They had known each other since their university days, had similar perspectives on life, and both knew they wanted to start a business. Again, just like Warwick Hill, Nick and Andrew didn't create something new. They spotted a tiny niche that had been missed and capitalised on it.

They saw the opportunity to take the kind of e-ticketing and e-voucher software being used extensively by event organisers and repackage it for the food and drink sector, and BookMyNight was born. It's worth noting that their approach wasn't just to spot a gap and go for it.

From the beginning, they had an eye on the future, and a plan to sell. They asked themselves who would be likely to buy the business further down the line, and they got there first, knowing that the big players in the market, who had simply missed the opportunity, would later approach and say, 'Okay. Nicely done! How much do you want for it?' And that also made the business more appealing to investors.

Since exiting the company, the pair have gone on to launch Horseplay Ventures, an investment playground that matches top startups to the investors best-suited to them. Nick is also the founder and host of the Pitchdeck podcast, which I highly recommend to anyone in the startup space. It's an incredible resource for finding out what investors are looking for and gaining insight into how to fund a startup.

## There's More Than One Way to Skin a Cat

. . . but I'd rather you left our feline friends alone and focused on building a fantastic startup. Ideation happens in lots of ways. As we've discovered through the stories of other founders, sometimes the problem is staring us right in the face, and all we need to do is acknowledge it and see if anyone's come up with a way to fix it. If they haven't, there's the opportunity.

We may be able to think up an innovative solution ourselves, as I did with Stakester, or we may hunt high and low for partners to fix the issue, as Brie Read and Tom Martin did.

It could be as simple a mission as spotting the solution somewhere else and successfully importing it to where the problem is, as Warwick did.

Or, to take a leaf out of Samantha and Mae's book, aim low and undercut everyone else by offering a no-frills, bare-essentials package. Sometimes the trimmings don't justify the extra costs. In Samantha and Mae's case, they were able to pivot quickly and meet the demands of their customers because they were fresh to the market and inexperienced. The established companies were catering for corporates that wanted to spend a fortune on flashy video commercials, not talking heads for social media posts.

They hit the high notes with ERIC because they understood the market they wanted to go into and learned from the mistakes of other event organisers. You know what they say, it's far better to learn from other people's mistakes than your own. Our own mistakes hurt more though, and that's what makes them more memorable.

Okay. I see you. Yes, you, the one who is thinking . . .

## Holy Fuck! I Have No Ideas!

Well, firstly, where have you been? Haven't any of the entrepreneurial stories we've looked at here prompted a single, creative thought? You have nothing to worry about because there are ways to kickstart the brain into action.

Remember my two favourite questions? 'Wouldn't it be cool if . . . ?'and 'Wouldn't it be better if . . . ?' Give it a try, especially when you encounter an obstacle. Let's say you always have to sit in a certain spot in your lounge if you want to use your laptop in the evening, because you can't see your keyboard unless you are next to a lamp.

The question 'Wouldn't it be better if I could see my keyboard no matter where I was sitting?' can throw up all kinds of ideas – LED lights for the edge of the screen that can be powered via a USB connection, or a super-lightweight lamp that attaches to the laptop. These ideas exist. I didn't make them up.

Start by identifying problems, and don't hold back. Throw in everything including the kitchen sink, and I can promise you two things: you will discover products and services already exist that you didn't know about but will find useful; and you will come up with some novel solutions that will seem so cool to you that you will strongly believe no one else has thought about them. They will have done. They just won't have done anything about it, *yet*.

### Great Minds

When it comes to brainstorming ideas, it's a case of the more the merrier, and even a crap idea's a good one. Why? Because even dreadful ideas provoke other thoughts. So, even if you are genuinely a desert in the original concepts department, all is not lost. Get together with potential co-founders. If they don't help you to reach a lightbulb moment, just maybe you will contribute to one of theirs.

## Know Your Strengths and Weaknesses

Many of the funders and investors that I have spoken to for my podcast have mentioned how cautious they are about backing a lone horse. If you are running a company on your own, you're going to need to be ultra-versatile, and you will be spread thinly for sure. Do yourself a favour by finding someone you get on with who has a different skillset from you, ideally someone who complements you well.

You might be the ideas person, and they could be a shit-hot developer. Perhaps they are one of those pains in the arse we all know who question everything to the Nth degree. Believe me, having someone like that on board can save a lot of tears later because they will spot the flaws that you don't. But whatever you do, don't fall short on self-awareness. It pays to know what your strengths and weaknesses are.

## Factory-Made Startups?

Megan Reynolds is an investor for Crane Venture Partners, an investment fund like no other. They have an accelerator programme[2] called 'Entrepreneur First', which is designed for people who have bags of intelligence, specialist skills and a boatload of potential, but who don't have an idea or a co-founder.

Think of it as *The X-Factor* for founders. As you can guess, competition to get onto the programme is fierce, and only the crème de la crème of applicants will make it. Founders are paired based on alignment – attitudes, interests, skillsets, passions, etc. – and then they are mentored through a six-month programme. And the best bit? Successful applicants are paid to go through the programme, and Crane Venture Partners invests in the startups they create.

Crane Venture Partners comprises two co-founders, one of which is Megan, and five operating partners, who each bring unique and specific knowledge and experience to the table – the investment committee (IC) – so if you're selected to go through the programme, your odds of success are high. You'll be in safe hands.

Megan's number-one piece of advice that she recommends to all founders is to learn to ask the right questions. People love talking about

[2] Accelerator programmes (also known as startup accelerators or seed accelerators) help new companies with funding, mentoring, training and events in exchange for equity.

their problems, so if you talk to the people you want to help and endeavour to truly understand their pain points, you are much more likely to create a commercially successful product.

## Execution – The Difference Between a Faux Founder and a Founder

Remember Sergei, who reneged on our bet? I had come up with a way of making sure nobody could ever do that to me again. Yet nothing changed; I was still wearing sweaty clothes in a smelly gym, and I didn't have my ten pounds. Me having a great idea didn't stop Sergei from nonchalantly turning away from his obligation to pay, strolling to the showers, and disappearing from my life (and this book – goodbye, Sergei).

> **'Here's a gap. I can do this. I'm really pissed off that other people are not doing it, and I know a whole bunch of people who might give me some money to do it. Maybe I should figure out a structured way to do that.'**
>
> *Eamonn Carey – Managing Director of Techstars*

Great ideas without action change nothing, so that idea you've had is not impressing me or anyone else. People have great ideas all the time. Great ideas are ten-a-penny. Great ideas don't matter. What matters is your ability to execute a plan and turn great ideas into great realities. Got it? Great!

Most great ideas arise when someone confronts an obstacle and comes up with a way around it. This happens every day. Anyone who leads an active life will meet problems all the time, and many of us envision solutions for them as well.

'What if all restaurants delivered; not just takeaways?'

'What if I could rent a flat as easily as a hotel room?'

'What if we had dedicated chatrooms for work projects?'

None of these ideas was complicated, and they probably occurred to thousands of people every day ten years or so ago, but it takes something particularly special to turn a simple idea into a Deliveroo, an Airbnb, or a Slack. That is what this book is about: execution – the difference between a faux founder and a founder. I should know because I used to be a faux founder.

That great idea that I had when that guy (see, I've forgotten his name already because he has left the book) walked away from our bet was not my first. I had tried and failed to get those earlier ideas off the ground, and I'd been unsuccessful because I didn't have a clue what I was doing. But I reached a critical moment when I had been burned enough by experience.

When I asked Megan Reynolds what, if anything, the best founders had in common, she came up with one word: productivity.

Before we move on, let's recap on the founders we mentioned in this chapter, and remember why they succeeded:

- Tom Fairey – got mugged by a Russian over a bet, and realised this was happening to lots of people and was easy to solve. Stakester was born.
- Brie Read and Tom Martin – provided the solution to a problem that people strongly cared about: ill-fitting tights.
- Warwick Hill – saw how to handle a problem in his native New Zealand and applied the solution in London where it was still needed. Thus, night buses for late shift workers came into being.
- Samantha Hornsby and Mae Yip – if Nike made founders, Samantha and Mae would be the brand's first success. They proved that sometimes it is better to 'just do it', first by stepping out and producing low-budget promotional videos for business clients – low-hanging fruit – and later by launching their first ERIC event with next to no experience in event management.

Don't forget the most important thing, though: productivity is key. Ideas on their own are ten-a-penny. Take action.

Got an idea? Yes? You'd better get busy, then, because the real fun starts in the next chapter when we'll be looking at how to sketch it out into something you can build. It's going to be non-stop from now on, so hold tight. Let's look at how not to fuck up a great idea!

# 3.
# WHO GIVES A FUCK ABOUT YOUR NEW PRODUCT?

Okay, I admit it. I considered 'Who Remembers the Sinclair C5?' as a chapter title, although asking who bought one would be the better question. The bottom line is whether anyone actually cares about the thing you want to create, because, if they don't, you ain't got a business. It's that simple. Don't waste your time developing something that people don't want.

We should give props where they're due. The late and much-loved Sir Clive Sinclair was a bit of a genius and a British national treasure, and some may even consider him one of the forefathers of home computing, in the UK at least.

After Alan Turing OBE FRS – that's *the* Alan Turing, whose team at Bletchley Park were responsible for cracking the Nazi army's cryptic Enigma code and changing the outcome of the Second World War in the process – developed the Turing Machine, a revolutionary milestone in the history of computing, other versions followed, but they were a far cry from anything we see today. Even by the 1950s, the old valve computers were the size of a room but weren't capable of much more than solving maths problems.

In 1980, Sinclair changed the face of computing forever when his company, Science of Cambridge Ltd, which later became Sinclair Research Ltd, built the first-ever home computer that people could buy for less than a hundred quid. Sinclair and his team beat the British Broadcasting Corporation by a year, although the BBC Micro, manufactured by Acorn Computers, was more powerful and looked more like the desktop PCs we see today.

The ZX-80 had a touch keyboard, which should not be confused with the touch screens we're familiar with today. Imagine a keyboard that's as flat as a pancake and having to push each key with two tons of pressure per square inch for the keystroke to be registered. Fun times, but we're talking four decades ago.

Sinclair Research quickly followed up on the ZX-80's success with the ZX-81 in 1981, and the ZX Spectrum, which was the UK's equivalent of America's Commodore 64, in 1982. The Spectrum offered much more gaming capability with an 8-bit processor, full-colour graphics, and a whopping 128 kilobytes (KB) of random-access memory (RAM). It may sound puny by modern standards, but that was a big deal in 1982.

If you were to give any of those computers to a young kid today, they'd throw it right back at you, but at the time people loved them and they were selling like hotcakes. Home computing was new, and these machines were on the leading edge of the technology of the day. They were exciting times, halcyon days when everyone was killing far too much time playing Pac-Man, Space Invaders and Donkey Kong on their Atari consoles.

I wasn't even a twinkle in my parents' eyes in the eighties, but anyone over a certain age will confirm that people cared about Sir Clive Sinclair's home computers because he had taken something that was not accessible and made it available to almost every household in Britain.

## One Wrong Move!

As well as designing Britain's biggest-selling home computer, Sinclair also invented a variety of other tech products, from pocket radios and TVs to electronic watches – cutting-edge technology that people wanted. He was at the top of his game, and for a while it looked like nothing could go wrong for the gifted tech founder. That was, of course, until he unveiled the Sinclair C5, a topless electric tricycle that looked like a three-wheeled go-cart.

The C5 was the sci-fi version of Del Boy Trotter's Reliant Robin from the iconic sitcom *Only Fools and Horses*. Strictly speaking, it was an 'electrically assisted pedal cycle', so drivers would need no helmet, driving licence or road tax to take one out on the road, although you might need your head testing for wanting to do so.

With a range of just 20 miles (32 kilometres), which is short by any standard, a top speed of 15 miles per hour (24 kilometres per hour), and no weatherproofing (did he think he was in California?), it was not a practical choice for most people and was given a very poor reception by the press. When critics weren't dismissing it as a joke, they were highlighting serious safety concerns, especially as anyone over the age of fourteen was legally permitted to drive one.

> **'If people get into it and in any way think that they're in a car because they're sitting down, then they're in trouble.'**
>
> *Sir Stirling Moss OBE (1929–2020) – British Formula One racing driver (Speaking about the Sinclair C5 in 1985)*

The C5 was not quick enough to keep up with a pushbike, let alone all the other motor vehicles on the road, and at less than 80 cm tall – shorter than the average five-year-old – it would be very easy for someone driving a car not to see it. Although it sported a futuristic Lexus-designed shell on the front and sides, it offered no protection to the driver and the lightest collision with a car or a motorcycle could lead to life-changing injuries or worse. Even the most seasoned adrenaline junkie would be screaming for their mum and holding on to the steering wheel with a death grip because taking a C5 onto the road was about as sensible as cooking up a barbecue in a petrol station.

There's no doubt that Sinclair was a visionary who was well ahead of his time. He had had his eye on producing electric vehicles since the 1970s and had set up Sinclair Vehicles Ltd in 1983 to make it happen. He meant business. The *Guardian* reported that he was projecting sales of up to a hundred throusand in the first year, and Sinclair was throwing plenty of money at the marketing; however, within the first three months of its launch, sales were proving to be no faster than the C5 itself, production was cut by 90 per cent, and by August of the same year, Sinclair Vehicles had gone into receivership. Only fourteen thousand C5s were made, and of those only five thousand were sold.

## Driven By Conviction Rather Than Demand

Sir Clive had the right idea. He was driven by the conviction that the world needed a new form of transport that was more efficient and significantly better for the environment. To be fair to him and his team, the C5 was only ever intended to usher in a new paradigm; and they had other, more practical, vehicles in the pipeline.

'You have a mission to do something.'

*Anthony Rose – Founder of SeedLegals*

Where Sinclair went wrong, disastrously wrong, was in not finding out whether anyone would want to buy his invention. He was driven by conviction rather than demand, and the C5 was later voted as 'the biggest gadget disaster of all time' in a poll of over one thousand tech enthusiasts carried out by organisers of The Gadget Show Live. Other candidates in the top-ten list of gadget disasters included Betamax video (outgunned by VHS), Sega Game Gear (blown out of the water by Nintendo's Game Boy), and a pair of strange scissors specially designed for cutting pizzas!

## I Love My Product, So Doesn't That Mean Others Will?

It's a start, but that's all.

The gadgets listed in the hall of shame found themselves there because they were considered too expensive for what they did, not very useful, or not as good as their competitors. There is no way of being certain a new idea will take off, but thinking about how it compares to other similar products, whether it does what it's supposed to do, whether people will want it enough to pay the asking price or give a fuck about it is a good place to start. Any investor would be concerned if you weren't in love with your idea, but you can't be its only fan!

## Customer Validation

In the last chapter, we considered the process of ideation, and we even looked at tactics to help the most uncreative people think up new concepts. We heard how other founders turned problems into opportunities. While the products were worlds apart, addressing a variety of needs in different markets, they all had one thing in common: people wanted them.

## How Do I Find Out If People Want My Product?

Look, I hate to break it to you, and I know it's tempting to ask your mother, but unless your mum happens to be called Cruella de Vil, she's probably going to tell you you're a genius and your idea is great, even if it's shit. If you're going to start with family, pick the sibling who has always wanted to beat you at everything and is guaranteed to pull your idea to bits. Honestly, that's the best feedback you can get.

There's a theme that's going to pop up repeatedly in this book because it's relevant to every stage of the startup process: networking. It's one of the easiest ways to turn things in your favour from the start. Whoever said 'it's not what you know but who you know' had a point, but not necessarily because of cronyism or favouritism.

## Your Mates Are Unlikely to Be Your Customers

If you are interested in crypto, and you want to launch a product that helps novices to make better investment decisions, knowing people who are interested in investment, or are operating in the crypto space, or are working in tech, and so on, will be extremely useful.

Friends and family, your mates from the local bridge club, and your buddies from the trainspotting society are all well and good – always value your friends – but most of them are unlikely to help you progress your tech startup. They are probably not your customers and are unlikely to be able to help you develop your product. That said, if your product is designed to make crypto investing as easy and accessible as buying a lottery ticket, then it could appeal to anyone you speak to, except for Audrey down the road who only has a landline and says the internet's the work of the Devil.

> **'You've built something, you think you've delivered the dream, but somehow sales aren't up month on month, or people aren't using it.'**
>
> *Anthony Rose – Founder of SeedLegals*

Remember what happened to Sir Clive? You can save yourself a lot of aggravation right from the start by thinking about who your product is for and speaking to as many of those people as possible. Just because you've had a superb idea doesn't mean you are ready to build it. You are nowhere near there if you haven't validated it. Validation is the first step to being able to provide proof of concept (POC), which is something you're going to need later if you want to attract investors.

Max Kelly, senior vice president of Techstars, says networking with the right people is not only an excellent way to find out what people think of your idea, but most people in the startup space, including investors, will be more than happy to offer help and advice. Furthermore, and we'll be looking at this later, networking with the right people will increase your chances of winning referrals for investment. Believe me, pitching to an investor who wants to hear what you've got is much more fun than going in there cold.

## The Mom Test

In his book, *The Mom Test*, Rob Fitzpatrick asserts that asking anyone – not just your mother – whether your idea is a good one is the wrong thing to do. Your mum's not the only one who will lie to you. Sure, you have to find the right people to speak to about your product, but you also have to ask them the right questions.

Anthony Rose put this well when he asked me to imagine I'd created this new, all singing and all dancing, hi-tech bicycle lock that's wifi enabled with a GPS tracker and an app. If I go up to someone and say, 'Listen, I've invented a new device that tracks your bike, so you can get it back if it gets stolen. What do you think? Does that sound like a good idea?' they're bound to give it the thumbs up because I've asked the wrong question.

Firstly, they won't want to offend me, but secondly, because of the way I've asked the question, it sounds awesome. Who wouldn't want to be able to help prevent the theft of their property? I haven't told them the price, the battery life, or GPS signal strength, yet any one of these variables could be a dealbreaker.

What I should have been asking was whether they had looked for a similar product before, how much they'd pay for it, and whether they were aware of any competitors. If they haven't looked for the product before, that could either mean you've come up with something revolutionary that no one else has ever thought of, or it's more likely (reality check) that they weren't that fussed about finding out how to protect their bike from theft. However, if they say they would only pay half of the selling price you had in mind (less than it would cost to make), you're in trouble because that gives you a clear indication of how many fucks they give – nowhere near enough.

## Feedback Is Useful

You need as much feedback as you can get, right from the beginning, my friends, and your potential customers will be able to give you that. What if your idea is met with raised eyebrows, tumbleweeds, or questions about your sanity? Great. You're a creative person. Your network has just saved you a ton of time, money, sweat and embarrassment. Darwin's Law has helped you with the least pain possible. Or it could mean you were talking to the wrong people. If you were talking to the right people, you know what to do. You will come up with other ideas.

More realistically, you are probably on to something that people want, but it might need some tweaking. Having conversations with the people who matter will help you identify what features need to change. Chatting with the people who care about your idea comes with a bonus. They might end up becoming your first customers.

## Win Customers While You Validate

The moment Brie Read shared her experience of having to take her ill-fitting tights off in the middle of Edinburgh's most trendy street, she got all the customer validation any founder could wish for. She didn't need to ask for people's opinions, carry out market research, or get stuck into any mind-numbingly boring data analysis tools to see if her findings were statistically significant. Anyone who had ever worn a pair of tights before – man, woman, Shakespearean actor, Superman – had their own experience of the same problem. With one social media post, she knew something that no one else had figured out: the bodies were not to blame for the tights not fitting; the tights were. More than that, she knew people cared, and they wanted to buy tights to fit them.

After spotting a problem that he had already seen the solution for, Warwick Hill validated his idea by asking potential clients if they would be interested even before he had formed a company. It was a smart move. It might seem like common sense, but seeing something work in one country doesn't necessarily mean it will succeed in another, and there's no harm in checking. In Warwick's case, he managed to bag four new customers as part of the validation process.

Here's another brilliant example of where a founder checked in with his customers and bagged business before building the product.

## The Birth of BASIC

Having read about the Altair 8800 minicomputer kit in the January 1975 edition of *Popular Mechanics*, the then-unknown programmers Bill Gates and Paul Allen saw an opportunity to make the new breed of home computers more attractive to everyday people. Back in the early 1970s, you'd almost need a maths degree to get your computer to do anything, so if computers were going to be used by the wider population, a simpler way to talk to them would be a bonus.

They approached Ed Roberts (who later became known as 'the father of the personal computer'), the founder of Micro Instrumentation and Telemetry Systems (MITS), which was the company behind the Altair 8800, and pitched software that they hadn't even created. Cutting a long story short, Roberts agreed, and Gates and Allen went on to develop Beginners' All-purpose Symbolic Instruction Code (BASIC) for the Altair. Gates and Allen went on to co-found Micro-soft (which later became Microsoft), and Altair BASIC evolved into Microsoft BASIC.

Why build something new when you know how to match a product someone else has built with the people they want to reach?

## Spotting a Product-Market Fit

Chris Smith, who gave up a successful career in law to set up as a venture capitalist, already knew a thing or two about startups. He had launched his first business after spotting an opportunity to grab a cut of someone else's gig when he was an undergraduate.

Sitting on a tube in London's Underground, he noticed an advertisement from a communications company that was selling pay-as-you-go, no-contract, international SIM cards. They were selling an excellent product, and Chris had access to an ideal market; he was surrounded by international students from every continent of the globe. He approached the company and pitched himself, boasting that he had access to ten thousand contacts. They believed him and gave him a specific access number for his customers to use and offered him a commission on all the calls that came through.

Initially, Chris was using posters on walls and fliers at university raves to generate business, but he went on to collaborate with a web developer who built a website for the business. What had started quite slowly – £2 in the first month, £6 in the second, £9 in the third – grew enough to give him an income of between three and four thousand pounds per month in commission. His 'hobby' had turned into quite the money-spinner.

There was no reason for him to approach his potential customers in the student union and check the demand before launching his venture. Their need was obvious, and he had nothing to lose because the product was already out there. All he had to do was make sure that if they were going to buy the SIMs, they would purchase from him. He identified an excellent product-market fit and capitalised on it.

## How Unique Does My Idea Need to Be?

If you are entering a huge market, you don't have to be producing anything unique as long as it does what it says on the tin and people want it. The more unique it is, the more vigilant you must be to establish customer validation.

One way of hitting the bullseye is by aiming for a small gap in the market that has been ignored by all the other players. There may be other products out there that are better than yours at doing the same job, but if they are not reaching their market, you have an opening. It doesn't matter how many are out there if the people you are targeting haven't heard of them.

## Everyone's Favourite Subject – Themselves

The online retail sector is massive. Walmart is in pole position as the biggest online retailer, followed by Tesco Direct. Where does that leave everyone else? There is always room for extra players. They just need to grab their niche, however tiny that is. Take Notonthehighstreet, for example. They have cut a perfectly shaped space to sit in by partnering with over five thousand other online retailers and offering personalised products.

If you want to buy a necklace that has Holly's name on it, a bracelet with Sophie's name on it, or a neck scarf for Rufus, your pet dog, with his name on it, you can get it from Notonthehighstreet. They can sell the personalised version of almost anything you can imagine. If it's not on the high street, it will be on Notonthehighstreet. Very clever. Oh, and that's a superb example of how to pick a great name. We'll be looking at how not to fuck up your brand name shortly.

> 'The big realisation was that I really do have everything I need to be happy right here.'
>
> *Hector Hughes – Co-Founder of Unplugged*

Another massive industry is travel and leisure, so how did a young entrepreneur who was barely into his twenties find a way to break into it? Hector Hughes was a go-getter who started his first tech business before he was old enough to sit a GCSE. While it lasted, Hector was enjoying a work hard to play hard, jet-set lifestyle, drinking to excess, taking drugs and partying to the max. It was only once his business collapsed that he realised how burnt out he was.

## A Retreat to the Himalayas . . . At Your Doorstep

Hector dropped everything and ran for the Himalayas, where he spent several months in silent solitude to reset. While he was there, he discovered the practice of transcendental meditation (TM), which involves chanting a short mantra twice a day for 20 minutes at a time. This sharpened his awareness and gave him improved clarity, which brought about a realisation that everything he had been focusing on up to that point had been bollocks.

When I interviewed Hector for my podcast, he said, 'My life up until that point had been so dictated by what people thought. I was such a people pleaser, a "yes" man. I had been living life on everyone else's terms.'

This insight led to the launch of Unplugged, a company that provides getaways with a difference. Unplugged owns several ultra-compact, back-to-basics, 'unplugged' cabins that run on solar power. They are each situated around an hour's drive from London, but once you've arrived, you may as well be on the other side of the world – no internet, no wifi, no connectivity. You must lock your devices in a box, take the plunge, and drop out of the matrix for three days and three nights.

According to Hughes and his co-founder, Ben Elliott, based on research they carried out before the first lockdown in 2020, 52 per cent of people were planning to increase their time holidaying in the UK, and 90 per cent cited escapism as their primary reason for travelling. What they needed to escape from was not the British Isles or even the county. Given that more than 75 per cent of us check our phones within 15 minutes of waking up, and more than half will check work emails on weekends and while on holiday, what we all need to escape from is not our geographical location but the online world.

The question is this: could you unplug your devices, turn your back on the world wide web, and focus on recharging in the wilderness for three days and three nights? Most people struggle to unplug for a day, let alone half a week, so our addiction to our devices could have been a tricky objection to overcome. Has anyone escaped at all if they don't post a couple of hundred photos and videos on Instagram on the way to, during and after a trip? Hughes and Elliott had already thought of that. There's a polaroid camera with plenty of film in every cabin and a cassette player with a great selection of relaxing music tapes to listen to.

If you're a Gen Z, I am guessing you are scratching your head and opening a browser to find out what, the fuck, a cassette player is. *Cassette player? Tapes? What, in the name of God's pet budgie, are those?*

Back in the olden days, not as far back as when people wore top hats and tailcoats, but it might seem like that for some of you, cool people used to buy vinyl records, and sound could also be recorded on magnetic tape, which was housed in a cassette. These were small plastic lightweight units that would easily fit in your jacket pocket.

For some, an Unplugged getaway will sound like a trip to Alcatraz, but that research carried out by the founders paid off. Within the vast market of people wanting to book a short break, Unplugged offers a unique experience that is tailor-made for a specific section of it.

## Catering for A Specific Need

Molly Johnson-Jones was a highly successful investment banker until she asked to take one day a week off work to cope with an autoimmune disease. She'd been living with the illness since the age of eighteen, but the stresses and strains of a very full-on occupation had taken their toll, and once a week she'd suffer from crippling pain and inflammation in her joints and even her eyelids.

Her employers referred her to an impartial occupational therapist, who advised that she register as disabled to protect herself from discrimination. She took their advice, but that didn't stop Molly from being handed a severance package and fired from her job shortly after.

Wow! What decade did this happen? Was it when dinosaurs were walking the planet? Surely, it wasn't recently? So much for being protected against discrimination.

It was 2016! There weren't any dinosaurs strolling in the streets, but there were plenty of alive and kicking ones in the firm where Molly used to work. Their attitude belonged somewhere in the 1960s and unfortunately, as Molly would quickly discover, they were not that unusual.

She applied for other jobs, only to find that, while some firms were more flexible than others, the onus was always on her to ask for it, and she was often made to feel like an ungrateful Oliver Twist daring to ask for 'more'. Employers usually asked why she wanted flexible time, and sometimes her reason didn't seem good enough to them.

> **'The problem before the pandemic was people really felt they had to have a reason to ask for flexible working, and even me, with a disability, didn't feel like my reason was good enough.'**
>
> *Molly Johnson-Jones – Co-Founder of Flexa*

Molly discussed the issue with other people who had disabilities or other reasons for wanting flexible work and found that many had shared experiences that were almost identical to hers. Why should anyone have to give a reason for wanting to work from home or for working flexible hours? Considering these questions led Molly to an opportunity.

Together with co-founders Maurice O'Brien, who also happens to be her partner, and Tim Leppard, the company's chief technical officer (CTO), Molly set up Flexa to provide 'much-needed transparency in the job-hunting process by verifying companies as truly flexible and increasing their discoverability through company profiles and employer brand marketing'. Fuck me! Even my editor couldn't have put it more succinctly than that. Great elevator pitch,[3] Molly.

## 'Flexification' – How Flexible Is Your Company?

The pandemic has ushered in a new era and a change in attitudes to working from home. Isn't every company offering flexible hours now?

[3] An elevator pitch is a condensed version of a presentation that packs enough punch to powerfully deliver the value proposition (the solution to a specific problem or the need satisfied) in the 30 seconds to one minute it typically takes to share an elevator ride with someone you want to persuade.

Flexible working benefits employers just as much as employees because of the gains such as increased productivity and reduced staff turnover. I had assumed flexibility was the new norm, but according to Molly, who has the data to prove it, I was very much mistaken.

Molly and her team conducted in-depth research, looking at thousands of data points, to establish how flexible companies were in the UK job market, and they used these findings to set a benchmark on what they considered true flexibility to be. To qualify as a truly flexible organisation to work for, companies must undergo a certification process, which Molly aptly refers to as 'flexification'. What an excellent word!

Any business that wants to work with Flexa as a client must fill in an online questionnaire as part of their application to see if they qualify. Hundreds of organisations have applied, which has provided Flexa with yet more data-led insight into the UK job market.

**'No one knows your business better than you do.'**

*Molly Johnson-Jones – Co-Founder of Flexa*

Molly told me that she had also assumed, as I had, that everything had changed since the pandemic and employers were now much more flexible. The statistics prove otherwise. A whopping 45 per cent of applicants fail the flexification test for two main reasons: firstly, because employees have to put a formal request in, explaining why they need it, and hope that the reason they've given will be accepted; secondly, because employers offer flexibility on condition that there is a specific reason for it, such as a doctor's appointment or home delivery. Neither of these is a truly flexible arrangement. In both cases, the employee is expected to justify it in some way.

According to Molly, and anyone who's worked with me will know I am with her 100 per cent on this, true flexibility is knowing that you have it without having to request it. That means a minimum commitment from the employer of one, two, three days, fully working from home, or whatever is agreed at the start of the contract. Once that commitment is in place, a staff member can stay at home for any reason at all as long as they put the work in – whether it's because they want to be close to their pet cat, they like to have a nap midmorning or because they are visited by the real-life version of the guy from the old Diet Coke adverts on Wednesday afternoons!

## Grab That Drop of the Ocean

How does Flexa succeed when most businesses are not even close to being on the same page where flexible working is concerned? As Molly discovered when she got ill, too many companies think they are doing their employees a massive favour by allowing them to go to the toilet without logging it as unpaid time.

'Roberts, where do you think you're going?'

'Sorry, boss. I need the toilet.'

'That's the third time you've been this week? Is it a number one or a number two because, if it's a two, I'm docking your wages?'

Holy Moly! No wonder job-hopping is so rife.

The reason that Flexa succeeds is that it is addressing a specific and hitherto overlooked candidate preference that will also greatly enhance a company's performance. It doesn't matter if most businesses are not prepared to offer the kind of flexibility that Flexa is looking for. It doesn't matter if 99 per cent of directors think Molly and her co-founders are as mad as a purely fictional, blond-haired prime minister who doesn't know if he is at a party or a work event.

Flexa only needs to attract those organisations that share Molly's vision because there are enough of those to guarantee a busy and profitable business. The recruitment industry is such a large ocean that even the smallest drop is more than enough.

> **'Ignore everyone's advice until everyone is telling you the same thing; then start listening.'**
>
> *Molly Johnson-Jones – Co-Founder of Flexa*

Not everyone is going to get you or your idea, and that's all right. When I asked Molly what mistake she felt she and her co-founders had made that she regretted the most, it was listening to people whom they perceived as more experienced or knowledgeable than they were. No one knows your business better than you do, so unless everybody you speak to says the same thing, stick to your guns and focus on the execution of your plan, except for one thing . . .

Creating a product that fits its market perfectly, effectively serving the needs of a tiny segment of a gigantic market or being the first in the universe to build the world's first voice-activated coffeemaker doesn't mean you're on to a winner. If your product is innovative, original, unique, slick, sophisticated, smart, useful, cheap or the best thing since sliced pizza but no one wants it, guess what? You haven't got a product, and you haven't got a business.

## You Want Me to Tell Others About My Idea? Fuck That! What If Someone Steals It?

There's a very common misconception that unless an idea is patented, it's not worth the paper it's written on. We hear it all the time on popular business programmes such as *Dragons' Den*. I am not going to piss on an entire industry built on the premise that intellectual property (IP) needs to be captured and protected, but you can't treat every idea with a one-size-fits-all approach.

> 'The biggest mistake that I've seen people make is going, "I'm going to build a white elephant because I believe that there are people who are going to buy it on the far side, and I'm not going to ask if there is anyone out there, if there is a market for it, because I'm nervous that if I say my idea out loud, someone will steal it from me."'
>
> *Eamonn Carey – Managing Director of Techstars*

Remember what I said in the last chapter? Sorry to burst your bubble and shatter your ego, but you are unlikely to be the first person to have thought of whatever it is you've invented. Whether you get a patent pending on it or not – in this country, across Europe, or around the globe (costly and time-consuming affairs) – as soon as it's out there, the hyenas will hone in and try to benefit from your hard work. Of course, there will be copycats, but you are light years away from having to give a shit about that right now.

The world of tech is fast, so you don't have any time to waste. If you are not spending every waking moment trying to either keep yourself fed, watered, rested, mentally healthy or working on your startup, you're not doing it right. Concentrate on bringing your idea to fruition and forget everyone else. Just focus on making sure you get there first and with the best product possible, by quickly and diligently following the process to get there.

The thing you are afraid of is possible. Someone you speak to about your idea might be tempted to steal it, or they may spill the beans to the wrong person. You can get people to sign a non-disclosure agreement (NDA) if you're that fussed, but there are plenty of ways to circumvent them if someone is determined enough. Don't forget this: if someone else is following you, that means you're ahead. You have to keep going to stay ahead. Move forward like a bat out of hell. RIP Meatloaf. God bless you, brother!

## Now What?

So, you've read this chapter, and you've concluded that people do give a fuck about your new singing mirror – hmmm, whom did you ask about that? – but what are you gonna call it? Let's find out how not to fuck up your name.

Even the best idea is going to be met with a slow clap if people don't understand how it will help them, and that starts with the name. There are a million and one ways to fail with a name. Names should roll off the tongue like the front-page headline of a tabloid newspaper, grabbing attention and telling the story in an instantly engaging way.

Trying to be too clever or drawing on an overused word that's almost become a cliché is likely to confuse or annoy. Being too technical and matter-of-fact – always a risk where techies are concerned – could turn off your end-user, who couldn't care less whether your product uses nanotechnology or gizmos that any *Star Trek* writer would be proud of. How is your product going to fix their problems? That's what they want to know.

**'It's the way I tell 'em.'**

*Frank Carson (1926–2012) – Comedian*

Choosing the wrong name for a first-class product is like destroying an excellent joke because you don't know how to deliver the punchline. When it comes to product names, remember Frank Carson's catchphrase. How are you telling 'em?

History is littered with product names that were bound to cause sniggers or irritation rather than buying transactions. IMuffs, D-Box, and Chumby are three prime examples from the world of tech. If they don't strike you as being crap product names, imagine being offered a hot drink of Urinal, or seeing Pet Sweat on the shelves of the local supermarket.

The people who came up with these names all had great products and the right intentions. IMuffs were Bluetooth earphones designed for iPhones. The D-Box delivers a 4-D simulator experience by moving and shaking viewers in sync with the action on the screen. The Chumby, which may be making a comeback, was a kind of bean bag with an integrated small screen – like a tablet but cuddlier!

Okay, I can hear you screaming at the page, 'Don't leave it there! What, the hell, is Urinal? Who buys Pet Sweat?' Urinal, my dear friends, is a medicinal drink designed to treat urinary infections, and Pet Sweat is an energy drink that you're supposed to give to your pet. I know, I know – you are now imagining one of those yappy Yorkshire terriers that raise the roof every time someone walks within a square mile of their home. Who would want to pump one of them up with caffeine? The mind boggles.

## Lost in Translation

One of the worst cases of a name-fail that I have ever come across was the i.Beat blaxx MP3 player. It was the latest in a series of i.Beat products that were sold by German vendor TrekStor. Unfortunately, no one in their marketing department checked how their new product name sounded to the English-speaking world. It didn't take them long to find out once the product was launched.

Online design, technology, science and science-fiction magazine, *Gizmodo,* was quick to alert TrekStor with an open email:

> *Dear Trekstor*
>
> *Your PR division sucks/may never have learnt how to read aloud. Given both of those possibilities are not mutually exclusive, we have a strong inclination to believe both statements are true. You are doing a great job at proving us right, all thanks to your new iBeat blaxx MP3 player. Do not get us wrong, the little fascist music playing device looks quite the accomplished gadget. We are confident it plays just as well as you promise, but we have a little problem with the name. We are guessing, (not being complete morons), that anything named 'iBeat blaxx,' is probably not going to go down well with anyone who is not an absolute jerk-off. What do we know? Still, if you see the light and would like to apologise to all those many, many individuals you have offended, please feel free to drop us a line at tips@gizmodo.com. Further, as your publicity department could*

*apparently not organise a piss up in a brewery with due competence, perhaps our trusted readership could assist you in the naming process? If you would like to take us up on our offer, please see below for suggestions.*

*Kind Regards*

*Gizmodo* [sic]

That was quite a restrained letter, wasn't it? Imagine if they had shared how they really felt about the name!

TrekStor's vice president (VP) and CTO, Gil Szmigiel, was quick to respond and take immediate remedial action:

*Dear Gizmodo,*

*TrekStor is shocked by the way our new MP3 player's name 'TrekStor i.Beat blaxx' is perceived. Of course the word 'Beat' is not meant as a verb, but refers to the beats of the music you are listening to. More than 4 years ago, TrekStor introduced the i.Beat MP3 player series that today consists of more than 25 different players – all named individually. 'blaxx' was chosen, because the player is designed with an elegant black piano finish.*

*As a reaction to the bad connotation of the name, TrekStor decided to rename the product 'TrekStor blaxx' – effective immediately. We sincerely apologize to everybody whom we offended by the initial name of this product and want to emphasize that TrekStor condemns violence and any form of racism.*

*Mit freundlichen Grüßen,*

*Best regards,*

*Gil Szmigiel*

*Vice President / CTO*

Well played. I'm not sure there was much else they could have done, but prevention would have been the better option. It should never have happened. For whatever reason, perhaps because sentences are constructed differently in German, with the verb being placed at the end, TrekStor's marketing team had failed to notice that the word 'beat' could be read as a verb.

## Knowledge Is Power!

Sometimes, disaster strikes when names are translated into other languages. Amusing examples include Sega, a slang word for masturbation in Italian; Mensa, which translates as 'stupid female' in Spanish; and Coca-Cola, which proved a bit of a headache for Chinese translators. The original Chinese version was 'ke-ke-ken-la', which means 'bite the wax tadpole'. In the end, they settled on 'ko-kou-ko-le' as the way to pronounce it, which kind of means 'happiness in the mouth' – and you can read that any way you want!

So, you've done some research and discovered that the super-cool name you've chosen for your new tech product translates as 'I'm stealing your moped' in Swahili. You might decide it doesn't matter because you are focusing on selling to the US and Europe. Fine. Then, you learn that it means 'daft penguin' in Greek. Is it the end of the world? Do you have to go back to the drawing board? Well, translation issues never stopped Coca-Cola, Sega or Mensa. Pick another name for your Greek market.

## Is Anyone Else Using My Brand Name?

> **'One of the most difficult things, when you start, is picking a name. You know, domain names, everything's taken – between that and trademarks.'**
>
> *Anthony Rose – Founder of SeedLegals*

When Anthony Rose had an idea to create an online platform where startups could gain easy access to the kind of legal documentation they would need, one of the first challenges he faced was finding a suitable name.

For every name you can think of, you first have to go online to see if anyone else is using it. There's no reason for an expensive trademark check. Just go and look for it. The problem with keeping it simple, uncontrived and as easy to understand as a 'Stop' sign is that you can bet your arse that someone's already taken it.

Let's say your intuition has delivered the goods, and you've come up with some excellent and perfectly appropriate names for your product. You might find that no one else in your industry has staked a claim to them, but someone in an altogether different sector has. If that's the case, you might just march on with it anyway, but it depends on what the other product is. Remember what I said about not wanting a title that gets attention for the wrong reasons? Sharing the same product name as an anal suppository is not a wise move.

## Is It Available as a Domain Name?

Even before you type your proposed names into the search bar, why not go to a web hosting service such as GoDaddy or Fasthosts, and do a quick check to see if it is available as a domain name?

'Oh, no! "Popquizdaddy.co.uk" has already been taken. I'll have to scrap that.'

Hold your horses. Perhaps you don't have to give it up. Have a look to see whether anyone's bothered to build a site or simply purchased the domain name. There are loads of reasons why they may have bought the domain – to block others, they had an idea (which they've now dropped), they are hoping to flog it to someone who wants it, just to name a few off the top of my head. Consider choosing a different domain extension.

Hey, you! Yes, you. You checked, didn't you? You went online to find out what Pop Quiz Daddy is. If you didn't, let me save you the trouble. It's available! I made it up, so if you've ever fancied building an app for pop quiz fanatics, the door's wide open.

## Validate, Validate, Validate!

Anthony Rose told me how the name of his startup, SeedLegals, came about. He'd stayed up until around one in the morning, conjuring up as many names as he could until he amassed around thirty of them. He was about to buy the domain names and had a vision of himself bouncing into the office the next day, turning to his three teammates, and saying, 'Hey, I bought these domains. What do you think?', only to hear them flatly tell him they were all crap. How could he be sure his ideas were good? User testing!

The first thing he did was approach a local cafe. He showed them a card that he had produced and asked them to give a free drink to anyone presenting it at the counter, and he promised to foot the bill. If he was going to ask people to help him choose the best name for his startup, the least he could do was offer them a thank you.

He went to all the people he could find in the shared office space he was working from and handed them each an A4 piece of paper, upon which was written a list of potential names for his startup. This list included such catchy titles as Claws.com, Lexmartyr, Docmotion, SeedLegals and a host of others. All they had to do to earn a free coffee was to look at the names on the sheet of paper and say which one they would be more likely to invest in if they were doing a funding round.

Responses ranged from 'That's too complicated' to 'Sounds difficult' and 'Sounds scary', but when it came to SeedLegals, one of them said, 'Ah, SeedLegals. I know what you guys do.' When Anthony heard this the second time within a short space of time, he knew he was on to something.

For guidance on how not to name your startup, follow the lead of banks, VCs and other financial institutions. Well, that's not strictly true. The kind of names they select – Smithers, Wilco, Bonner LLP or Franklin Thomas Finance – are what we expect them to be called, a combination of surnames of the partners who first founded the firms.

## Ready to Start Building?

We've been thorough, so far, to ensure there's no way for anyone to fuck up their startup. By this point, if you're still reading, I'm guessing you have a pretty cool idea that you have taken steps to validate (not just by asking your mum), and you've come up with an original, interesting and clear name.

So, does that mean it's time to build a minimum viable product (MVP)?

Don't jump the gun just yet, my friend. You're going to have to sketch it out first, and you'll need a team to help you do that. In the next chapter, we're going to look at how to avoid building something people don't want, how to map out the journey and reach a point where you can either bootstrap your startup or find investors.

# 4.
# WHAT THE FUCK AM I GONNA DO WITH MY IDEA NOW?

If you have done everything right up until now, you are at a critical three-way roundabout. The first exit is for those who choose to bow out, which is fine. Founding a startup isn't for everyone, and you should give yourself a solid pat on the back. Getting this far is further than most do. You got in there but decided it wasn't for you, and that makes you infinitely more heroic than the chap sitting next to you who is too afraid to even try.

That said, if you're feeling that way, I want to persuade you to stick it out because we've all felt that way. Believe me. I have. On the other hand, come on! What the fuck happened? You found out your idea's shit, and no one wants it? You were laughed at? Is that it; that's the extent of your resilience and determination?

If you're feeling that way now, so early in the game, you either missed the part in the first chapter where we discussed how hard it is to be a founder, or you didn't believe it, or the path of the entrepreneur is not for you, and you should choose something safer that makes you feel more comfortable instead.

The second exit, which takes you straight ahead, is called 'Shit Gets Real Avenue' because this is where the fun starts. You're going to need everyone on standby – your mum, your partner, your best mate, the dog, your priest, or that shrink you see on Thursdays – because here, my friend, is where the faeces will become so tangible and will smell so strong, you will almost be able to taste it. If you're meant to take this avenue, though, it's fucking worth it! But it's good to have a support structure in place, and that includes the measures you're going to take to keep you mentally and physically strong – enough quality sleep, a healthy diet, 'you' time spent in meditation, painting goldfish, or going for a brisk walk, and all the people that give you a boost when you feel like crap.

And the third exit? Well, that depends on where you are now and what you encounter from now on. Sometimes, you have to go back to the drawing board. It doesn't mean you've failed. It just means that the project is not a goer, the idea is not a runner, or, as Grolsch's Dutch spokesperson, Ronald, might say, 'Shhtopp! This plan's not ready yet.'

I don't know about you, but I'm ready to go straight across that roundabout, but before we do that, let's check where we are.

You should have:

- A solid idea that solves a genuine problem
- A sound understanding of the pain point(s) your product will address
- A clear knowledge of who is experiencing those pain points
- A keen sense of your product's value
- Enough validation to know other people will pay for the product
- A great name that is simple, memorable and says something about what your product does
- A steadily growing business network

Furthermore, and just as importantly, you will need:

- At least one mentor, coach or both
- Supportive friends and family, or, failing that,
    - a vicar, imam, rabbi or another religious/spiritual guide you can turn to
    - a shrink or counsellor, or, failing that,
    - a pet you can cuddle that loves you!
- An exercise regime that includes a healthy diet and plenty of sleep, and you might want to consider something as adventurous as cold-water therapy and breathwork such as the Wim-Hof method. Works for me!

## You're Still Here?

Some have gone home, some are rethinking their plans, and some are feeling hesitant, but you, my dear readers – yes, you who are reading this line – are made of the stuff that makes great founders, and that's enough for me. Let's march forward together.

Why did I big you up so much? Because you deserve it, and that's what you need, but not from me. You're going to find plenty of reasons to doubt yourself, so be ready to dig deep and counter those negative voices that spring up from nowhere when the going gets tough.

You would not have come this far if you did not believe you had something of value to share with the world. Hold that thought. You have something of value to share with the world. Isn't that fantastic? Better still, being an entrepreneur is like being a professional helper, so not only are you going to make life easier for people in some way, but you're going to make money in the process. You're a superhero waiting to happen. Break open the champagne!

No! Not yet. That champagne shouldn't even have left the supermarket yet, but it's good to recognise your value, so you can remind yourself of why you are doing what you are doing when things are not going according to plan. Sometimes the greatest things happen when you're at your lowest ebb. Did I tell you about the day my annoyingly loud voice saved my arse?

Really? I didn't? Okay, here goes . . .

## The Day My Annoyingly Loud Voice Saved My Arse

I hope you read that subheading in an annoyingly loud voice because despite what people who don't like annoyingly loud voices have always told you, shy kids don't get the sweets, and getting noticed will get you places.

Remember that idea I had for a gaming app that would act as a digital stakeholder? Well, I did everything I was supposed to do, and I felt as though we were well positioned to get the funding that we needed to take the plan forward.

As you will find out later, fundraising is not for the faint-hearted. You will experience more rejection than at any other time in your life. I did. Some investors give one reason why they won't bet on you, while others will say the opposite. You may not be given any reason at all, or a potential funder may just ghost you.

It's like the worst dating experience ever except the stakes are higher. After putting so much blood, sweat and tears into your startup, being told it's bound to fail or that you are not investible hurts even more than a blind date saying you've got the personality of Genghis Khan, the body of Quasimodo, a face like a cat's arse, and the intelligence of a tadpole. And that's pretty much how I was feeling with Stakester.

I was at rock bottom and wanted to quit, so I did what any self-respecting person would do: I met up with a friend to moan about it. That person was Emma Davidson, whom we chatted about in the first chapter.

Emma and I met up in a cafe in the centre of London. Now, the thing about cafes in any city, but especially the capital, is that you never know who's sitting at the table next to you. The person on the right of you may have just been released from prison, and the one on the left could be the founder of a global brand. London's a melting pot of different lives, cultures, histories and attitudes, and it's a massive leveller. In a city with a population of over nine million and where around three hundred languages are spoken, you're a tiny atom just like everyone else.

While I was bending Emma's ear, letting her and the whole world know why Stakester was such a cool idea and how dreadful it was that I was being so badly done to by all these heartless, visionless investors, who were 'clearly' too blind to recognise the 'obvious' genius of my plan, I was seated a couple of tables from an investor. Half the room was probably wishing I'd shut the fuck up and go home or up my game, but this guy had other plans.

'Sorry to interrupt you. I wasn't deliberately earwigging, but I couldn't help hearing about your idea. Here's my card. I'm willing to invest in you. Give me a call when you're ready, and we can arrange a time to chat properly,' and with that, he bid us an excellent afternoon and strolled out the door. I was back on the Stakester roller coaster, Emma got a break from my whining, and I became even more annoyingly loud than ever.

## Never Underestimate Yourself

Don't undervalue your business because the value you place on it will impact everything you do; how you talk about it to others, how you expect others to think about it, how you interact with investors and your level of confidence. The value you place on yourself and your business is almost like a gear that you choose. Are you going to stay in first gear, or are you going to put your foot down, and get yourself to top gear where you belong? Be confident!

Don't underestimate your position. To have come this far, you have the market validation, so you know you have something that people want and will pay for. You know why your product is unique, superior or offers more value for money than everything else that's out there. Never let go of that thought and know that you belong at the table regardless of who else is sitting there – investors, potential partners, customers or suppliers.

## Value Your Experience

Don't underestimate your experience. Far too many people confuse experience with skill set or experience with tenure. They are not the same. I have always loved sales. I love everything about the process – finding the ideal prospects, making the approach, gaining that first spark of interest, growing it, and gently guiding them to a place where they can see they have a problem that has to be solved and that I can fix. Friend, I loved (and still love) closing!

Forgive the humble brag, but I twice had record-breaking years where I blew the competition out of the water. Succeeding wasn't an accident. I had a process that worked, and part of the process was meeting people. The more people you talk to, the more decisions you get, so no matter who you are, you will get more sales by the law of averages. I went through more face-to-face conversations in each of my record-breaking years than other people were having in four. Who do you think had more experience?

Tenure without context is meaningless. It could just as easily mean dead wood as valuable experience. It is not the time you spend doing something that counts, but what you do with that time. Every time I met someone, I encountered a slightly different challenge, and I learned from the experience. I found out new things about people, what problems were out there, and how my product could be adapted to address pain points.

Through experience, we gain tacit knowledge, which is priceless, because you can't get it from the classroom or a book. Think about the last time you saw an experienced plumber, electrician or another specialist tradesperson. They have a work-around for every situation. Get it? Your skill set is your toolbox. Experience teaches you how to apply the best tool for any task and how to come up with a work-around for the more unusual challenges.

### They Need You as Much as You Need Them

Don't underestimate your value to investors. They need you as much as you need them. They are not meeting founders for the fun of it. They are searching for the right people and businesses to invest in because they want as large a return as they can get. If they have asked to see you, that means a lot, so embrace it and appreciate what it means. They are hoping you will be their next magical investment just as much as you want to be invested in.

Never forget that programmes such as *Dragons' Den* are there to entertain as much as to give insight into the mindset of investors. Unless you go into a meeting and tell your potential investor to fuck off, you are highly unlikely to be scowled at or spoken to harshly.

Think *angels*, not *dragons*, at all stages of the investment merry-go-round. They want your pitch to be music to their ears, and they want to invest in people they can have a great relationship with moving forward. They're not there to kill your dreams. Know your value, own it and have the confidence to ask for the deal that reflects how valuable you are. The more confident you are, the more money you will attract and the less equity you will lose. Trust me. Investors love confidence.

## Don't Be Naive!

If you're a new founder, as intelligent, innovative and determined as you are, you have a lot to learn, and when you've learnt what you need to learn, there'll be other stuff to learn; and that will continue forever. But don't be naive.

**You are not a genius.**

Don't think you're the smartest person in the room, because even if you were, that wouldn't be a good thing. Rule number one: always try to surround yourself with people who are cleverer than you.

**You're not the only person to have thought of that product.**

I know I have said this already, but it's worth mentioning again: you don't have to be the only or the first person to have conceived the product. You need to be the first to build it, create the best version, have a better route to market or, ideally, meet all three of those conditions.

**You can't do it all on your own.**

You might think you can, and you might be able to up to a point, but eventually you will have to bring in others, or you won't have a scalable business. It's almost impossible to do it all on your own, no matter how much energy you have, how much of a control freak you think you are, or how determined you are. Who are you going to talk to, who are you going to bounce ideas off, and who are you going to share the burden with? Who's going to build the product, and who's going to win the customers? People tend to be better at one or the other.

**If you, because of your experience and expertise, are the product, you don't have a scalable startup.**

This should be common sense, but sometimes even the brightest, most innovative people are lacking in it. You might be able to solve problems that no one else can, and that will make you a highly valuable and sought-after resource, but your service is not scalable. The only way you will have a scalable startup that can grow indefinitely is if you can package your skills in a way that hundreds, thousands or millions can access them simultaneously.

**Saving the planet's great, but that can't be the only reason your startup exists.**

At some point, you have to make money. If you can't show how that's going to happen, you're not going to win investment no matter how positive your purpose is. Maybe you're not looking for investment because you plan to bootstrap. How are you going to do that if you don't make money? We will look at what investors want in more detail in a later chapter, but, for now, note that you must be able to show the potential to grow in terms of revenue and customers, even if you are not profitable in the early stages.

It's time for another disclaimer:

***Making the world a better place, having a social conscience and caring about others are all remarkable things for a startup to be involved in, and they certainly won't drive investors away, but you're supposed to be a business, not a charity. They want to know what you're going to do with their money and how you're going to grow it. If you plan to help spiny lumpsuckers, pink fairy armadillos, or***

***strange-tailed tyrants at the same time, and your investors give a shit, that's a bonus.***

And, yes, those animals do exist.

**Investors won't back you just because they love your product.**

> 'Show me the money!'
>
> *Fictional character Jerry McGuire, played by Tom Cruise in the film,* Jerry McGuire

They'd be more worried if you didn't. Fuck me; if you don't love your self-cleaning microwave oven, a revolution waiting to happen in kitchens around the world, how can you expect anyone else to get enthused? Money makes the world go round, so you have to show how you and your team are going to make it.

**Being a founder can't be a side hustle.**
It's pretty difficult to start a business when you're homeless or haven't got the basics. Founders tend to be in well-paid jobs or have the capacity to make money as consultants. It pays to build a nest egg before you start a business, and that's what I did, but you'll find that whatever money you have runs out quickly. You must treat your startup like a full-time job, and if you must do any other work to fund your business, that other work is the side hustle.

> 'If you're not yet full-time on your thing, how committed, really, are you?'
>
> *Max Kelly – Senior Vice President of Techstars*

This will sound harsh, but if you can't afford to give up your time to work on your startup without expecting other people to fund your existence, don't start a company. It's that simple because you've got to commit, so only do it when you can. Besides, if you're trying to blag some angel to pay for you to put the time in, they will see through you.

**Investment doesn't come cheap.**
Did I mention Tom Cruise's film character, Jerry McGuire? 'Show me the money!' Investors are not interested in throwing money at a venture

for the chance to win peanuts. They can find safer bets for lower percentage growth.

Startups are incredibly risky, no matter how much you believe in yours, and at a guess, around eight out of ten of them fail. If you were going to place a bet, knowing there was an 80 per cent chance you would get your money back at best but probably lose most or all of it, what kind of pay-out would you be hoping for? You're not going to do it for a measly 10 per cent more than you put in, are you? Or even 50 or 75 per cent.

> 'As soon as you get into the VC world, you've decided to get on a treadmill because each VC round, they're giving you enough to fund you for the next eighteen months, they want to see significant growth, so they want you to spend that money, and then you have to raise your next round.'
>
> *Max Kelly – Senior Vice President of Techstars*

Depending on the stage that they are at, angel investors are more likely to know what you're going through because they will have experienced it themselves, so you can expect them to be more supportive. At the VC level, however, you can forget about the touchy-feely bit. It's all about the money. Not only will they want to take their slice of equity from your business, but you will be expected to use their money to grow quickly until the next round, and the next round, and so on. They want to see their investment growing by factors of 100 per cent. And where does that leave you?

Capshare analysed five thousand cap tables to look at how much equity co-founders have between them. According to their research, by the time you've gone through several rounds, you and your co-founders will be lucky to still own one-fifth of the business you started. You may come out with only 15 per cent between you. Assuming you have one or two co-founders, you're going to own as little as one-twentieth, just 5 per cent, on exit, so you can probably kiss goodbye to the island you were going to buy in the Pacific. Sorry to piss on your dreams.

**You are not the fountain of all knowledge, and you shouldn't be.** Most first-time founders are naive in one way or another, so if this is your first time, and you feel guilty for entertaining any of the naive thinking I've highlighted, don't. Where do you think I got that list from? We've all been there, my friend. Let's recap on how not to be naive.

- **You're not a genius**. Okay, Mr IQ of 160, I'm not talking about you. Happy now?
- **You're not the first person to have thought of that product**. Except you. Yes, you, the person who invented the gizmo for running cars on toilet water.
- **You can't do it all on your own**. Well, there's probably a one-in-a-million chance that you can, but, eventually, even you will need other pairs of hands.
- **If you are the product, it's not scalable and you don't have a startup.** No exceptions. You cannot be the product. You might be at the heart of it, as the source of knowledge, but you are not the product.
- **Your noble mission can't be the only reason for the business to exist.** Make sure you're in it to make money. If not, read the other book that I've not written yet, *How Not to Fuck Up Your Third-Sector Organisation*.
- **You should love your product, but your investors don't need to.** They need to believe in you and your business model.
- **Investors won't invest in you just because they love your product**. Will anyone pay for it? That's the question.
- **Being a founder can't be a side hustle**. It takes 100 per cent commitment. You can take your mum out for Mother's Day, and that's it. The rest of your time belongs to the business.
- **Investment doesn't come cheap**. They'll want everything except your soul, and even then . . . never mind. That's a different story.
- **Don't think you know it all**. Except you, again, smarty-pants, but had you heard of spiny lumpsuckers, pink fairy armadillos or strange-tailed tyrants before I mentioned them? I thought not, but one out of three is not bad.

With all of that in mind, don't forget to ask for help.

So, now you know not to be naive, what's next?

## Don't Forget to Be Naive!

I know; you call it self-contradictory, but I call it Zen. See it as rules needing to be broken. It's the same gig.

When the odds are stacked against you, but you believe you can succeed because you just know it in your heart, that's naive. It's incredibly naive, but it's great. Don't lose that feeling.

> **'I love seeing people who have that really strong kind of founder-market fit, that real passion for what they're doing; people who, when you go and meet them and you have that initial coffee, you can feel the energy fizzing off them.'**
>
> *Eamonn Carey – Managing Director of Techstars*

When you believe that you are the first to have thought of your new levitation device – or that it is going to work when you build it – that's naive. It's the best kind of naive. Go for it, but don't miss the steps we've covered – remember validation, validation, oh, and validation.

When your family and friends tell you that you're crazy for giving up a full-time job and a great career to follow your dreams, they're probably right, but don't listen to them. Embrace your naivety and do it anyway. Don't forget to hit them with the glorious 'if that job's meant for me, it will find me again'.

I was not a gamer, but it didn't stop me from diving into the gaming space with Stakester. How could I possibly dare to imagine I had something to offer gamers? Wet-behind-the-ears, more-enthusiasm-than-sense, cheeky, cocky, inexperienced naivety – that's how!

To put it briefly, because I want to write one book, not twenty, all those wonderful qualities we see in children – the sense of wonder, appreciation for small things, a hunger for adventure, the feeling of being indestructible, the belief that anything's possible, the open mind, and the lack of social conditioning – are all slightly naive, and they are the attributes you should be embracing as you enter the brave new world of founderdom. Hey, Mr IQ of 160. Yes, you, again, you haven't heard of that word because I made it up. I love it, and I hope the editor loves it too.

## Just One More Thing . . .

It's time for us to take our first steps down Shit Gets Real Avenue, but before we do that, in the words of the great Columbo, 'Just one more thing, sir/miss' . . .

We've spoken a lot about winning investment, and, for most of you, that's how things are going to pan out, but that's not the only way to build and grow a startup.

## Finding Investors Isn't the Only Route

There's a myth that to be a successful entrepreneur you have to go through an accelerator, go through funding rounds, and grow the business to the point that you can sell it, make your exit and earn a few million in the process. That's all well and good, but you don't have to take that route.

Surprisingly, perhaps, given that he's the Senior Vice President of a tech startup accelerator, Max Kelly recommends that founders aim for the bootstrapping route if they can. One way that you can fund the development of your product is through consultancy work, using your intellectual property (IP) to serve clients while simultaneously building up your knowledge for the product you want to build and gaining product validation.

> 'If someone is paying you to develop the thing and also validating the thing at the same time, it's like, "This is awesome."'
>
> *Max Kelly – Senior Vice President of Techstars*

Once your product is ready, your customers will already be waiting for it, and you will have gained a 'clearly validated market recommendation'. If you can't get that validation, you will have a strong indication that there's no market need, and you will have to decide whether to pack it in, pivot or go back to the drawing board. Of course, if you can, it truly is 'awesome' because it means you have cash flow from day one, which you can use to take on other people, bring in a part-time or full-time developer or outsource some development work, and you will have a client base to build on.

> 'When you have it, you don't need to ask the question as to whether or not you have product-market fit. When you have product-market fit, you know you have product-market fit.'
>
> *Paul Murphy – Partner at Northzone*

### Bootstrapping versus VC

Max made a superb comparison between jumping on the VC conveyor belt and bootstrapping. The median exit amount for companies that have used VC investment is around £20 million. The mean average is much higher because of statistical outliers that have compensated for the vast majority that come out with nothing. If you bootstrap your business, you might only need to reach between three and four million in revenue for a £20 million exit. Assuming angel investment costs you 20 per cent, you and your co-founders will have £16 million between you. That's still not private island money, but it's going to pay for a lot of goodies. As Max pointed out earlier, however, you might be able to grow your company from scratch without any investment at all, from angels or otherwise.

British entrepreneur Oliver Cookson, from Manchester, founded the sports nutrition brand Myprotein when he was twenty-three years old. When he started, he was hand-making orders from a lock-up. Seven years later, at the ripe youthful age of thirty, having fully bootstrapped his company without any loans or investments, he exited for £58 million on the table plus shares in the group that bought his company. These days, he's worth hundreds of millions and is well on his way to becoming a billionaire, so he probably could buy a private island in the sun.

To get the same kind of exit with VCs on board, you'd have to go through many rounds to get your company to the point where it could be sold for £100 million, and you and your co-founders may come out with £20 million between you. You'd be marginally better off, after a long haul, and it may feel as though you are working more for them and their interests than you are working for yourself along the way. Bootstrapping is doable but extremely tough, especially if you intend to do it on your own, so don't beat yourself up for wanting to find investors.

## Are You Sure You Want to Do This Alone?

I always say every startup begins with one founder. Someone has to have the idea and the vision to take it forward, but most founders very quickly find another one or more co-founders to join forces with. The big question is whom to join up with, and that's one of the things we are going to look at in the next chapter. We're also going to look at proof of concept (POC) and how to get it; minimum viable products (MVPs) and whether we need to build one; and, the mother of all conundrums, how the fuck we're going to build our product, and how much is it going to cost. We've got work to do. You wanted Shit Gets Real Avenue, so let's do this thang.

# 5.
# WHO THE FUCK AM I GONNA WORK WITH?

Well done for making it this far. It's good to know you're finding the book useful, and my dreadful sense of humour hasn't deterred you. Jokes aside, you must ask yourself an important question before reading any other chapters: are you sure that you can launch and build your company on your own?

There are benefits to being a sole founder. You have full control, so you can be as tunnel-visioned as you want. If your plan works, you will enjoy all the glory. The financial rewards will be greater because you won't be sharing them with co-founders. Those benefits will be significantly magnified if you can grow your business without external investment and pull off a lucrative exit in a few years. Others have done it, so it is possible. Therefore, nobody can tell you not to. It is up to you, but make certain that is what you want and know what you're getting into before you do. Since you're here now, let's consider the advantages of bringing in co-founders.

## Why Join Forces With a Co-Founder?

There are several reasons why you should consider taking on at least one co-founder. Have you ever freelanced before? If so, you will recognise that sole traders wear many hats, and you will know that being your own boss isn't as much fun as it sounds.

**Being your own boss can be a shit job.**

We all need a kick up the arse occasionally. It's human nature, and when we do, it's the responsibility of our boss to do the honours: 'Smithers, is there a reason you're leaning back in your chair, picking your nose? Just remember, your monthly review meeting's happening on Friday.

Make sure you've cleaned out both nostrils by then, please, and if you get the time, you might also get on with the report you're supposed to have completed yesterday!'

As a sole trader, it's on you, and it takes a lot of discipline. A fifteen-minute lie-in can easily evolve into regular late starts, and then you have the pull of the kitchen, your pet hamster and social media to contend with. Every action has consequences, and if you slacken, you will quickly know about it as the to-do list gets bigger, the pressure builds up, and it starts to feel as though you're losing. To make matters worse, the only person who can fix it is you, but you've already failed as the boss, and your self-esteem is crawling on the floor. You started this, so you must finish it.

**You're responsible for everything.**

When you work for yourself, you are not only responsible for providing the service, but you also have to deal with everything else that goes with it – marketing, business development, invoicing, customer service, chasing payment, accounts, maintaining customer records and so on.

These are all mammoth tasks when you break them down. Marketing alone can be a very time-consuming exercise as you juggle content creation with maintaining a presence on social media as well as online and offline networking. I've told you how much I love sales, but it still takes a lot of time and effort to source prospects, pitch them and close them. Don't forget that you're the boss, so it's your responsibility to inspire and motivate your team – you! Where are you going to find the energy to do all of that, and are you the best person for every job?

There's even more fun at the beginning because you will be responsible for building the product, testing it, tweaking it, and so on, and if you need investment to do that, that's on you as well.

> 'If you are not talking to customers; if you are not building the product; if you are not thinking and spending time working out how to explain what it is that you are building, which goes back to talking to customers; or eating, sleeping or exercising, you are doing something that is not necessarily moving the needle.'
>
> *Eamonn Carey – Managing Director of Techstars*

As the founder of a startup, there is always something to do, and if there isn't, you should be asking yourself what you can do to 'move the needle'.

**Lighten the load.**

At the very least, co-founders will lighten the load, and you will no longer be your own boss. Some people pay a fortune for accountability partners, but you don't have to because you have each other. When one co-founder is slowing down, one of the others can give them the push they need. Your workload will be halved or reduced by a third or even a quarter. Can you imagine how much more productive you can be?

**Focus on what you're good at and what you enjoy.**

You're a founder, right? So it's a given that you're smart, innovative and super cool, but everyone has strengths and weaknesses, and you're unlikely to be excellent at everything. Sales and administration are worlds apart. People tend to excel in one or the other, and even those who are great at both will have a preference. Having co-founders on board will allow you to focus on the jobs you are good at and the ones you enjoy.

**Increase your potential.**

In the early stages, there is a lot to do, and you want to avoid having to outsource to others. Outsourcing will inflate your costs and could lead to other problems. Increasing the size of your founding team will broaden your skill set and reduce the need for outsourcing.

**Strengthen your position.**

Having a few people on board at the start strengthens your position in a variety of ways. Two, three or four minds are better than one for strategic planning, problem-solving, and for 360-degree awareness of the opportunities and threats that may emerge in your market. Collectively you will have a broader set of strengths and, therefore, fewer weaknesses.

> 'What are the things that, as a founder, they've experienced before – problems they've experienced before – that most other people don't know about?'
>
> *Megan Reynolds – Investor at Crane Venture Partners*

The more combined experience you have between you, the more versatile and adaptable you will be. Consider the words of Megan Reynolds at Crane Venture Partners. She wants to know what problems founders have experienced (and navigated a way past) before. Think of anyone you take on as a co-founder as being an encyclopaedia of extra knowledge and experience. Keep this in mind when deciding whom to bring on board.

**Lone founders are less investible.**

Angel investors and VCs are more likely to invest in startups that have more than one founder. The only thing that gives them the heebie-jeebies more than a startup team of one person is co-founders who are best mates. Why? Because they want to know whether they can trust the team to execute the plan and make money for them. Co-founders who are besties is a concern because the future of their company depends on their relationship, which is going to be severely tested by the road ahead. That doesn't mean you can't start a business with your best mate, especially if you are aligned in every way. I've already mentioned Mae Yip and Samantha Hornsby were good pals when they founded their startup, and there are plenty of other examples to come. But don't be under any illusions; co-founding with a mate or spouse has its risks and, whatever else happens, play down your friendship when pitching to a potential investor.

Looking for a co-founder demonstrates a higher level of self-awareness. When I was starting Stakester, despite my perfectly healthy, some may say massive, ego, I needed someone to see the things that I didn't, including my weaknesses, someone who would get me back on track when I was feeling wonky.

Philip O'Reilly is head of deal execution at Draper Esprit, a specialist in funding startups at the series A[4] and series B stages and setting those companies on a trajectory of major exits. He told me that, putting aside the product, market fit and the numbers, the thing he pays most attention to when deciding whether to invest is the people. He has to assess how effective the team is, how well they work together and what they are capable of.

A team of one can spook investors because you are not only expecting them to believe there's a market for your product, but you are also asking them to trust that you are one of those rare individuals who can do everything on their own without burning out or having a breakdown.

---

[4] A series A round (also referred to as series A financing or series A investment) refers to a startup's first significant round of venture capital financing. It usually happens once the product is built, you've got traction and are looking to scale.

When they see a solid team of two or more founders, the whole is worth more than the sum of the parts. They see a well-oiled machine that will get more done, find more innovative solutions to problems (hive mind), and is more likely to go the distance (strength in numbers).

Have second thoughts about going it alone? Let's find you a co-founder. Read on, partner.

## What Makes a Great Co-Founder?

**A shared sense of purpose and a passion for fixing the problem.** The strongest teams are bound by a shared sense of purpose, so try to find people who understand the problem you are solving, are just as passionate about making it happen, and share your values.

> 'Every case that I've invested in, the founders are absolutely amazing, they really, really understand the problem that they're going after, and they've just got this incredible product sense, and so even their initial versions of the concept or the product, as rough as they might be, are just really impressive.'
>
> *Paul Murphy – Partner of Northzone*

It's a bit odd that the previous pages don't recommend co-founding with a mate, but working with your best friend is exactly what the following three examples show. Nick Telson and Andrew Webster, founders of DesignMyNight, were best mates at university, and both went on to become high achievers in the corporate world. The thing that made them so compatible as co-founders was their shared dream. They knew they didn't want to spend their lives working for corporates, and they were determined to achieve financial freedom by their thirties.

Mae Yip and Samantha Hornsby, who founded ERIC Festival, were great friends driven by the same mission. They had a problem that they were determined to solve, and they wanted to solve that problem for other people.

Paul Murphy first showed tremendous entrepreneurial promise as an undergraduate. Paul and a mate of his had been coding for years, so they started doing web design for people to make money. At the time, the only way to get websites built was to go to expensive digital agencies that were charging five-figure sums. Paul and his friend were arbitraging student talent to create websites that they were able to sell for three times what it cost to make.

They went on to create a content management system (CMS) six years before WordPress was a thing, which meant they could build sites quicker for their clients while charging the same amount of money, increasing their margins. The dot-com crash happened, but their business survived, and they eventually sold it to a competitor for parts.

After finishing his degree and having learnt a few lessons from his stint as a techpreneur, Paul knew where his strengths lay, so he followed his instincts and joined what was then the most technically advanced company on the planet, Microsoft. He started as an engineer before getting involved with product development and strategy, later overseeing the technical giant's acquisition of Skype.

Following his stint at Microsoft, Paul went on to join forces with a group of other technically minded entrepreneurs, and collectively they brought companies such as Giphy (which they sold to Facebook) and Aviary (a photo-editing app for mobile, which was later snapped up by Adobe) into existence.

Patrick Moberg was one of the other members of the group who, like Paul, loved games and had a passion for design. They were both frustrated with the games available on their mobile phones, which were limited mostly to kids' games and casino games. Surely they could create something better, and they were confident that many other gamers were just as bored with mobile games as they were. They set out to build beautiful games and launched a company called Playdots, and they built a gaming platform called Dots, which was a big hit from the get-go.

There are a few takeaways from Paul's story. Firstly, even though he and his buddy outsourced work when they launched a web development company at university, they were both skilled coders, which meant they could tell the difference between a decent coder and a dabbler.

Teamwork played an important part throughout Paul's career, from his early days at university to his time at Microsoft and later when he got together with other like-minded individuals. The hugely popular Dots came about not only because of teamwork but because of the shared vision of co-founders Paul and Patrick – their love of games and design and their frustration with the poor choice of games for mobile phones. They both shared a problem that they could solve and that they knew other people would want them to solve.

**You're still determined to join forces with your best friend?** Ideally, you should try to avoid starting up with your best friends for the reasons I mentioned earlier. Putting aside what investors think, starting a business together will test any friendship. Do you want to jeopardise your most important friendship? Well, I did! Okay, let's look at some exceptions to the rule.

*You're not friends anymore. You're family!*

Family means forever, or it should. By the time they've become adults, siblings have been through numerous trials and tribulations together – countless rows where every kind of insult may have been flung in all directions, the most precious shared experiences, tears, laughter, estrangement and maybe even fistfights. If they are still getting along after that, their relationship is indestructible.

How indestructible is your relationship with your best friend? Be prepared to have the fiercest, most passionate, heated disagreements – fracas that may lead to screaming at each other from a metre away and jousting with pencils – and then be prepared to park those events and act as though nothing happened . . . just like happy families do! My co-founder and I have had plenty of disagreements since we started Stakester, but our friendship is more solid than ever, and Stakester's going strong.

Mae and Samantha both admitted to having had issues when they started in business together. They describe the first two years as 'weird' but have completed the transition from being friends to being family. They got through the rough patches by reminding themselves of why they had embarked on the journey together. It wasn't about the money. It was about being two best friends who wanted to solve a problem together. Their friendship comes first, closely followed by the shared mission, and they deliberately allocate a couple of days every month to put aside the business and spend time together as mates.

*Set clear boundaries*

You will get on better and get more done if you set clear boundaries, so you both know who is doing what within the organisation. Samantha and Mae complement each other perfectly. Mae keeps her eyes on the here and now, paying attention to what needs to be done in the short term and ensuring no balls are dropped. Samantha is a visionary who is constantly looking well into the future. What Samantha lacks in design skills, Mae more than makes up for – and to think, all that talent would have been wasted had she stayed at PwC (apart from fantastic-looking spreadsheets, of course). They know how to work as a team, and when they both feel strongly about an issue, they meet in the middle.

Sometimes, even married couples start businesses together, and they make it work, so there's hope for everyone. That said, if you're planning on bringing in your hubby or your wife, they already own half the business, so you have nothing to lose!

## What Role Am I Gonna Play?

Look, you came up with the idea, so it's your party, right, and I'm guessing that you want to be the one to run things. Correct? It's fine. Embrace your craving for global dominance. The world needs leaders, and to have come this far, you've already proven that you're made of the right stuff. But who are you going to get to help you, and what roles will they play?

> 'Maybe think about it like a marriage. You're going to be in this for a long time, so pick your partners wisely.'
>
> *Philip O'Reilly – Head of Deal Execution at Draper Esprit*

### Every Team Needs a Strong Leader

Your co-founders will appreciate a strong leader, but that doesn't mean bossy. It means someone who knows the territory inside out, understands the mission and has the vision to steer the ship. Sometimes it is difficult to see a clear path, or you may be pulled in different directions at once. Someone has to decide what to do next. Co-founders will want to be included in decisions, and it would be foolish for any leader not to consult with their teammates, particularly if they have partnered with people who are smarter than them in some way (as opposed to 'yes' people).

Eamonn Carey, MD of Techstars, says he loves to see teams that elicit excitement, ooze self-belief and fill him with FOMO. This happens naturally when a team is united, and everyone knows their place.

### Every Startup Needs a Strong Team

On the flip side, when I asked Philip O'Reilly what his red flags were, he mentioned founders who cut across each other in meetings and openly criticise each other's ideas. If you can't work as a team and mix well when you are meeting a friendly potential investor, how will you cope when the seas are rough?

### Make Sure You All Get On

Philip warns founders to pick their partners wisely. You need to consider not only what skills and experience your co-founders are bringing to your startup, but how well you are going to get on together. If someone is a tech genius but has a talent for starting arguments, you might be better off steering clear of them as a co-founder. You can always hire them as a staff member or outsource development work to them. Put people in the environment that suits them best.

### Team Dynamics

When I asked Max Kelly at Techstars for his thoughts on choosing co-founders, he advised founders to consider several factors:

- How long have you known the person?
- Have you worked together before?
- What problems have you worked on together?
- Have you been through tough times?
- Who is going to be the boss?

Even though Max also believes that joining forces with your best friend is a terrible idea, if that friendship has developed from a working relationship, the boxes listed above will probably already be ticked, and that will set you up for success.

> **'The beauty of startups is basically you have a super-ambitious team that's trying to do something that nobody else is doing and then getting it to work. If you have those three things in combination, that's where the magic is.'**
>
> *Jens Lapinski – CEO of Angel Invest*

One of Stakester's investors, Jens Lapinksi, the former managing director of Techstars in Berlin and now the CEO of Angel Invest, makes around twenty investments every year, ploughing anything from £100,000 and upwards at a time. This is a guy who knows what he's talking about when it comes to startups.

What counts for Jens is team, team and team. He's looking for high levels of intelligence, a strong work ethic, and a commitment to doing things right. Is the team tight, or does it look like they were pulled together last week like the members of an *X-Factor* boy band? He is looking for strong individuals who work well together and have the capabilities to build a product and get it into the hands of customers.

In Jens's opinion, one of the biggest killers of startups is a team that fights. Don't pick the wrong people, don't have gaps and ensure the skill level is there. Remember, funding is the fuel, not the engine. Your team is the engine.

## Who's Gonna Be Your CTO?

Remember, the more that you and your co-founders can do to avoid having to outsource, the more control you will have over the business, the lower your overheads will be, and the more potentially profitable you will be. If you do have to outsource, you don't want to end up depending on an outsider or freelance for your company to run.

Paul Murphy was an experienced coder when he started up a web development company. He knew the difference between a chancer, a bullshitter, and someone who knows what they are doing, and he doubled his chances of getting it right by working with a co-founder who was as into coding as he was. Had anything gone wrong with a piece of work they'd outsourced to students, they would have the power to fix it. They were effectively acting as the chief technical officers.

Jens Lapinski refused to fund a company because although they had a core team in place, they'd brought in a CTO as an external hire, so the most important person for their project was not an integrated member of the team. Whether you have a CTO or not (and if you're a tech company, you definitely should), you might need to hire others to help with the build.

> 'I optimise for two things: serendipity and optionality. If I look back at my thirties, I think what I've done is I've tried to meet as many people as I possibly can who are interesting, cool and good people, and by increasing my surface area of connections and serendipity, interesting things just end up happening.'
>
> *Alex Dunsdon – Partner at Saatchinvest*

If you're building a product, you need a CTO. There are no ifs or buts. Either you are the CTO, or you must find someone you know well, trust, and have worked with before to take on the role. You could also do with a chief finance officer (CFO) as businesses are built on numbers, and when it comes to trying to convince others to invest in you, it will show that you're not making the numbers up as you go along even if you are. Having someone on board who understands sales and marketing is a bonus, but you can hire these people later.

If you have already built a strong and broad network, it will be a lot easier to put together a core team of people you know well, but remember, networking shouldn't be like collecting Trump cards. You have to engage with the people in your network and get to know them. Take note of what others have said and done, and make sure you have worked with your co-founders before.

Alex Dunsdon puts it beautifully when he says that he optimises for serendipity and optionality. If you have not been doing that so far, start now.

In the chapters that follow, let's assume you have your co-founders in place. It's time to look at building your product.

6.

# WHAT THE FUCK AM I GONNA BUILD?

You've pulled together a core team of co-founders, and they're happy for you to be the boss, so pat yourself on the back. Now it's time to look at building the product. Or is it?

What if you haven't got the money? Perhaps you're the bootstrapping type, and you have the time, determination and skills to build your product without any outside help. If that's you, brilliant, but if you are going to need investment to get your startup started, what are you going to do? Build a minimum viable product (MVP) or see if you can win investment with nothing more than a team, a great idea and some data that suggests you're building something that people want?

> 'To build or not to build? That is the question.'
>
> *Wrote Shakespeare at no time ever*

Had Shakespeare been interested in writing a play about startups, maybe he would have used that line somewhere. What would the twenty-first-century Bard of Avon write? *Mac Death*, *Twelfth Byte* or *Much Ado About Data* perhaps, or even *How Not to Put Thine Enterprise in a Pickle*? Dreadful, I know. That's why I am a tech startup founder and not a comedian or playwright! But the question remains: to build or not to build?

> 'The problem that you find with a lot of tech founders, coming from a tech background, developers mainly, they try to solve a problem by building something, and that is not necessarily always the case; so, I always say, "First things first, you have to know your customers. Try to speak to them as much as possible."'
>
> 'How many times do you hear of founders that say, "Oh, I started this, it didn't work, do you know I actually had to start from scratch?"'
>
> *Sara Simeone – CEO and Founder of Digital Oracles*

The CEO and founder of the online deal monitoring platform Digital Oracles, entrepreneur Sara Simeone, points out that her team spent two years thoroughly researching their market and speaking to potential customers before they put together a single byte of code. What they lost in time, they got back ten-fold by creating a product that worked first time, did what it was supposed to do, and that customers appreciated and wanted.

> **'How much money is wasted, pre- and post-seed, by people pivoting, by not building the product correctly first time, by iterating two or three times before they get it right? It must be a good 80 to 90 per cent.'**
>
> *Warwick Hill – General Partner at Supercapital Partners LLP and CEO of Electricboxx.com*

The three most common challenges for founders are cash, cash flow and time. Whether you get investment or not, you will have a finite amount of money to play with. Cash flow will tend to move in one direction – outbound – and it may feel as though you haven't got time to keep up with the simple things like cooking a meal, washing the dishes or taking the dog for a walk.

Time and money are precious, and you have to be careful how you spend yours. Building the product yourself is going to take time, while outsourcing will seriously eat into your cash reserves. Outsourcing can also be risky.

(NB: if you're focus is *not* on tech, please feel free to skip the rest of this chapter.)

## Don't Become Part of an Outsourcing Horror Story!

If you've got a superb idea to build something that's streets ahead of anything else on the market, you are sitting on some very valuable intellectual property. The last thing you want is to have any of the unique features that you have thought of being leaked to your competitors or, worse still, being built for them. What are you going to do?

### Protecting Yourself From IP Theft

Most of the code you need won't be unique or cutting-edge. You just want it to be neat, tidy and functional. If you are not technical, think of coding as building a home; every house is unique, but they are built from the same materials. If you've seen one doorway, you've seen a thousand, although every door will be slightly different. The same applies to the other fittings and fixtures, and so it is with coding.

You can buy a lot of the code you need 'off the shelf'. Only outsource what you have to and, even then, if you are paranoid about an unscrupulous individual selling the code to the highest bidder, don't outsource the most sensitive part. Use your trusted, well-paid, carefully hired in-house talent for that.

### Out of Your Hands Means Out of Your Control

Anyone you hire in the UK or the US is going to be pricey, so it's sometimes tempting to outsource to a company based somewhere overseas, where you can enjoy a meal at a Michelin three-star restaurant, consume half the stock in the bar, and get a taxi back to your apartment all for less than a fiver – and if you're still broke, you can sell your kidney for a couple of thousand pounds.

If you are outsourcing to another country, forget everything you know about British law and assume that you have no IP protection whatsoever. Non-disclosure agreements (NDAs) are worthless, and remember that in any country, its laws are only as useful as their enforcement. No enforcement means no law. It's that simple, so don't outsource the bit that makes your startup so special.

### NDA Fuckups

CAD design software company SolidWorks thought it had covered all bases when it asked the employees of the Indian company it was hiring to debug its source code to sign non-disclosure agreements. What no one at the company realised until it was too late was that they had no legal relationship with those staff members and the agreement should have been signed between the Indian company and its employers.

A disgruntled employee stole a copy of the code and tried to sell it to a competitor of SolidWorks. The suspect was arrested by Indian police when he allegedly attempted to sell the code to an undercover FBI agent from Boston, Nenette Day. The problem, according to Day, was that the NDAs 'weren't worth the paper they were written on', and for them to have any teeth at all, 'the employees would have had to sign the agreement with the Indian company, not the American one.'

Even though the code thief had been caught red-handed, prosecutors in India were unable to convict him, and he continued working in the industry. The code in question was worth $300 million.

## 'Fork Handles?'

Other problems that can arise with outsourcing overseas are time zone differences and communication issues. They could be the most technically gifted people in the world but if they don't understand what you want them to do, and you don't understand them, you're going to run into difficulties. Communication becomes even more tricky when you only have a small window of opportunity for a real-time chat at stupid-o-clock in the morning. A lot can go wrong in twenty-four hours.

Two of our most well-loved comic geniuses, Ronnie Barker and Ronnie Corbett, hilariously illustrated how communication can fail in a sketch that has had people in stitches since the seventies and will never go stale. Barker plays the part of a customer on the lookout for a list of odds and ends, and he walks into Corbett's old-fashioned 'ironmongery shop' that sells almost anything you can imagine, which, incidentally, was based on a real shop that had been trading since the 1700s. I kid you not.

'Fork handles?' asks Barker.

'Four candles,' Corbett confirms, 'Yes, sir,' and off he goes to get four candles from a drawer. 'There you are,' he says as he places them on the counter.

'No,' Barker says. 'Fork handles!'

'Four candles. That's four candles,' protests Corbett, sounding slightly confused.

'No. Fork handles; handles for forks,' adds Barker for clarity. Unfortunately, things go from bad to worse for Corbett as every single item on Barker's list can mean one thing or something entirely different. Next time you take time out, go look up that sketch. You won't regret it. That script was conjured up by a pair of comedians, but sometimes reality is funnier than fiction. This is a real tweet that I found on the internet:

> 'At 8, I ordered my entrée and the waiter asked if I wanted Super Salad. I said yes. He said Super Salad? Yes! He then asked Salad or Soup. Ohhhhh.'
>
> *Tweeted by an anonymous Twitter user*

There are some things that you can't make up. Clarity is everything.

## How the State of Florida Fucked Up Its Outsourcing

The State of Florida ran into problems when it hired the services of Convergys Corporation to work on its People First payroll and human resource system at the beginning of the new millennium. The nature of the project meant that Convergys was being trusted with highly sensitive employee information. That didn't stop them from subcontracting the indexing to GDXdata, and it didn't stop GDXdata from improperly outsourcing to a development team in India, potentially creating the perfect storm of data breaches.

GDXdata had been forbidden from outsourcing work offshore but did it anyway, and Convergys only found out when two former employees of GDXdata filed a 'whistleblowing' lawsuit against their old bosses and court documents were made public. Convergys put out a statement at the time, saying they'd been misled by GDXdata, and they cancelled their contract with them.

Although Florida's Department of Management Services (DMS), which was overseeing the People First system, reported that no known cases of credit card fraud or identity fraud had occurred, they admitted that the breach had affected up to 108,000 people who were working for or had worked for the State of Florida.

That's a fuckup that no company wants to be responsible for, so if you're handling sensitive information, keep the process as simple and as tight as you can, so you know exactly who has access to what. What kind of data are you dealing with? Data always needs to be protected, but some information is particularly delicate. Remember Ashley Madison, the dating site for people looking for extra-marital affairs?

The international community of cheaters were crapping themselves for months, and possibly still are, as they wondered whether Stavros from Transylvania was going to send them an email threatening to tell Sandra about Michelle, Antonio about Eduardo, Abdul about Sajad, Philip about

Brian, and Christina about Ted, John, Paulo and . . . Helena! 'You have twenty-eight days to place a Bitcoin in this wallet!' Protect your data as fiercely as you protect your code.

Sometimes the issue isn't the risk of data leaks but sloppy work. I found that out the hard way.

## Don't be Naive! Check, Check and Check Again!

When we were building Stakester, we didn't have the in-house skills to make the product, so I went through a process to find someone or an organisation that did, and I used LinkedIn and other platforms to ask for recommendations. I identified a few that I believed could do what we needed and narrowed the list down to three, then two, and finally, to the company that I hired.

The first problem was that we were small fry for a company that was dealing with much bigger fish, so we were way down on their list of priorities, and they passed our work to their least talented and least experienced resources to deal with. The second problem was that I didn't have enough knowledge or expertise or experience to accurately judge the quality of the work they were doing for us – how long it should take, how much it should cost, how robust it was, etc. When they told us it was good quality work, I assumed it was good quality work.

As time went on, deadlines were slipping; they were saying it was going to take extra hours and people, and we were being asked to dip our hands deeper into our not-so-deep pockets. Eventually, something wasn't sitting right with us, so we hired someone to review the work, and that's when our fears were confirmed. We'd been taken for a ride, and they'd played us for months. There are a couple of lessons here.

### Check it out. Don't assume.

Even when you go through a solid and robust process to find the best candidate to outsource work to, you might still end up with a raw deal. Don't assume that because you've shown due diligence in the hiring process or because you are spending a lot of money with a large and reputable company, you're going to get what you paid for.

**Know the difference between the good, the bad and the ugly, or hire someone who does!**
Secondly, if you don't have the skills to tell the difference between high-quality work, mediocre work and outright shit, don't leave it to chance. Ask for help. There'll be someone in your network who's qualified and experienced enough to know. For the price you'll pay for them to spend a couple of days reviewing the stuff you've paid for, it's worth it. Don't let yourself throw money at the wall for months on end as we did.

### Who Owns the Key to Your Code?

Developers have been known to withhold access to code for spurious reasons, effectively holding their clients to ransom. You can avoid this pitfall by agreeing to pay on delivery after full access has been granted.

### The Devil's in the Detail

Don't let any of these horror stories put you off outsourcing. While you should consider money, cash flow and time, the one thing you must, absolutely must, do is move quickly and without cutting corners. Someone else could be working on the same idea, and outsourcing will save you a lot of time. Sure, there are risks – being ripped off, poor service, betrayal of trust, data breaches, IP theft, and even denial of access to your code – but there is plenty you can do to mitigate them, and most of it is not rocket science.

Nail stuff down before work commences. Ask a would-be supplier what precautions they are going to take to protect your idea and your data. Keep your IP in-house if you can. Check the quality of the work at the beginning and throughout the lifetime of the project. If you're not qualified, make sure you have someone who is. Oh, and if you're buying fork handles, write it down, present them with a diagram, do whatever you want, but make sure they know you want fork handles. Clarity is everything!

## Hold On! Does This Mean We Are Building?

Erm . . . No, not necessarily but kind of. Look, you've done loads of research, asked friends and family, business contacts, potential customers and your friend's pet chihuahua what they think of your idea. All the signs are there that you have something that people want and will pay for, so you have some proof of concept (POC), but wouldn't it be great to put your idea to the test and learn how to make it better at the same time?

Building is going to be costly however you look at it and regardless of whether or not you end up being part of an outsourcing horror story. Therefore, you should only build what you have to build at this stage, so you might consider an MVP.

> **'If you have got your community, these are most likely your first customers, so test whatever idea you've got with them and make them a part of the evolution of your product.'**
>
> *Sara Simeone – CEO and Founder of Digital Oracles*

## What's an MVP?

It's a minimum viable product. M. V. P. Does what it says on the tin, mate!

Okay, I will stop being a smart arse. What does that mean? What makes something viable, and what does 'minimal viable' mean in plain English?

Just to be clear, an MVP is not a half-done, unfinished or in any way sloppy product. It must be a complete piece of kit that you should feel comfortable giving or selling to a customer, and it should work in the way it is supposed to work and achieve the objective it is intended to achieve. It's a product, so it needs to be designed, built, tested and tweaked until it works every time all of the time. Let's look at the invention of the car as an example.
What are the essential features of a car?

- Does it need a sunroof? No.
- Electric windows? No.
- Radio? Behave.
- Heated seating? GET OUT OF HERE!
- Automatic transmission? Who said it had gears, mate? It goes. It stops.

For it to be a car, it needs three or four wheels, an engine to drive them, brakes, a steering mechanism, indicators, windscreen wipers, brake lights, headlights, reverse lights – you get the picture. On reflection, the essential stuff is what you need to pass an MOT test – that's a Ministry of Transport test of roadworthiness if you're not British, otherwise known as 'take a deep breath and hope you don't get robbed blind by an unscrupulous mechanic'.

Think about your product. How many features could you scrap before your thing stops being the thing it is supposed to be? A car is a motorised vehicle, and its purpose is to enable the user to get from A to B. Agreed? If we were to cut the number of wheels down to two, it would no longer be a car. It would be a bike.

## What Can We Learn From an MVP?

Once people are buying and enjoying your single-geared automobile, you can learn from your customers.

- 'Hey, this is great, but wouldn't it be lovely if we had an extra window above our heads to let the sunlight in?'
- 'It drives fine, but it revs so hard, I'm surprised the engine hasn't blown up. Is there any way you can make this quicker by giving it gears like my pushbike?'
- 'You know what this car needs? Music, that's what!'
- 'I don't know what it's like where you live, but I was shivering in that vehicle, Tom. How's it working? A combustion engine? Surely you can pump a little of the heat into the carriage?'

Every piece of feedback you get shows you a way to improve your product.

### Iterate, iterate, and iterate again!

You might come up with an idea of your own.

'All our vehicles are fitted with smart governors that make it impossible for you to go past the speed limit. When you exit a motorway, the onboard computer knows and reduces the vehicle's maximum speed accordingly. Not only does it make your car safer, but you also will never get a speeding ticket again!'

It seems like a great idea, but you find out that no one wants the feature, so you don't need to build it. Later, you learn that some people like the feature, so you install a button to give the driver the choice. On the other hand, you have acted on the comment about gears, and all your cars are made with five gears as standard. You get a great idea:

'We are going to make driving easier than ever. Our new vehicle still has five gears, but you will never have to change gears again. It's automatic.'

And so it goes, iteration after iteration, allowing your product to evolve into the best it can be.

## The Art of Building Without Building

Let's say you're still not sure whether your idea is viable, and you need a little more POC before you will risk building anything. We'll look at the car again. The car was different from a horse and cart because of the engine. If you were around when everyone wore top hats and tailcoats, carried walking sticks, got around by horse-drawn carriage, and discussions on how much horse shit was littering the streets was a thing, how would you obtain a POC for your yet-to-be-built automobile?

We've got to prove to Sherlock Holmes and Dr Watson that our new invention is better than their deluxe, chauffeur-ridden, horse-drawn 'sleuth mobile' and, more importantly, we want to be convinced that if we build a 'proper' one, they will buy it.

We could make a smaller version of the carriage, with front and rear windscreens, and instead of having it pulled by horses, it could be pushed by a couple of people to create the illusion that it is being driven by an engine. The only bit of additional technology the POC would require would be a basic steering mechanism to give Sherlock a feel for driving it, and even then, if push came to shove and we didn't want to build that tech, we could have another two guys using pulleys to turn the front wheels whenever Sherlock 'steers' the car one way or another.

This isn't quite an MVP unless you intended to sell something that would be pushed and steered by extra helpers, but it would give your customers a chance to visualise what you wanted to make for them.

I am guessing you want me to cut the bullshit and share some real examples. Thanks to Anthony Rose, I have a couple of absolute belters.

> **'Don't build anything until you've worked out that people really want it.'**
>
> *Anthony Rose – Founder of SeedLegals*

Anthony sees building stuff too soon as a failure. The goal is to get knowledge without building, and he asks founders to consider whether they can get more by doing less. You can outsource physical servers, use open-source software, and leave the building until after you've got some traction.

Before setting up SeedLegals, Anthony was the head of iPlayer at the BBC. They were competing against ITV, which had just launched a new pay-to-download service to keep up with the likes of Netflix. It cost them around £12 million to build the new service, but after eighteen months they realised that nobody was buying. What could ITV have done differently?

A better idea, according to Anthony, would have been to have built a button that would display the following message when pressed:

'Thanks for clicking this button. If enough people click on this, we are going to build the product.'

Had they done that, the lack of presses of the button would have told them everything they needed to know. No POC. Hmm . . . coulda, shoulda, woulda.

Okay, here's another, and it is a perfect demonstration of how to fake it to make it and another example of the art of building without building. Friends, Romans and countryfolk, have a seat and enjoy what follows.

When they were starting up, Anthony and his colleagues built a simple website, which was nothing more than an attractive front window. None of the back-end code had been installed, but it looked the part, and visitors were able to use an online form to provide all the details that the proposed software would need to process requests and generate the appropriate legal documents. This was a shiny, new motorcar without an engine.

For every set of customer data that was collected with the form, Anthony and his team had to go and process it manually and create the documentation by hand. They had created an MVP using only a fraction of the code they would need to build the full product. This fake set-up would be impractical and time-consuming in the long run, and impossible to scale, but it was sufficient to find out what customers thought of it and to learn how to make it better.

We've considered whether to build and what to build if we are going to build, and we have considered who should build it, but how much is it going to cost? How much is everything else going to cost? Whether we are looking for funding or bootstrapping, we still want to know how much money it's going to take, and that's what we're going to look at in the next chapter.

# 7.
# HOW MUCH MONEY AM I GONNA NEED?

If you think I'm going to give you a forensic breakdown on how to calculate your costs, you can forget it. I'm an entrepreneur on a good day, not a fucking accountant. Don't be naive. Make sure you have someone who understands the business of numbers or hire a professional to help you with the fine-tuning. I am not here to give you a paint-by-numbers guide to putting together a business plan either. You don't need one, no matter what they've told you at the Chamber of Commerce or that business networking event you attended at six o'clock this morning. I'm not an expert in anything, by the way; just another founder like you.

Am I suggesting that we throw planning and cost calculations out of the window? Not really, but you might want to leave the spreadsheets and number-crunching to someone qualified or enthusiastic about it. Besides, even if you wanted to do it, it's as boring as hell. Ask Mae Yip!

Look, you either want to build a profitable business that you and your co-founders are in total control of, which you can grow slowly and carefully and eventually sell, or you want to find backers to invest in you to help you grow as quickly as possible regardless of profit, so you can sell to a bigger fish that knows how to make the most from what you've built later on.

This chapter is about considering what you're going to need to spend on, recognising the worst-case scenario, and thinking about how you can save on expenditure, so you can focus on growth instead of panicking about making payroll.

## Start With the Basics

This may seem like common sense, but how powerful is your computer or laptop? Is it fit for purpose? Could you do with something faster? What antivirus are you using, and what's your plan B if it packs in? Have you ever thought about backing up your documents, or are you one of the millions that count on your machine starting up the next time you turn it on?

It's time to professionalise your approach. If your computer dies, it's no longer a case of having a moan and accepting that you have lost your most recently saved curriculum vitae, last year's holiday pics, and those naughty videos we won't talk about. That's fine for a home computer, but if you're using it for business, you have to be prepared for shit like the blue screen of death. You need to be able to carry on with minimum disruption. These things happen, and when they do, they can destroy your startup if you have not planned for them. I don't want to sound like an IT service provider, but you are backing up all your important files, aren't you? (Billy, blushing intensely, puts down his copy of *How Not to Fuck Up Your Startup* and types 'Cloud storage' into his browser's address bar. It's okay, Billy. We will pretend not to notice.)

Then there's software to think about. It's probably time to stop using the dodgy unlicensed stuff you got from Gary down the road, and think about switching to legitimate packages. Look on the bright side: it will work better, and you will be entitled to all the latest updates. It's worth investing in a suite of essential business software that will enable you and your team to work more efficiently.

## Dress to Impress?

What other things are you going to need? Will you be meeting lots of people? You should be. How will they expect you to present yourself – smart casual or well-heeled and dressed to kill? And looking fantastic doesn't have to mean splashing out on the most expensive brand names.

Okay, if you are selling a financial service and claiming to help your clients jump from seven to eight figures, and you turn up with a fifty-pound watch from the high street, they might not take you seriously (*if* they can tell the difference). If that's you, dare to be different and don't wear a watch, but most of us don't need a high-end timepiece that's going to set us back hundreds or thousands of pounds.

Are you going to be using your vehicle, or will you be travelling by public transport? How much are you going to need to spend on fuel or fares for all those networking events you can't wait to attend? Apply the same logic here as you would to how you dress. You don't need to invest in the latest prestige motor. I still drive a Hyundai i10, and I fucking love it. Sexy it is not, but efficient at getting me from A to B, sure; it does the job perfectly well, and my wife likes it. Remember what The Bard said about all that glisters not being gold. Appearances don't always match reality, and being a successful founder has nothing at all to do with posting crap on social media from a yacht in an exotic location or being filmed in a Bentley.

Provided you show people the respect they deserve by turning up on time, showing up fully, and presenting yourself professionally, they shouldn't care whether you bought your handmade shoes from Church's or you're wearing a factory-made, plastic-soled pair of beetle crushers from the local supermarket. They should be more interested in you and your investment proposition.

## It's Time to Tighten Your Belt

How much do you need to live? We've talked about this. If you want your startup to survive, you have to give it everything you've got, which you won't be able to do if you have a nine-to-five, processing data for Rogers and Spencer Financial Solutions in Barnsley, a fictional company that I made up on the spot with no intended link to any real financial organisation that exists or has existed, before you start looking for a lawyer, Messieurs Rogers and Spencer, whoever you are!

> 'I was quitting my job, I was putting my savings into doing the company and then, effectively, we, on day one, kind of had to start generating revenue to sustain ourselves. From very early on, we had to generate revenue to keep the lights on because there wasn't going to be any external investment, or certainly we never believed that there would be. If I didn't think there'd be people on the other side of that equation, I wouldn't have started the company.'
>
> *Eamonn Carey – Managing Director of Techstars*

Giving up a full-time job is harsh, I know, but your startup needs you. Can you survive on a part-time job, or can you make money doing something related to your startup? I'm sorry. I don't want to sound like either of your parents on your first day at university, but you need to look at how much it's costing you to get by each month. If necessary, you can probably pack in that cup of coffee from Expensivebucks, Costoomuch or Cafezerochangefromafiver. Buy one of those machines that make strange noises, and get a fucking flask for hot drinks on the move! Better still, cut down on your caffeine intake and drink green tea or water instead . . . with some of those brain nutritional supplements from Dan Murray's company, Heights. I take them and, believe me, they make a difference. **Disclaimer: I have not been paid to promote Dan's products.**

## Where Are You Gonna Work From?

Your front room-cum-office may have been enough until now, and it still will be for a little while, but if you are serious about building a startup, you're going to need people and, ideally, access to a place for you to work together. 'The world's changing,' I hear you say. 'The pandemic has shown us another way of working. Who needs offices when we can work from home?' You might be right. Society has undoubtedly glimpsed a new way of operating, but it's too early to kiss goodbye to offices, my friend.

For a start, not everyone wants to work from home. Terry, the introverted developer, might love nothing more than gluing himself to his gaming chair in the darkness of his den, the bedroom, staring into a screen the size of a small cinema and communing with his machine like a member of the fictional Borg species from *Star Trek*. Meanwhile, poor Frank is experiencing severe mental health difficulties and getting cabin fever because he's been stuck in the house for two days, and Charlene is missing the buzz and the banter of office life.

The working environment has changed significantly over the years, especially over the last decade, so it's important to think about an office space that will work for you and your team. You *will* need an office. And that's going to include spaces for your team to unwind and, when you can afford it, luxuries such as a full-sized pool table or similar recreational device.

> 'Did we do things that were optimised for success or for the wrong reasons? "Hey, if we find an office space out in, you know, NW73, we will save £85 a month on office space." Great, but VCs aren't going to visit you there.'
>
> *Anthony Rose – Founder of SeedLegals*

Offices can be costly. There are three main things you need to think about. Location, location and location. Why? Because you have to assess how easy it is for you and your team to get there, how easy it is for you to get to other places from your office, and even more importantly, you must make sure you are making it as easy as possible for others, especially clients, not to mention VCs, to come to you.

How big do you think your office needs to be? Whatever you've got in mind, double it, double it again, and probably again. How many people do you think you're going to employ? You might not have them now, and you probably don't have the money to take them on, but if you're going to go down the investment path, you have to think growth, growth and more growth, and it has to be fast. What about IT infrastructure? It's too late to think about these things after you've signed a three-year lease!

## Fuck Profit! It's Gonna Be About Growth

Every single penny you plough into the business, whether it's your money, financial support from friends and family, or cash from your investors, has to work for you. It must contribute towards growing the company. On Investment Avenue, growth is more important than profit. Look at any big tech company you want, and you will find that most of them were running at a loss for years.

Twitter launched in 2006, and by 2012, the platform was being used by more than 100 million users, who were posting 340 million tweets a day, and it was handling an average of 1.6 billion search queries a day, but guess what? According to reports in the *Guardian* at the time, Twitter didn't record its first profitable quarter until the end of 2017, after managing to reduce its annual loss from $457m in 2016 to $108m through a strategy of rigorous cost-cutting.

Notably, the tech company's share value immediately grew by 20 per cent. Growth: that's the love potion, not profit. If you had shares in Twitter, and you suddenly saw their value rise by 20 per cent, would you give a fuck whether the business was profitable or not? You might even be able to afford a proper coffee at MegaBucks.

Let's look at Facebook. It launched in 2004, but when it IPO'd in May 2012, its most recent earnings report had shown a loss of $59 million against total revenues of $1.26 billion, according to *The Atlantic* at the time.

Yes, it was losing tons of money, even after eight years of trading, but its revenue was up 36 per cent on the previous year. Growth, my friends.

Finally, just to drill down the point, we'll consider Uber. Having launched in 2009, the mobility-as-a-service provider recorded its first profitable quarter in 2021, as reported by *Reuters*. They posted EBITDA earnings of $8 million for the quarter ending 30 September, compared to a thunderous loss of $625 million for the same quarter twelve months earlier. Along the way, according to a report by *CBS News*, they managed to record a heart-stopping loss of $5.2 billion in the second quarter of 2019, the company's biggest loss ever. That would be enough to make anyone choke on their banana! 'Honey, cancel that trip to the Bahamas. We're off to Butlins.'

## You're Gonna Need the Best People

We'll be considering recruitment strategies in more detail later, but for now, just know that you will need to hire the most qualified, experienced and skilled technicians that you can find. You need to build a team of staff who are dedicated to your project, not freelancers. You want to attract the best talent and keep them in-house. Freelancers are a turn-off for investors.

> **'Once you have these great computer scientists, great product managers and great marketers, they then attract other people around them into their orbit.'**
>
> *Rob Kniaz – Partner at Hoxton Ventures*

You have an idea, and it's going to cost shitloads of money to build it, but don't cut any corners. If you are going to go for it, you need to give it your best shot. Every pound you spend increases the size of your risk, but by spending it well, you push the odds in your favour. Yes, I know I mentioned off-the-shelf software in the last chapter, but that's more of a reason to make sure that the process is overseen by the most technically gifted developers you can attract.

You have to think about how much money you're going to need, so don't account for a half-arsed effort, even if you're operating on a budget. Imagine there's going to be no shortage of dollars and you're going for gold. It is better to overestimate how much you'll need than to run out of money later.

## Don't Attempt to Eat the Whole Pizza With One Bite

I haven't lost the plot. I'm being metaphorical. No one in their right mind would try to stuff a whole pizza in their mouth in one go. And yet, that is exactly what a lot of founders try to do with their startups.

> **'Dude, there's no way you're gonna build all this shit. You're gonna run out of money first.'**
>
> *Anthony Rose – Founder of SeedLegals*

Let's say you've come up with a smart app that intuitively knows what dishes will grab your attention when you walk into a restaurant. It listens to your conversations, pays attention to every word you type, and every Google search, and effectively stalks you for the sole purpose of knowing what you love to eat. Or maybe it just mines that information from a well-known social media app that's already monitoring your every micromovement. Wow! It sounds scary as fuck, I know, but humour me for a few minutes.

As you stroll into Eddie's Steak House, you don't even need a menu. You sit down, tell your smartphone to open 'Chef's Recommendation', and you are presented with every meal available, listed according to how well it matches your gustatory preferences. That's a fucking great idea, actually. I wonder if anyone will take the ball and run with it.

But you want to build on it. You decide you want users to be able to order their food through the app to help it better understand their food preferences. Oh, and while you're at it, it will record how many calories they're going to load up with, what the nutritional values are, and it gives a colour-code health rating based on their age, lifestyle and medical history. And so it goes. Use your imagination. We could go on forever adding features until it's calculating what time you're going to need a taxi and ordering one for you ten minutes before you leave the restaurant.

There's nothing wrong with letting your mind wander and exploring all the possibilities, but it is better to take things one step at a time. Split your big project into small bite-sized chunks. Anthony Rose advises founders to think about growth in terms of stepping stones and to stagger their investment rounds accordingly.

### Stepping Stones

The first phase of development for Chef's Recommendation would be to build an app that fulfils its primary purpose, which recommends the most appropriate dishes from the menu of wherever the user has gone to eat. The next phase might be to add the healthy-eating functions, and so on. Focus on your key driver. If it's a business-consumer app, focus on that. Later, there may be an opportunity for business-to-business – think of all the data you're collecting – but you don't need to think about that when you're trying to get your startup off the ground.

As Rose puts it, you promise to deliver 'thing one', which may be something boring (as far as you're concerned), show how that will lead to 'thing two' and how 'thing two' will take you closer to 'thing three' where it begins getting much more exciting. When you build it this way, in a more structured manner, you have more control over the growth of your business, you can adapt quickly to changes in the situation – events that could lead you to change course – and you also show potential investors that you know where you're going, but you're not running at it like a kid in a sweetshop.

## Hidden Costs

Try to think of everything, and don't forget those hidden, hard-to-spot issues that can seriously fuck up your plans and eat your money. Take release cycles, for example. Until you start building, you don't know how long it is going to take. Scrum methodology will get you so far and make the process more efficient but the more innovative your idea, the more you are dealing with unknown variables.

### Original Tech Puzzles

If you're a coder, you don't need me to tell you what a monumental pain in the arse it is when the software doesn't do what you want it to do. It should work, you can't see anything wrong with it, and yet it is doing something so strange that you are totally mindfucked as to the cause of the problem. Even the mildest mannered programming Zen ninja can start screaming at their screen, trying to pull out the hair that would be there if they weren't already bald, and coming out with original expletives any hardcore shock jock DJ would be proud of – 'Youuuuu fucking, soup-slurping, twatty WOBBLE BOTTOM!'

'You need some air, Derek?'

'Fuck you, too, you big turnip!'

'OK, I'm just going . . . to go . . . over here . . . ' [slowly retreating from the situation]

'Good idea, pumpkin head.' [giving 'pumpkin head' the finger without taking his eyes off the screen]

If your relationship survives that kind of stress, you will, one day, laugh at such cortisol-charged outbursts. 'Did you really call me a "turnip" and a "pumpkin head"?' Don't forget what's been said about co-founding with your best mate or even romantic partner. 'Wobble bottom' can be a relationship killer. Also, what happens in the office needs to only happen in the office and stay in the office. Never – no, seriously, I mean it – ever have such outbursts in front of clients. 'She's so passionate about her work' or 'He's not neurotypical' are not going to cut the mustard.

## Bugs, Bugs and More Bugs

Then, you finally get it to work, and it is doing what it's supposed to do, plus a bunch of other crazy shit that you never asked for. Yes, you've created the buggy version, and now you've got to iron out loads of weird and wonderful quirks that appear to have been created just to fuck you off. You're wondering when someone with a hidden camera's going to show up and admit that they've pranked you. And all the while, you're running out of runway. Yes, just as Anthony Rose warned, 'dude, you're gonna run out of money.'

## It's Adding Up, Isn't It?

Already, we can see how the costs start to add up – IT equipment, the office, people, networking expenses such as travel, clothing, entrance fees and refreshments – even before you have compiled a single piece of code. Add in the unknown expenses that will come with trying to build something that works, and you can already see that the short answer to the question of how much money you're going to need is 'fucking loads, mate'.

You're also trying to be as efficient as you can, or you should be, so you don't want to hire in people that you're not going to use – more reason why you should be thinking about breaking down your long-term plan into smaller, more realistic, achievable phases – and you definitely don't want to pay huge rent on a massive office for three people. Yes, I know that flies in the face of what I said about imagining what you think you need, doubling it and doubling it again. There lies the rub. You have to account for the worst scenario, but that doesn't mean diving into unnecessary expenditure head-first.

I wish I could tell you that's all you need to account for, but there's more. What about your marketing costs? We'll be considering the myriad of ways you can market your product without having to sell the house and your family of Alaskan Malamutes.

### How Long's It Gonna Take to Get Customers

This is a key question because the longer it takes to bring in the bacon, the longer you are going to be haemorrhaging moola and not replacing it with anything – running out of dough, my friend. Not being profitable is one thing, but having no money to pay for the things you need means the end of the line.

How long it is going to take to win business will depend on the product and whom you're selling it to. If you are building an enterprise product for banks and other large financial institutions, you can expect the process to take years rather than months, from the first effective contact with a decision-maker to seeing your product purchased and implemented. Looking to sell your technology to a mobile provider? It takes eighteen months to embed it in their network, and that's once you've sold them the solution, according to Warwick Hill.

Warwick points out that most startups don't have a clue what they are getting into when they try to sell to enterprise-sized organisations – there will be security protocols, not to mention the vigour and scope of work to integrate their software, and the issue of legacy software.

> **'You have to be able to show the product is useful, will work, will add value and is deployable.'**
>
> *Warwick Hill – General Partner at Supercapital Partners LLP*

Put yourself in the shoes of a procurement manager. You're tasked with paying for tech that will make the organisation more efficient, improve capabilities, or increase its profitability. If you can do that without too much aggravation, they're going to be interested because it will make them look good. That's what they're paid for. However, if you sell them something that still needs tweaking or doesn't do what it's supposed to do, or if something goes wrong during the onboarding process, what do think you is going to happen to them?

There's no way they are going to risk letting your fuckup fuck up their career prospects. Now, with that in mind, imagine what kind of questions they might ask you, and know the answers to these questions and as many others you can think of as possible. As Warwick Hill would say, they are not there to provide free proof of concept. If you're going to sell to them, you'd better have done your homework and be prepared for the long haul.

## It's Gonna Cost a Fucking Fortune, So What Now?

You're going to need more money than you had first thought? Brilliant. That's a result because it's better that you know that now. Investors don't expect you to be word-perfect superheroes. A lot of them have been there, remember, especially angels. But there's a point when not knowing your shit stops being endearing and pleasantly naive and becomes coughs-on-a-mouthful-of-doughnut absurd, so it's far better to overestimate how much money you're going to need than fall far short. Think big, think structurally, and think thoroughly. No one's going to laugh at you for not knowing the unknowable, but they will expect you to try to factor in the unknown variables credibly.

## Still Thinking About Bootstrapping?

If you're still thinking about bootstrapping at this point, well done. You must have a solid game plan and a very comprehensive set of skills and talents. From here on in, we're going down Investment Avenue, and you're welcome to join us for the ride. We will also be looking at how to successfully exit, so you might want to hang about.

## I'm Gonna Need Some Help

You've done the maths, and you've realised you're going to need a lot more money than you can beg and borrow from your mates, your family, and the local vicar, and you have enough self-awareness to know that bootstrapping's not for you. What now?

I'd like to say, 'Go get 'em, Roger', but that would be unfair. I've been there, and I have learnt the hard way, so hopefully I can save you from a few of the fuckups I made. Enjoy the ride.

# 8.
# LEARNING THE HARD WAY

By now, if you've been keeping up and paying attention, the idea that was hastily scribbled out on a napkin or recorded as a voice note as you sat in the car park of a motorway service station on the M1 (a great time for conjuring up new concepts, by the way) has evolved into a fully fleshed-out plan. You've got the right team together to help you take things forward, and you've figured out how much it's going to cost.

Great! You haven't felt happier and more satisfied with yourself since the time you won the 100m sprint on your high-school sports day. The only problem is, you can't raise more than a few thousand pounds, even if you sell the motor, the sofas, the flat-screen home cinema and the pet dog. So, what are you going to do?

## Where's The Money Gonna Come From?

I'm willing to stake a three-course meal at the Ritz that you've been considering how to raise funds from investors. You may have already spoken to a couple of banks, and you will have got the same kind of offer most startups can look forward to – a current account with no fees for the first year and, if you're lucky, an overdraft facility of a few hundred quid, maybe even a grand.

Did you apply for a loan? Even if a bank is willing to put faith in you, you'd be unlikely to get more than a few thousand pounds, and you'd be expected to pay it back – with interest – within the first year. If you haven't been down this road yet, I appreciate it doesn't sound like fun, and it isn't. For those who have, it's fair to say they want to find investors.

In 2019, having never pitched to an investor before, I went out to the market to raise money for my three-month-old company, Stakester.

Launching a startup can feel intoxicating. For maybe the first time in your life, you are in complete control of your destiny. Inspiration fuels you like a performance-enhancing drug, and you scribble down ideas faster than an actor playing a genius in a biopic. You are the hero of your own story, and you're going to slay that age-old nemesis, mediocrity.

I felt incredible, high on my entrepreneurial vision and a dream of running through an open-plan hipster office, high-fiving scores of beaming employees. It was easy for me to feel so optimistic because not only did I have a great idea, but I was fortunate enough to be able to fund the very early stages from my savings, and I didn't need to draw a salary straight away. That's not the case for a lot of founders, so I appreciate how blessed I was.

Things were rosy until, like every other person with a great idea, I crunched some numbers. The sums didn't add up, and I felt as heartbroken as any *X-Factor* contestant who has ever heard that they didn't make it to the live shows. I had a little cash in the bank but nothing like enough to make it happen, so to get the company off the ground, I was going to need some external investment – money – and way more than I could hope to get as a bank loan or from friends and family.

## Calling on Angels

One way of getting the kind of investment I needed was to embark on what is technically known as an 'angel round at ideation stage',[5] which is a bit of a mouthful. The more commonly used expression is 'pre-seed' which, in investment terms, is the earliest of the early.

Going for an angel round would mean crafting a pitch deck, hunting down investors and throwing out one pitch after another. It was going to take a lot of work, and it wouldn't be plain sailing, but if I was going to get the cash I needed, this was the route to take, so I rolled up my sleeves.

For the first round, I called on about one hundred different investors, presenting to some of them three or four times. It amounted to around two hundred pitches in total, tapping through the same deck, spinning the same story, and selling the same vision. I repeated myself so often

[5] An angel round at *ideation stage*, also known as pre-seed, is the earliest possible opportunity to raise capital from private investors.

that I started to dream my pitch, slide by slide, line by line, and noticed my mind drifting away in meetings even while my mouth rattled on word-perfectly. I felt like an actor in a long-running West End show, except there were no curtain calls and there was no applause – because nearly all those pitches ended with the words 'Thanks, but no'.

It was a full-time job, being rejected, and it hurt as much as I'd imagine being smashed in the face with Conor McGregor's left fist would. Now, I'm good at pitching, or as Jay-Z might put it, 'I've got 99 problems, and a pitch ain't one.' I have taught people and companies around the world how to do it and won global pitching competitions; however, pitching is much like cooking, and just because you know how to bake a cake, that doesn't mean you can cook a roast, and that's where I was going wrong. Although I was used to pitching products to companies, I was inexperienced when it came to speaking to investors, and I made mistakes, lots of mistakes, the kind that cost time and money – time and money that I was running short of.

The low point came a few months in when I was rejected by my top three preferred investors at the final stage, all on the same day. Utterly sapped, I retreated to a dingy coffee shop, finding myself mindlessly sipping the cold dregs of my third cup as I brooded on how to tell my family and co-founders that the jig was up. The dream I had sold them, the vision I had conjured up, the concept that I had risked everything to back was finished. It was all over.

It was two weeks before the bills were going to be due, and I would have to pay people with money I didn't have. Before I could summon up the nerve to make those calls and explain the situation, I dialled my mentor, who told me to retreat to the gym, sweat out the tears and get some focus. He was right. I hit those machines like a madman, and after punishing my cardio-vascular system till my entire body screamed, I crashed into a broken heap on the changing-room bench.

## A Second Wind and a Fresh Approach

As my mentor had predicted, the effort stiffened my resolve, and I decided not to give up straight away but to give it one more week. 'The definition of insanity is doing the same thing over and over again and expecting different results', is a famous witticism, usually attributed to one of the world's most well-loved geniuses, Albert Einstein. I don't know who said it, but it's true . . . most of the time – you have to give an approach a chance to work before scrapping it, and nobody could say I hadn't done that.

It had taken me a couple of hundred attempts to realise I had to change my approach. With a clear head, I asked myself a few tough questions and got back to my laptop. I tweaked the deck a little, changed the wording of my covering email, and spent two solid days smashing emails out.

The simple changes I made had an immediate effect. Some replies came in straight away, and a couple of days later I received an offer; not for the full amount but enough to regain some momentum and keep the Stakester show on the road.

In the end, it took nine months to get to $650k on that round, but I remembered the lessons I'd learned – those changes that I had made to the email, to the pitch deck and my attitude – and when I put them into action, later on, it took me just two weeks to secure over $3 million in our second raise.

## Lessons Learned?

In the next chapter, I'm going to tell you exactly why my previous attempts at fundraising had failed and what I did differently to turn things around. Yes, it's time to discover how not to fuck up your pitch!

# 9.
# THE GAME-CHANGER

In the last chapter, you discovered that even with rock-solid effort, determination, resilience and hard graft, you can still end up in a grim cafe, with your head down, staring at an Americano, wondering where it all went wrong. It doesn't have to be that way.

I'm going to share the changes that made the difference, to save you from experiencing your equivalent of the nightmare that I endured in the coffee shop. You will also get to learn from the host of savvy investors and founders who shared their hard-won fundraising wisdom with me when I interviewed them for my podcast.

To get the most from this, you must be ready because I'm going to assume that:

- You have a promising idea
- You have an effective team
- You have thoroughly thought through the problem that you are solving
- There is a market for you to tap into
- You are willing to work your socks off

If you've got any lingering doubts about any of these five points, you need to do a little homework now, so go back over the last three chapters of this book, ask yourself a few difficult questions, and get yourself pitch-ready.

## What I Discovered After My Third Coffee

What was the simple change that I had made to the pitch that turned our fortunes around? What had I done to my emails, my pitch deck and my patter that made everything fall into place – in less time than it has taken me to type this sentence? What was the tweak, why was it so easy to implement, and why was it so effective?

If this were a Hollywood blockbuster, I would not tell you, here in Chapter 9; I would tease you for a few more chapters, building up the suspense, making sure you were sitting keenly on the edge of your seat and increasingly impatient until all these ingredients reached a critical mass. Only then would I deliver the big reveal, everything you thought you knew about the story would be turned on its head, and you and the rest of the audience would gasp as one . . .

An amusing thought but not fair on you, my reader. You're not here to have your emotions played with. You are here to get your startup running with the minimum amount of messing around, so here it is, in two bullet points:

- I started by spelling out how amazing our product was, how big the market for it was, how quickly we could build it and how scalable it would be. Those things were all true, but the approach was unsuccessful.
- I pivoted to selling the company, by emphasising how amazing the team was, how well we understood our product and our market, and how ready we were to grow. All of this was true, and the approach was successful.

If that's two bullets too many for you, the impatient startup founder, here it is in one:

# DON'T PITCH YOUR PRODUCT. PITCH THE INVESTMENT OPPORTUNITY!

(Just to make absolutely sure that we're on the same page)

That's it, and it is that simple, but let's look at what that means in practice.

## Roadmap

Create a killer pitch deck
Perfect your profile
Network like crazy
Research your leads
Send out the deck
Follow up
Pitch meeting

# BE READY
# BE PATIENT

Give this useful rule of thumb a try: Think about how long it's going to take you to raise the money.

Now double it!

From the first pitch to the last contract, our pre-seed round took nine months – the perfect period to bake a baby but way, way longer than we wanted. Fundraising doesn't happen overnight. Building a profile, finding investors, speaking to them, answering their questions, updating your deck, and re-engaging with ones who have gone quiet, all take a ton of time. It's slow, frustrating, repetitive and eye-wateringly hard. Startups are like dogs; they age differently from the rest of us so, in startup time, that round took something like ten thousand years.

You would think the hardest thing about the pre-seed process is dealing with rejection, but it isn't – it's the slow pace of progress. When I started, I thought I could close it out in two months. I had seen other founders' seed rounds and series A rounds go from pitch to term sheet that quickly many times, but there are lots of reasons for people to be slow. It could be the summer holidays; it could be coming up to bonus season, and they want to wait; it could be that they have other jobs and commitments; it could be that they are waiting to see how their other investments perform; or they may be testing you subconsciously to see if you survive. In the end, the reasons don't matter. The fact is, they don't have the same time pressures that you do, so they won't work as fast. You are expected to move mountains within seconds, your investors take months to move pebbles, and that's just the way it is.

It's better to play the long game. That way, you will be delighted if it's quick, and you won't become another 'failed due to cash issues' statistic. Ensure everything under your control runs as fast as possible. Simple things, such as responding quickly to emails, or being available for meetings, cost nothing but can make a significant difference. Treat the process as part of your job and allocate structured time to it with specific goals, making sure you take full ownership of the trivial tasks and pay as much attention to them as you do for everything else.

## Manage Your Expectations

Those nine months were brutal, as the whole team was put through the agonies of chronic uncertainty and heartache. Expect it, learn to handle it, and keep each other sane. If you retain focus, maintain diligence, keep outreach activity high, take feedback often and refine your pitch accordingly, you will win, and those conversations that have thus far begun with the words 'Wouldn't it be cool if' will open with 'Wasn't it cool when'.

## Manage Your Time

Raising money is time-consuming, physically, and all-consuming, cognitively, and all the time that you're chasing funds, you're not running the company. You need to improve your efficiency, or you are going to ruin all the hard work that you put into making something incredible.

Don't take your eye off the ball. Consilience Ventures, a new early-stage fund in London, reached out to a large sample of founders and analysed how they were using their time. They discovered that the typical founder could spend up to 60 per cent of their time on fundraising, which only leaves 40 per cent for running their business. Your startup cannot afford for you to be dedicating only two days a week to it. There's a reason you're the captain of the ship, and if you're not at the helm, no amount of money is going to get you out of those stormy waters. And yet fundraising needs doing, doesn't it?

So, what's the solution?

Don't do anything that doesn't require your specific knowledge and skill. Doing it all yourself is a false economy. Your time is precious, and your company needs your focus. Therefore, the objective is to delegate, automate, prefabricate or outsource every task that doesn't specifically need your attention.

Make a list of all the activities that need to be done for a round: making the deck, finding investors, writing follow-ups, producing and providing due-diligence information, and so on. That's the easy part. The more difficult step is addressing each item and asking yourself whether another member of the team could be doing it instead of you. Don't be a control freak! If you have the shit-hot, world-beating team that you claim to have assembled, someone will be able to help you out. If you don't feel that's possible, something's not right; either your team isn't as talented as you think, or you have self-destructive trust issues.

Delegate appropriately and share the load and remember that if you're having trouble delegating at this stage, you'd better watch out; it will only get worse when your company is growing like crazy, so learn how to hand off work, fast.

Some things *do* need you. These include:

- **Pitch meetings** – If a founder isn't at the pitch, it raises questions, and the chances of raising cash are significantly reduced. Make sure you are there.
- **Pitch deck content** – This is your company and your vision, so you need to own the deck. Get people to check it, and get designers to make it look amazing, but remember that the core is yours.

Some things *don't* need you. These include:

- **Everything else** – You, the founder, don't need to be managing the email list. You don't need to be scraping websites for contact names. You don't need to be searching LinkedIn. You don't need to be picking fonts, formatting PDFs, or booking the photographer . . . you get the picture.

Give reliable people a clear brief, be available to answer their questions, and they will surprise you with the results; and because they will be dedicated to the problem at hand – rather than multi-tasking, which you would have been – they will be faster, more focused and more productive.

Getting these things right will help to ensure that stay on the road to victory, but there's still plenty that can go wrong, starting with the pitch deck. There are a hundred and one ways to fuck up a pitch deck, so in the next chapter you're going to find out how to avoid the pitfalls.

# 10.
# DON'T FUCK UP YOUR PITCH DECK

Putting all other factors aside, your pitch deck can make or break your chances of winning investment. If you fuck it up, you're not even going to get a phone call, never mind a face-to-face, so let's look at how to get it right. Your startup is counting on you.

The best decks are simple, straight to the point and (you remember what I told you in the last chapter, right?) tell a story that's not about the product but the company – in other words, the people. Of course, that story must feature the product and has to be brilliantly presented, but don't forget that people are at the heart of it.

## Investors ≠ Customers

For 99 per cent of pitches, your investor isn't the same person as your customer, so they won't necessarily understand the problem that your product solves, and they almost certainly won't understand your market.

Consequently, investors – at this point – don't care about the intricacies of how your product works, and they don't care about its features or how cool it looks. What they want to know is that your product is better than everyone else's, that you have an unfair advantage, and that you will outperform your peers and be fantastically massive, which will give them a huge return on their investment. What does that mean in practice?

## What Points Does the Pitch Deck Need to Prove?

### You're in a Massive Market

The size of the market that you're selling into is critical. Creating a new market is incredibly hard. That doesn't mean it can't be done, but it's tough. Therefore, it's much easier for an investor to put money into something that will be part of an already massive market because there is space for you. Having a small piece of an enormous pie is more likely than having a gigantic piece of a tiny pie.

A great example of this is Peloton, a global manufacturer of bikes, which currently only has about six per cent of its market. For those who invested in the early stages of Peloton's development, I'd say the company's proved itself to be a shrewd bet. If you want people to invest in your startup, show there is a huge market and that you have found a gap and a way to exploit it.

A huge market can look daunting from the outside but like many other challenges, once you've taken the plunge, you will wonder what took you so long.

> 'Find a very big ocean to surf in because you might be a really shitty surfer, but if you catch a big wave, you're going to have a great ride. If you're in a small ocean, it doesn't matter how good a surfer you are, the waves are all a foot tall, and you're going to have a shitty surf.'
>
> *Rob Kniaz – Partner at Hoxton Ventures*

### This Works at Scale

Startup investors are not interested in something becoming two, three or four times more valuable. Surprisingly, they're probably not that interested in you moving to profitability, either. They care about building the value of your business to the point where it will either float or get acquired for at least ten times the value they invested at. This kind of growth is a product of scalability, so you must articulate that your business *can* scale effectively – *if* your investors put in the money.

### You Move Fast

Investors will always be attracted to pace. Of course, some investors are in things for the long run, and they want to invest for ten years, but most venture investors want to see a return within three to five years; so, your vision of scalability and huge growth must fit in that timeframe.

### This Isn't a Fair Fight

Investors get pitched a lot, and most of the pitches they see are quite clever ideas. What's more, and I hate to break it to you, other people have almost certainly had your idea before. It's even worse if you are in a big market, where there are probably lots of other companies aiming to exploit the same gap as you are. To attract a savvy investor, you must show them that you've got an unfair advantage; whether it's a different distribution channel, a rockstar team or a fantastic network, it's the secret sauce that makes you more likely to win the race.

**Top Tip – Know Your Market Inside Out**

This might sound like common sense, and you may think you have it sussed, but here's what seasoned investor Warwick Hill had to say on the matter:

*'The sad fact that I have seen is a lot of people start companies thinking that they have understood what the problem set is and that they understand how to integrate the problem set into the market, and then they get there and they don't.'*

Food for thought? If you haven't thoroughly checked your market, start now; and if you think you have, you probably haven't done enough.

## How Are You Going to Present Your Ideas?

Now you know the points you need to put across to potential investors. Let's delve deeper and explore how to create a deck that does the job.

### Don't Judge a Book by Its Cover?

Bullshit! If you've ever had an interviewee turn up late in sweat-stained gym clothes, you'll know how much first impressions matter. Another example: I once asked a friend of mine, who works at Tinder, which profiles get the most success. 'Easy,' she said, 'the ones with the most effort.' By this, she didn't mean the users with the most mindless right-swipes. She meant the users who took the time to pick striking photos and write compelling profiles.

Investors are people, not robots made of cash, and, like all of us, they experience immediate emotional responses to what they see. An angel investor will receive hundreds of pitch decks each year – an accelerator programme will be sent thousands during every cycle. If your pitch deck looks cruddy, your perfectly planned path to profit is at risk of remaining unread. After all, if you can't be bothered to get a few slides right, you're hardly likely to deliver the amazing product that you promise in the deck itself.

A professional format and great design will make the right first impression and show investors that you care about the project and are serious about your venture. Let's not get too carried away, though. A flashy deck won't save your business if it doesn't have the potential — you can't polish a turd – but following these tips should at least make your pitch deck stand out for the right reasons.

### Hire a Professional

Perhaps you know your way around the latest graphic design software, and you may be a dab hand, but as is the case for most things, although it's possible to do it yourself, you'll get better results by hiring a professional. While you can also find good-quality templates online to get you started, you run the risk of your pitch deck looking too similar to others to stand out. A designer may seem like an extravagant expense for one document, but when the future of your business is relying on it, going the extra mile to make sure it stands out from the crowd might just be worth it.

Websites such as YunoJuno can connect you to freelance designers who can spend a day or two making your pitch deck shine. Just remember to tell them that you need it in a format that you can edit later. An experienced designer will work with you on the format, colour scheme and fonts to make sure that it looks appropriate for you. In our company, we had the right expertise in-house, in the shape of Andy, our head of product, who is a great designer. Here's his advice:

### Choose the Right Format

Before you go jumping into PowerPoint, take a minute to think about how your pitch deck will be consumed. If you plan to deliver the pitch personally, a presentation with strong visuals and simple bullet points is probably the right format choice; however, if you're sending it via email or application form, you might find it useful to know that according to the document sharing solutions company, DocSend, 12 per cent of pitch decks are viewed on a mobile device. Armed with this information, it makes sense to ensure your presentation looks great on a phone, or, at the very least, you must make sure it can be opened and read on a mobile device.

At Stakester, the first pitch deck we designed featured a lot of high-resolution mock-ups of the app. It looked great, and I sat back waiting for the investments to roll in, but we soon realised we had a problem — the file size was huge. Our emails started bouncing back, and potential investors gave up trying to load it over their 4G network. Even the smallest bit of friction can cause your deck to be discarded, so get the format right to make sure you don't fall at the first hurdle. That's something that you can control.

### Be Consistent

If you're pitching for seed investment, you probably don't yet have a brand or visual guidelines to draw from. Consistency is the key to producing a deck that looks professional, so make some choices and stick to them.

Choose a base colour that is appropriate for your business, one that captures the overall essence and spirit of your company, and then you can use a website such as Colormind to create a harmonious, balanced colour scheme around it. Use your base colour a lot (for backgrounds and titles) and the others sparingly. Apart from white and very dark grey, don't be tempted to stray from your colour scheme. It's there to make life easy, so you don't have to think too hard about colour, and to ensure consistency. Never use black – it's too harsh on screens and will jar with the rest of your colour scheme.

Once you've got your colours, pick a pair of fonts. It looks slicker to have one 'display' font, which has more personality, for titles; and a 'body' font, which is more functional, for the rest of your text. Display fonts project feeling and look better when they are large, while body fonts are for clear communication and must be easy to read when small.

Web development company Reliablepsd can help you choose a pair of fonts from its free Google library. Do not use Comic Sans, Arial or Times New Roman for your pitch deck. Do not use Comic Sans for anything, ever. Just in case you missed that, do not use Comic Sans for anything,

EVER! Beware of gimmicky, over-designed display fonts, which usually wear out the viewer's eyes faster than staring at the sun. There are thousands available for free download . . . and there is usually a reason why they are free; as far as free fonts go, you usually get what you pay for.

> 'Keep It Simple, Stupid!' – (KISS principle)
>
> *A methodology developed and adopted by the US Navy in the 1960s*

Once you've chosen your fonts, don't mess about with size, *italics*, **bolds**, UPPER CASE and SMALL CAPS. The more variation you introduce, the messier your deck will look, so display no more than three or four different font styles on a slide.

If you want to include additional visual elements, such as icons and stock photos, you can easily find free ones on the web; however, as with colours and fonts, the trick is to stay consistent, so find a library of images that suit the overall style of your site and stick with them.

Whatever you do, don't underestimate the importance of brand consistency. There are lots of great books on why brand is a big deal, and they'll all tell you that consistency in style across all things from your website to email signatures is important, so always be mindful of this. The goal is to ensure that every time someone sees anything relating to your company, they know it's your brand.

### Go BIG or Go Home

Slides containing large blocks of small text are unlikely to be read, so resist the temptation to cram everything you love about your company into your deck. Instead, pick out the most impressive aspects of your pitch – the elevator pitch – and display them in a clear, legible and confident way. Large, bold text that sharply contrasts with the background will always stand out and look smart, particularly on smaller devices.

Now you know what your deck should look like, but what about the content?

### Dazzle Them With the Content

You must grab attention and create the right impression from the first page, which is why it's so important to . . .

### Excite Them With the Cover

The cover is the first and only time an investor will make an emotional snap judgement about your business. Get it wrong, and it might also be the only page they read. Get it right, and you can hook them in, excited to get stuck into the details.

> **'Many investors are going to make up their minds about whether they are interested or not from slide one.'**
>
> *Alejandro Cremades – Author of* The Art of Startup Fundraising *and a Serial Entrepreneur*

Keep your cover simple. Include your brand name (or logo if you have one) and a hook that creates intrigue – it might be a question that leads the reader to think of the pain point that your app addresses, or the promise that it will fulfil. Successful cover page hooks include:

- *Book rooms with locals, rather than hotels.* (Airbnb)
- *What's buzzing on the web?* (BuzzFeed)
- *Changing the way we game.* (Stakester)
- *Next-Generation Car Service.* (Uber)
- *Do what you love.* (WeWork)
- *Organizing the World's Business Information.* (Mattermark)
- *The Best Way to Move Money.* (Dwolla)
- *Take Back Your Wallet.* (Mint)
- *Make America Great Again.* (Trump)*

* I'm not saying this is a great product, but it is a memorable brand. There's a lesson here.

You may have immediately spotted several things they have in common. They:

- **Use fewer words** – Aim for about five and no more than eight.
- **Use verbs rather than nouns** – Nouns bore, whereas verbs hook readers . . .
- . . . **except** for the verb 'to be', which bores readers too, so avoid 'to be', 'is', 'was', 'are' and 'were'.
- **Shout 'CHANGE'** – Humans find change irresistibly fascinating.

And there is something else that they don't do that you shouldn't do either:

- **Don't spell out what the product does in fine detail** – We're attempting to pique their curiosity.

Do this instead:

- **Share one core idea** – That's where the real juice is.

Once you know what you are going to include for your first slide, you need to think about how you are going to place the content on the page. Choose a large font size for your display text and compose a sentence that will get people excited about your business, and you will have yourself a great-looking cover. You can use a picture, but an eye-catching logo and compelling hook can also work well on their own. At Stakester, we used a photo of gamers to communicate the competitive, tongue-in-cheek tone of the brand.

## Follow Up With Substance

If your cover page has done what it's supposed to do, and you've whetted your potential investors' appetites, you must meet their expectations and follow up with meaty content.

**Tell them what your product will do** – Now you've hooked them, it's time to start giving them some answers. Use the second slide to tell them what the product *does* – not what it *is* – and how it will improve the user's life.

**Tell them how big the market is** – The metric might be the number of users in the market, the number of transactions, the revenue total for your sector worldwide, or a combination of some or all of those – it doesn't matter – but make it simple, make it clear and use a graph or a diagram if necessary. If the market's growing, show that too.

**Show them your faces** – Entrepreneur.com calls the team slide 'one of the two most important slides in your pitch deck'. That's because an investor is usually buying into you, not just your product. A straightforward way to make the team slide look more professional and relatable is to include headshots of you and your team.

Consistency is just as important here as it is for other aspects of the visual style of your presentation. If you need to include photos of more than one person, use the same format for every shot: the same place, the same setting and even the same time because that will ensure other factors, such as the lighting, remain constant as well. If this is not possible, you may be able to create some consistency by styling the photos with a graphic treatment.

At Stakester, some members of our team were in the States, and we couldn't all get together in the same room for a headshot session, so each photo was coloured with a gradient wash, which made them all look as though they were part of the same set.

**Tell them about your traction** – Are you growing as rapidly as an early Facebook? Or will you? What indicators are there that you will be able to turn your idea into something that grows fast?

**Explain your unfair advantage** – Are you a fourteen-times world whittling champion and making a new knife? Or do you have some other specialised knowledge, expertise, opening or talent that your competitors don't have?

**Top Tip – Dedicate a Slide to A Key Takeaway!**

Pull out one of your key takeaways and dedicate a slide to it. This will not only help to make your idea stick in the mind of a potential investor, but it will improve the rhythm and flow of your deck, giving your reader a moment's breather from the denser pages.

**Added Bonus**

When you're presenting in person, it gives you a natural opportunity to pause and register the reaction, respond to questions, and so on.

**Test it** – Don't send out your deck until you've run it past several intelligent and (constructively) hostile testers. Don't tell them how great you think it is; ask them to rip the shit out of it. Offer them drinks in exchange for every mistake they point out, and more drinks for every improvement that they suggest.

**Polish it** – Practise the patter that will accompany the show. Ideally, you want a story that perfectly complements the slides, one that you can tell without looking at the screen. You should be watching the audience for their reaction. Make sure that they are focused, that they are following what you're saying, and that they are enjoying the journey. Where you find the same questions popping up repeatedly for a specific slide, fix the deck so those questions are answered by the preceding one.

**Check it, double-check it and check it again** – If there is a spelling mistake in there, investors will spot it. If there is a font inconsistency, investors will spot it. If something is difficult to read or has unclear grammar, or if the image of the graph doesn't match the numbers captioning it – you get the picture – they will send your pitch to the trash.

Once you've tested, polished and practised your presentation, don't send it to investors until you have proofread it on paper. Print it out! No one knows why, but mistakes leap out at you when they are on paper and are harder to spot on-screen. Cut out unnecessary words. Keep sentences short and punchy.

**Iterate. Iterate. Iterate** – Don't stop designing as soon as you've sent out your first deck. Get feedback, tweak and repeat. Always continue looking for better ways to communicate your idea. If you gradually improve with each iteration, it won't be long before you've got a killer pitch deck.

### Top Tip – Treat it Like Dating!

Chris Smith is the managing partner at Playfair Capital, an angel-stage fund, so he has seen his fair share of pitches. He also spent ten years as a lawyer, so he knows a thing or two about putting together strong arguments. Chris's top tip for pitching?

*'Treat it like dating. Don't tell everything on the first date.'*

> If you come in with a forty-page pitch deck, you'll never get to have a real conversation about what it is you are doing, and you will never learn about the investors.

## 'Who the Fuck Are You?'

That might sound brutal, but I'm unapologetic because, to every investor out there, you're just another desperado looking to stick your hands in their pockets and that's exactly what they will be asking themselves about you. They want opportunities to invest, but investability starts and ends with the people. The big question is this: are you investable?

You might think you are, and maybe you are, but in the next chapter you're going to learn how to make sure that potential investors know that, too.

# 11.
# DON'T FUCK UP YOUR PERSONAL PROFILE

Unless you've randomly dipped into this book for the fun of it, you haven't come this far in the journey to go and blow it all by fucking up your personal profile. One of the most basic errors you can make as a founder is not having any presence at all.

## Raise Your Personal Profile

If you are one of the grey people on social media, whose profiles tell visitors almost nothing about them, not even what they look like, then you are missing out on the opportunity to be noticed for the right reasons – that's less damaging than being known for the wrong reasons, but it is still not optimal.

Social media is only one face of personal branding. You also have to consider how you present yourself on your website. Have you distributed any press releases recently? Have you appeared on any other websites because of something good you've said or done? How discoverable are you?

Humility's a commendable quality, but shy kids don't get the sweets, so if you have been lurking in the shadows, you need to change that, urgently.

Hold on. Stop! If you're thinking about sharing a stack of dinner selfies, boasting about how you refuse to tip waiters or blaming everything that's wrong with the nation you live in on sick people claiming benefits, you might want to reflect a little before you dive in.

## Don't Make Yourself a Persona Non Grata

Did you skip the start of this chapter? If so, I know what you were thinking: 'I don't need to read this bit. I'm all over LinkedIn, my Insta is well cool and I'm the king of Facebook. You don't need to tell me to raise my profile, mate.' I'm guessing you missed the bit about reflecting before posting, so I'm going to invite you to consider a couple of questions.

**What do you think is the first thing an investor will do if they like your pitch deck?**

- Invite you for a meeting?
- Make you an immediate offer?
- Tell you how fabulous you are?
- Take you for a drink?

All those options are possible, but not before they type your name into the search bar. Hmm, Mr 'King of Facebook', Ms 'Queen of Insta', or righter of all wrongs on LinkedIn, I wonder how comfortable you're feeling right now. That brings me to my next question.

**If someone Googles your name right now, what will they find?**
You can be sure of one thing: even if you don't know the answer, someone else already does because they've done it. That's a sobering thought, isn't it?

Now, imagine this:

You've judged your approach perfectly and produced the perfect killer deck. Your ideal investor opens it, loves it and decides to look you up, but what do they find?

Your LinkedIn profile shows a picture of you getting pissed on a beach in Barbados and proudly declares that you're still working that summer job you quit five years ago, a glance at your public Instagram presents your passion for tequila slammers, and your Twitter shows nothing but flame wars with fans of other football teams, and you're fucked because that investor who loved you minutes earlier now thinks you're an idiot.

That's right; of all the pitch errors you could have made, you've made one of the worst, and it didn't have to happen. If there is one opinion that every investor I have ever met, pitched or interviewed has shared, it is that the people are what matter most, and that makes complete sense because, in the early stages, your people are your only asset.

## You're Right, But Where Do I Start?

That's easy. Put yourself in the mind of the investor. Try looking at things from their perspective and, while you're doing that, ask yourself a couple of questions.

> **What would you want to see?** – Relevant experience? Subject matter expertise?
> **Where would you look?** – LinkedIn? Google? Twitter? Crunchbase?

The answer is yes to all of those, so you need to make sure that your platforms are in tip-top shape and present a fair reflection of what a good bet you are. Does it look like you're taking your startup seriously, and is an investor going to trust you not to lose their money?

In the same vein, do you share subjective opinions on sensitive matters such as politics, religion and other potentially divisive topics that are part of the zeitgeist? Unless being controversial serves your purpose and aligns with your brand values, tread carefully because the same opinions that make you a few new friends on social media could be a turn-off for your perfect investor.

If it genuinely matters to you so much that a difference in opinion could be a deal-breaker for you, go ahead and share yours because you will attract the people you want to connect with and deflect those you might clash with. You could call that opining with purpose or adopting a Marmite strategy, but if you're ranting for the sake of it, you might want to reconsider your approach.

Your brand is everything, and it is critical that your company looks and feels credible, so make sure that your social media is either on-brand or private, and check that your LinkedIn profile, company website and pitch deck are bang up to date and all agree on the details of what you're doing. Don't forget to set up the company on LinkedIn, taking care to include your logo and well-crafted 'About' copy.

## Network Like Crazy

> 'Serendipity is a superpower.'
>
> *Alex Dunsdon – Partner at Saatchinvest*

You know that lovely feeling of meeting *exactly the right person* at *exactly the right time?* It might feel like it happens by accident, but have you ever noticed that it seems to happen to some people all the time?

Serendipity happens when you have a great network; when you put yourself in front of people, listen to them and talk to them. Yep, it can be painful, especially if you're shy, but a broad network is priceless . . . and the only way to build it is to meet more people, formally, informally and – if you're at a wedding – very informally indeed.

Attend startup events, go on podcasts, and talk about your company. Spotaguest.com is great for discovering shows that need guests. Talk about your company to everyone you meet – we did, and, in a rather clichéd moment, were offered investment on a golf course. If you'd seen any of us play golf, you'd know that was quite remarkable. Ask to join panels at events, write on online publishing platforms such as Medium, and so on.

I used the online platform Meetup, where like-minded people can come together to discuss topics, and yes, some of the meetings were terrible, but one yielded me an investor, so it was worth it. If you can't find a good Meetup with a topic you care about, make one.

When you do meet other founders, listen to what they have to say, and don't be afraid to ask – politely – for help. Every founder who has raised money has also been rejected (probably many times) because they weren't the right fit, which means they have a solid list of investors that could be the right fit for you. Having been through what you're going through, they get how hard it is and will likely be sympathetic. I regularly introduce founders to investors whom I like but who have said 'No' to me, and (humblebrag) they have subsequently done great deals. Most people are more than happy to give you a little time and advice, share a contact or make an introduction. We are social animals at heart.

### Be Everywhere

Networking will throw up some leads, but to get your pitch out there effectively you need to be systematic about finding names and email addresses (for active approaches), listing yourself (so that you get discovered) and getting personal referrals. Our money came from direct email, angel syndicate platforms,[6] a podcast listener, and a chap who overheard me pitching to another potential investor in a coffee shop.

The lesson is clear: you can't predict where the money will come from, and if I hadn't tried all of those channels, we may not have hit our target. Be everywhere; write a blog, record videos, launch a podcast, interview people, appear on other people's podcasts, and post your deck on all the platforms you can. Network. Network. Network. Don't stop! It's a long game, so keep going.

### List Yourself

Your investors could come from anywhere, so to maximise your chances, list everywhere. There are plenty of places where you can list your pitch; some free, some not. Investors regularly scroll through these sites for deal flow,[7] so make sure that you can be found there.

There are loads of platforms available, but here's a list of the ones that have worked for me:

- 'The Brief' (Part of NfX.com) – US-focused platform that features more funds than angels.
- F6S – 90 per cent of accelerators now come through here.
- Angel Investment Network – Largest database of active angels in the world.
- AngelList – De facto site for angels to list their investments and profiles.
- Decksender – Free, simple and a cool idea.
- Connectd – More for finding a non-executive director (NED) but features some good profiles.
- Odin – UK and EU version of AngelList. I'm an investor, so let's just say this is the best site and leave this here: https://joinodin.com/

---

[6] An angel syndicate is an investment vehicle that allows a group of investors to pool their funds together for the purpose of making one carefully chosen, larger investment. Startups can gain access to a much greater amount than they would have been able to win from any one member of the syndicate, and angels benefit because the risk is shared by everyone in the syndicate.

[7] Venture capitalists, angel investors, private equity investors and investment bankers use the term 'deal flow' to refer to the rate of flow of business proposals and investment opportunities they have access to and the flow itself.

### Ask for Introductions and Referrals

When I started raising, I had no network of early-stage investors. There was no super-rich father-in-law, generous grandparent or investment-savvy former colleague I could call on to kick-start the journey either. I had to graft, just like most founders, and I can tell you this with 100 per cent confidence: your failure rate is going to be massive. Huge! But you can significantly improve your chances by getting referrals.

Half of the money I raised came from cold approaches but the other half, which came from referrals, was so much easier to obtain. It's not rocket science. When someone you trust tells you something is interesting, you are more likely to believe them than the person selling it. The best strategy for generating referrals is to search LinkedIn for angels, see who they are connected to in your network, and ask for an introduction. It's that simple. The next best approach, as previously mentioned, is to ask funded founders for connections.

Some people will tell you that you can't reach out to an investor without a referral, and – yes – it *is* true that a referral will improve your chances; however, if someone tells you this is the *only* route, please politely tell them to . . .

'Do one, and stop perpetuating your closed-community, elitist agenda!'

If we don't let new blood in, we'll never see change, and right now we need a little change.

### Actively Approach (Carefully)

Anyone who has ever worked in sales will tell you that nothing beats direct outreach. Yes, the conversion is low, but there is no better way to get direct contact with investors. The annoying bit is that building a list of people to reach out to takes . . .

SUCH

A

LOOOOOOOOooong

TIME!

Don't let that put you off. Get someone else to do it for you! *Who?* You may be wondering. Well, let's look at the options.

First, set some criteria for your potential investors: location, industry, job role and keywords. They should be based in your industry (or investment if not), working either within it or adjacent to it. Go for CEOs, board members, managing directors and so on, as the more senior they are, the more disposable income they will have. Keywords should include *investor*, *angel*, *early stage* and *pre-seed*. If they use these words on their profiles, they want you to contact them. This is important because it helps you to avoid reaching out to people who don't want to be approached, which will make people less likely to report you to the Information Commissioner's Office (ICO)[8] if they think you have fallen foul of the General Data Protection Regulation (GDPR).[9] If you are worried about stuff like that, seek relevant legal advice.

Use LinkedIn or AngelList to find five examples of the ideal investor. Remember that if you are based in the UK or a country that's part of the European Union, you will be subject to the General Data Protection Regulation (GDPR) and similar legislation.

The more time you put into writing the brief, describing the ideal candidate, picking search terms, and providing some LinkedIn/Angel.co profiles, the better the results you will get. By painting a more detailed picture of your ideal investor, you make it easier for a freelancer to find stronger matches, which may also help them to work quicker. You should ask for more than you think you need. It's better to be oversubscribed than under.

Now that you've created a detailed brief that outlines the kind of people you want to approach, including five examples of your ideal investor, you can outsource the tediously time-consuming part, so visit Upwork or Fiverr and search for 'lead generation' or 'list building'. Pick two freelancers, give them your examples, and get them on the case. Two should get the job done twice as quickly, and if one of them doesn't

---

[8] The ICO is the UK's independent body set up to uphold information rights. It has its own website – https://ico.org.uk/

[9] The General Data Protection Regulation (GDPR) is a set of rules created by the European Union (EU) to govern the protection of personal data in EU member states. Although the United Kingdom (UK) has now left the EU, it has retained GDPR rules in their entirety. The ICO offers guidance on how to adhere with GDPR rules here – https://ico.org.uk/for-organisations/guide-to-data-protection/guide-to-the-general-data-protection-regulation-gdpr/

do a great job, you still have the other as insurance, and they shouldn't charge more than $0.35 per name.

Ask your lead generators to place everything into a Google Sheet, using column headings for the key information that you are looking for (First Name, Last Name, Company, Job Title, Location, Email, LinkedIn, etc.). This will save time and ensure you get the data you need. Remember to vet the list thoroughly before you send anything. I emailed my old boss. We are not friends. It wasn't a great moment.

## Background Checks

Once you've compiled your list of names, carry out a little research on each of them to glean useful background information. Have they ever been interviewed? Have they made any public statements about the kind of investments they look for? What non-executive roles do they hold? Does their Twitter tell you anything? Look for angles that you can use in your approach.

Finally, bear in mind that once you've completed all the preparation, carefully crafted your message and pressed send, up to 10 per cent of the emails will bounce. No list is going to be perfect, but if you take the steps outlined above, you're less likely to receive any angry complaints.

We've looked at how to raise your profile in a way that's going to help you look worthy of investment, and we've explored more proactive ways for making sure you are seen by potential investors – without fucking up your personal brand!

I can hear a question. What's our email going to look like? It's a great question, and in the next chapter you're going to find out exactly what steps you need to take.

# 12.
# DON'T FUCK UP YOUR EMAIL

## The Art of Email Pitching

Email pitching is an art. Yes, it is! You have to catch people *immediately*, or you get nowhere. To find out how it works, I asked investors what they want to see, and I asked funded founders what they wrote. Would you like to know what they told me? I bet you would. The answers varied, but there were some common threads, which I am happy to summarise for you. Feast your eyes on these rules of thumb, and make sure you absorb them fully before you write a single email.

**First of all**, though, don't forget that you're pitching your company, not your product. Then, make sure that you cover:

- **What?** – What do you do, and why are you awesome? This needs to be tight. Whatever you're saying right now, it's not tight enough. Make it better! (Look at the tips I mentioned in Chapter 10 for punchy deck copy and apply them to your email.)
- **Who?** – Seriously wow them with the quality of your team and show them why you have the people to blow everyone else out of the water. Every investor you speak to will say, 'It's all about the people.' That's because . . . it's all about the people.
- **Killer stats** – Traction, market research, partnerships, opportunity size . . . whatever the sexiest numbers you have are, get them in – but don't overdo it. If you have smashed it on one metric, don't dilute the effect by including something weaker. Always play to your strengths.
- **The BIG question** – What are you asking for? Do you want them to invest? Then say so!
- **The need** – What are you going to use the investment for? As a rule, if it's not product development or growth, people get grumpy.

- **The deck** – Don't make them email you for the deck. Attach it as a reasonably sized PDF, in a format that means they can read it on their phone in the back of an Uber. Make it easy for them and you. You don't have time to respond to everyone who comes back to you with an impatient 'Please can I see the deck?' Who wants long and dull and repetitive and long and dull and repetitive? Stay sharp and efficient. Assume they will want to see the deck.

That's what you've got to fit in. Oh, and I did mention to pitch your company first, not the product, didn't I? Now, let's look at style. Here are some pointers:

- **Keep it brief** – The shorter, the better. Make it punchy. *Nobody* reads long emails, apart from people who work in HR. Need some inspiration? The movie pitch for *Talladega Nights* was six words – 'Will Ferrell as a NASCAR driver.' Vroom, vroom.
- **Don't overdo it** – Be clear, honest and calm. Words like 'awesome' and 'amazing' work in live pitches but in an email they feel phoney, which isn't what you want. You are proposing a valid investment opportunity, and you're deadly serious about it.

I've turned the email I used into a template that you can use to win investment for your startup. Look!

**Hey* __________,**

I'll be brief. I'm the founder of __________. With our product, __________, we enable __________ to __________, and we're seeing solid early traction. I previously worked at/for __________, and my co-founder, __________, was __________ for __________. We have partnered with __________, who are __________ in __________. [and . . . ] We launched our product last month and already have nearly __________ sales/downloads, putting us ahead of our original plan.

We have raised __________ of a __________ target, and I'm reaching out to you as a potential investor. ** This investment will further develop the product and drive customer acquisition.

I've attached our deck for your review.

It would be great to have a Hangout/Zoom to discuss further if of interest.

All the best,

Tom
[Contact details, website, etc.]

* It's up to you which greeting you use but choose one that's polite and familiar. Formal words and phrases such as 'Dear' and 'Good morning' create an imbalance of power and should be avoided.
** This is where you personalise – briefly, but enough to show that you've done your homework and that this isn't a generic cut-and-paste job. Say why you've picked them and why they are a good fit. Something like:

You've had an amazing career that shows you know how to hustle and scale, and I can also see you've worked at __________, which is super relevant to us because of ____________, so we would love you to join us for the ride.

Including a personalised touch will greatly increase your chances of engagement. If your list is hundreds of names long, it may not be feasible to do it for everyone, though.

Try to leave the 'To' field empty while you're drafting your email. You don't want to send anything to an investor that you haven't checked and proofread out loud at least a couple of times. Just as printing stuff out makes it easier to spot errors, so does reading text aloud.

## Emailing the Pitch

You've assembled a killer deck, built a database of a hundred or more email addresses, and you've drafted punchy, personalised, opening messages for as many of those people as you possibly can. Sending these works of art takes a long time, but luckily there are plenty of great mail-merge tools that speed things up without making your emails look like a mailshot. I especially like GMass, which links directly with Google Sheets and offers plenty of personalisation options. GMass Premium gives reasonable value and is moderately priced. You can send emails without the GMass label at the bottom, and you can automate your follow-ups.

Now it's just about hitting 'send', right? Wrong. Not quite. There are two more pieces of the puzzle, and these are crucial if you want to get it right: the subject line, and the time of day.

**Subject line** – People spend a lot of time thinking about this, which is understandable, as it is prime real estate. It's possible to overthink it, though. I find it's usually best just to put the name of your company.

**Time of day** – Pick your time carefully. I cannot stress this enough. If you send it in the middle of the morning, people are in meetings or buried in project work, and they are not going to give your email the attention it deserves.

## When Can I Hit Send?

Ask yourself what time of day you would be most likely to read an email in full and look at the pitch deck of some random startup. Or . . . look it up online. There is a ton of studies out there, conducted by people far smarter than me. They've crunched the data relating to when emails get opened and read, and others have boiled down their findings into simple rules of thumb that we can all consider:

- Don't send it at the weekend.
- Don't send it on Monday or Friday, either.
- Thursday is better than Tuesday, which is better than Wednesday.
- The best times of day are the periods when people tend to be actively 'doing their emails' – roughly 8 a.m., 1 p.m. and 5 p.m.

Don't forget about time zones, public holidays, half term and so on. 'Big news days' are a bad idea, too, as people's attention will be elsewhere, so avoid sending emails to coincide with elections, budget announcements, terrorist attacks, invasions and major breaking news.

**Responses** – A good response rate to a cold e-shot is around 10 per cent, once you've taken out the slightly aggressive 'No's. Look at my stats as an example.

| | |
|---|---|
| Unique opens: | 58 per cent |
| Did not open: | 41 per cent |
| Unique clicks: | 6 per cent |
| Replies: | 13 per cent |
| Bounces: | 13 per cent |
| Blocks: | 0.23 per cent |

**Follow up** – If you don't get a response, there's no harm in sending a follow-up. Notably, on one of my pitching rounds, *every single investment* came from a follow-up email. When it comes to timing, I'm a big believer in the 2–1–1 rule. Send a follow-up email two days after the initial mail, one week after that, and one month after that.

Here's the follow-up message I used:

> Hey ___________,
>
> Checking in on the previous note. Things are going well with the round, ***, and it would be great to have a conversation if you'd like to be involved.
>
> Hope to speak soon,
>
> Tom

*** If you have something cool to add that didn't fit in the first email, such as a partnership, a big-name team member, a record sales period or a cool new feature, slide it in here.

**Prepare for frequently asked questions (FAQs)** – Often, you will be sent a bunch of follow-up questions. A lot of these will be the same, and they're not always things you want to include in your pitch deck or opening email. Writing a new response every time is time-consuming and inefficient so every time you get asked a new question, add that, along with your response, to a document that you can refer to later.

When the question is raised by someone else, and it will be, you can cut and paste it from the FAQ document.

Common questions include:

- Can you tell me more about your team? (I am sure I mentioned pitching the company rather than the product)
- Can you share the name of some of your top investors?
- What's your go-to marketing strategy?
- How do you deal with data protection?
- What are your predicted financials for Year 1, Year 2, Year 3?

These questions can be an invaluable source of feedback and may well point up something that's not right with your deck or your cover email. It's also healthy to see questions as buying signals. If the investors weren't interested, they wouldn't be probing you. Anything that sharpens up your understanding of the strengths and weaknesses of your pitch and facilitates a process of improvement has got to be useful.

Investors don't waste their time on meetings with people they're not interested in, so when you get an invitation, allow yourself to feel confident. You've earned that meeting and, if you play your cards right, you could convert it into investment. Whatever you do, though, don't let confidence manifest as laziness, arrogance or poor preparation.

In the next chapter, you're going to learn how not to fuck up your pitch meeting.

# 13.
# DON'T FUCK UP YOUR PITCH MEETING

Hey, how are you getting on? Have you been invited to a pitch meeting? If so, well done, my friend! If not, don't let it stress you out. An essential ingredient for not fucking up your startup is the ability to accept rejection, brush yourself down, sharpen up your approach and try again and again. And when you make it to the next stage in the process, expect the same thing to happen again. It is not over until the dotted line's signed and the money's in your business account and, even then, the fun is only just beginning.

Let's not get ahead of ourselves, however. You need to know how not to fuck up your pitch meeting, and I'm here to help you by sharing the wisdom of all the great people who have helped me or appeared on my podcast.

## Know Who's Going

As the founder, you must be there. You don't want to be alone, but there's no point bringing a crowd of other people just because you want a sympathetic audience. Take one or two others but only if you expect them to speak during the meeting. They must serve a purpose.

Bring in your chief technology officer (CTO) to explain the science behind your great idea, your chief marketing officer (CMO) to share your unique marketing advantage, or invite your new, enthusiastic rockstar hire to come along, so she can say how this is the most excited she's been since her early days at Google.

Before the meeting, prepare as a team. This doesn't mean scripting the meeting, but you should agree on who will speak about what areas, who will field the investors' questions, and how you'll introduce yourselves, for example. This will ensure you come across as slick and well organised as a team.

## Know Your Pitch Like the Back of Your Hand

If you're not confident at speaking off the cuff, list the main points and memorise them. You can script them, if necessary, but your presentation will sound more natural if you don't. Practise your delivery in front of the team and have it recorded, so you can critique it afterwards. Make sure that every point you make flows logically from the one before. When you're moving from one topic to the next, ask a rhetorical question to keep the listeners involved: 'So, that's how the app works . . . but what's our traction been like?'

## Know the Value of Your Offering

Have a figure prepared for the value of the company and be ready to justify it. Know how much equity you ideally want to offer immediately, and think through other possibilities, so that you're ready for a meaningful conversation; that kind of nitty-gritty discussion will probably happen after the pitch meeting (more on that in the next chapter) but be ready – just in case.

## Know as Much as You Can About Your Potential Investor

You had already researched the investor before you emailed them, right? Do it again, now, but dig deeper this time. Read every press release they've put out in the last year, look at all the investments they've made; and dig out all the blog posts, podcasts and interviews that you can. This is the time to use social media to find out if there's something you can connect on. You both support Doncaster Rovers? *Amazing!*

## It's All About the People

Your idea probably is fantastic, but every founder has a great idea, and the people sitting opposite you in that investor meeting see around five hundred wonderful ideas every year. They're not contemplating how amazing your innovation is but whether you can turn it into a reality and give them delicious returns. That's why, when I was pitching, I was asked more questions about myself, my background, my co-founders and my team than anything else. At any given pitch, being interrogated about our people typically took up half the meeting.

The experts at Techstars, arguably the best accelerator in the world, say it best when they list the six most essential elements of any startup: **people**, **people**, **people**, market, traction and idea. What does this mean? Be ready and willing to talk about yourself. Tell the story – in brief – of how you picked up your impressive skill set and the knowledge that makes your company a winning bet. Make sure that you know the stories of your team, too.

**Take a long look at yourself** – This is where self-awareness becomes critical. Ask what gaps you have in your skill set that will deter an investor. Are you a marketing expert? Are you technically capable? Can you get traction? Do you have proven experience? If you have gaps, that's fine. Everyone does. Bravo for having the humility and the self-knowledge to admit it openly. If your co-founder doesn't fill that gap, recognise that you have to recruit someone who does. It's much easier for an investor to put their money on a group of people than just one. And, of course, many investors will be happy to offer their knowledge and experience.

> 'Don't be scared, homie.'
>
> *Nick Diaz – UFC Legend*

As you approach the investor, who can make your dreams come true, it's natural to feel butterflies. It's an incredibly exciting moment, and the outcome could be beautiful and life-changing. Excitement brings a special kind of energy that can supercharge the pitch, but fear is a problem. It will cause you to stumble, make mistakes and not be the best version of yourself.

I appreciate that being the founder version of Nick Diaz[10] and saying, 'Don't be scared, homie' is not overly helpful, so let's rationalise why you don't need to be. Here's the mind-blowing secret that you need to know: *Investors want to invest*. They don't want you to mess up. They want you to be superb. They are on your side, not against you.

---

[10] Nickolas ('Nick') Robert Diaz is an American professional mixed martial artist who, following a defeat to fellow MMA star K. J. Noons in 2007, famously said, 'Don't be scared, homie!' The phrase became a part of MMA folklore immediately and was quickly memefied.

## Read the Room

Don't focus on the pitch. Keep looking at the audience. Make plenty of eye contact, stay alert and take notice of how your listeners are responding. Watch their body language; for example, if someone is leaning forward and fidgeting, they probably have a question, or if two people are exchanging looks, they may have something in mind that they've previously spoken about – find out what it is.

## Be Ready to Go Off-Script

No matter how much background research you do, checks you run on your forecast, or times you rehearse your pitch, you cannot predict all the questions that will come up, or foresee all the holes in your model. You're talking to sharp people who depend on their ability to spot the fatal flaws in sexy-looking startups. They will see the things that you don't.

One venture capitalist (VC) highlighted a major gap in our strategy while I was chatting with him at a wedding, and I'm grateful that he did. Whether something like that happens to you or not, you have to be ready to deal with it. Show flexibility, show a willingness to listen and be open to feedback. I have seen pitches collapse due to an inability to pivot and respond to being thrown a curveball or to take criticism as a gift. It will make your business stronger if you can accept advice, and it will make you more attractive to investors if you can adapt.

## It's a Two-Way Street

Would you ask someone to marry you after three dates? I hope not, but you are planning to ask someone you may have only spoken to twice and exchanged a dozen emails with to be a major part of your life for the next three to ten years. Although it feels great when someone completes their due diligence on you and decides to invest, it's equally important for you to apply the same level of scrutiny to them. I've been through the experience of taking the wrong money (not, I hasten to add, with Stakester) and it is not fun – not fun at all. A private investigator shouldn't be necessary, but you should meet your investors face to face at the very least.

Ask yourself some difficult questions:

- Can I trust this person?
- Can I see myself wanting to celebrate my victories with them?
- Will they trust me, and let me do what I do?
- Will they bring any value to my business over and above the money?
- Do they have skills and a network that the business can leverage?

Don't be afraid to raise issues such as these and discuss them with your investors. If they are right for you, they'll understand why these are worthwhile conversations to have. It's not worth the risk of getting something like this wrong, so if you have any doubts, thank your investors for their interest, politely decline any offers they've made, and move on.

## Make FOMO Your Friend

Never underestimate the usefulness of the fear of missing out (FOMO). Even if you have just one backer, you can leverage them to conjure the most powerful investor emotion that exists – FOMO! VCs often tell me that the costliest decisions are the missed opportunities, not the ones that went wrong. There is no stronger validation for your opportunity than others investing, so make sure other investors know about it.

## Did I Mention . . . ?

As is the case for the pitch deck, you're pitching your company, not your product.

**A Summary of Common Fuckups (from the people who know best)**

I asked my usual panel of experts about the worst fuckups they see in pitch meetings. Here's what they said:

**Don't say you're seeking funding for extra runway** – This suggests that you're in trouble, either because you're not controlling costs or because your project is more difficult than you expected.

**Don't spray product ideas at the wall** – Focus on the one thing that your product does best, and how big it will be. Your CTO is probably incredibly excited about adding functionality, which is great, but this is not the time or place. You want to show focus and concentrated effort.

**Don't be leaderless** – It should be clear from your pitch who is in charge and that the rest of the team are happy to follow their lead.

**Don't say that you're funding a major pivot** – For an investor, this translates as you launching another business because the first one hasn't worked.

**Don't forget that now is the best time for your business** – The world is changing all the time. Demonstrate that you understand this and show that you're neither too early nor too late.

**Don't be a smart arse** – They understand their business, you don't, so ask them questions and find out what they need. Don't assume that you already know.

**Don't forget that venture is about growth** – You may be on the fast track to break even and modest profitability, and that's great, but it's not what VCs are interested in. They want to see a company get *big*. Amazon was trading for eight years before its first profitable year.

Don't let the pitch get cold – Let's say that it went well; you pitched like a Viking, they asked intelligent questions, and it became clear that they could mentor you to grow as well as pump in cash. No decision was made, but you walked out of there buzzing with anticipation . . . already dying to call them to follow up? Don't lose that feeling. Make it clear that you're enthusiastic, and don't let them get bored of the concept.

## Dealing with Rejection

Winning feels great, but what happens when you get rejected? You weren't thinking that would never happen, were you? Don't be in any doubt that you will get rejected, a lot. I wish I had been told how frequently before I started, so I could prepare myself.

After the ninth straight 'No!', I started to doubt whether we'd ever get funded and whether I had what it takes; maybe I just wasn't investment material, maybe I should have done an MBA instead of studying theology, maybe I should hand the reins over to my colleagues and get a regular job . . . so many maybes.

**'Don't take it personally.'**

*Warwick Hill – General Partner at Supercapital Partners LLP*

But then a wizard of the startup world, Warwick Hill, reassured me: 'There are ten thousand reasons someone might not invest, and you may only be one per cent away from "yes". Don't take it personally.' You can apply the same logic to being dropped after one date: it's not because you're a loser; you're just not right for them.

Prepare yourself for rejection, don't take it personally and don't give up hope. People will still want somewhere to put their money. Provided you can make a solid case for why it should be in your business, you'll be okay.

**Top Tip – Get advice!**

The most incredible thing about the startup community is that there are lots of great people who are willing to help, primarily because they have been through it themselves. Ask people for a coffee, get them to check your deck, and practise your pitch with them; and when you're a Basquillionaire[11] and ringing the bell at the New York Stock Exchange, make sure you pay the favour forward to others.

[11] A Basquillionaire is someone who has so much wealth, they can retire to the beautiful Basque country and spend the rest of their days off the grid. Okay, I admit it: I made it up because I wanted an excuse for a random footnote. 'Billionaire' and 'trillionaire' are so 2020s, so let's make a new threshold. Don't judge yourself by loser standards. I hope someone at *Oxford English Dictionary* is reading this.

## Now What, Tom?

Good question, reader! Remember what I said at the start of this chapter about the fun starting once the money is in the account? Yes, winning investment is only the beginning. Once you've acquired that pot of gold, you will have to deliver on your promises, build your product and show those investors the money that you said you were going to make for them.

14.

# WHO THE FUCK SHOULD I HIRE? (AND WHY THE FUCK SHOULD THEY WORK WITH ME?)

It's been one hell of a journey, hasn't it? Have you started with any of the stuff we've looked at over the last few chapters yet? Perhaps you've even won some angel investment, or are you waiting to see what happens next? Whether you have the money now or you don't, and you probably don't, you are going to need to build a team. We looked at this in an earlier chapter, but it's time to knuckle down and find out how to attract the best people you can.

Throughout my entrepreneurial journey, I have interviewed around two hundred people, and I have learned some valuable lessons along the way. Before I share those lessons with you, here's the science bit.

## Look for the Best People

Common sense says that the best people get the best results, but how much of a difference does it make? The analytics and advisory firm Gallup studied a hundred thousand teams to find out, and the results showed that hiring the right people makes a major difference to performance.

The data from the Gallup study indicates that companies that select from the top 20 per cent of people achieve a 10 per cent increase in productivity, a 20 per cent increase in sales, and a 30 per cent increase in profitability. As your company grows, the impact of hiring the best people will become increasingly attractive.

## What Will a 10 per cent Increase in Productivity, a 20 per cent Increase in Sales, and a 30 per cent Increase in Profitability Look Like?

If you have a team of ten people, a 10 per cent increase in productivity means they are doing the work of eleven people. Grow that team to a hundred, and they will be doing just as much as 110 people. By hiring people from the top 20 per cent, you have the equivalent of ten extra staff on a team of a hundred. Think about that. How much does it cost to hire one person? Now times that by ten. You are saving huge amounts and getting a lot more bang for your buck from the people you have hired.

Growth is going to happen significantly quicker if you are hiring the top people because of the 20 per cent increase in sales, and again this becomes increasingly juicy along the way – £20,000 more on £100,000 worth of revenue and £200,000 on a £1 million turnover. Add that to the gains you've made from improved productivity.

Did you notice the bit about 30 per cent improvement in profitability? Fuck me! Do the maths on that. Let's say you've hired a team of average people and made a profit of £35,000 on a turnover of £100,000. If you had hired people from the top 20 per cent, the 30 per cent increase in profitability would mean an extra £9,000 in profit. PROFIT!

That's £9,000 that you can plough back into the business for extra growth or money in your pocket for a rainy day. What's that going to buy you? A decent second-hand car, a new kitchen, or a full tank of petrol; take your pick. Just in case change destroys my one-liner, have you forgotten how rapidly fuel prices were rising as we approached the second quarter of 2022??? You get my point, though. Provided inflation doesn't mean we need to take a bagful of used notes to buy a packet of bog roll, nine grand's a lot of money.

Now, scale that up for a £1 million business, a £10 million business and beyond. It all adds up, doesn't it?

## Improved Staff Retention

Hiring the best people also leads to increased retention of staff. Businesses that take on people from the top 20 per cent will notice a 10 per cent decrease in staff leaving. If you've not run a business or managed people before, you may be wondering what all the fuss is about. Never take a happy team for granted. Any business owner will tell you that losing people is one of the biggest pains in the arse for several reasons.

First, hiring anyone is an investment. It takes time and energy to attract them, onboard them, bring them up to speed and get them started.

If they leave, not only do you have to face losing your investment, but you also know you are going to have to start the process again from scratch.

Secondly, any lessons they have learned along the way, which is important knowledge, may also be lost unless you can take on a suitable replacement before their notice period runs out – and that's if they work their notice period. Then there's the knock-on effect to the people who stick around. People leaving often means everyone else must work a bit harder, especially in a tight ship such as a startup, and a quicker turnover of staff is terrible for morale. No founder wants to go through the aggravation of replacing people who have left. It's tedious, expensive and unhealthy for everyone.

It's bad enough if someone isn't fitting in or delivering on the promises they made at the interview, but if you have hired a toxic person who is determined to toss it off until their last day, you will have a bunch of other issues to contend with. Will they distract others? Are they going to sabotage what you're trying to do, steal intellectual property or just make you want to kill them? Don't kill anyone in your company. That's particularly bad for business.

Why stick with the top 20 per cent? If pulling people from the best fifth of the job market brings those results – 10 per cent increase in productivity, 20 per cent increase in sales, and a 30 per cent increase in profitability – wouldn't it be cool if you aimed for the top 10 per cent or even the top 1 per cent? Did you see what I did there? 'Wouldn't it be cool if' delivers excellent results in all areas of life and business.

## What Planet Are You On, Thomas?

Wow! It must be serious if you're addressing me by the name my mother uses when she's telling me off for swearing at the dinner table or going over the speed limit by two miles per hour. What's up with you? Why are you asking me what planet I'm on?

'Thomas . . . ahem, Tom. Me and the CTO are working remotely from our spare rooms. My desk cost less than a hundred quid from Ikea, my desktop is on its last legs, and we're both broke. How the fuck do you think we're gonna hire *anyone*, never mind someone good?'

Hmm. Good question, and it's one that I can answer, my good friend. Here's something I prepared earlier. Prepare to be persuaded.

## Great Minds Love Startups

Startups to great minds and talented individuals are like ice cream to a wasp. They don't want to be just another number. They want to put their superpowers to effective use by being a part of something special, something that will put their name and their skills on the map. If you can show them the path to greatness and convince them that you have a plan that's going to get them there, you will have them eating out of the palm of your hand. You must know how to sell the dream.

## Sell the Vision

If you know how to sell the vision, people will quit their careers at superb companies, take salary cuts and work all-nighters to impress you, and they will thank you for letting them. How can I be so sure? Because they've done it for me. I've hired people from Google, Deloitte, Deliveroo, PwC, MTV and King at a startup with no traction, no funding and no sexy PR, just an idea and a promise. What's the vision? According to the great Reid Hoffman, founder of LinkedIn and author of *Blitzscaling*, it's this:

> 'Your role as a founder is singular when it comes to talent. You are there to convince the very best talent in the world that if they join your startup, there is a very clear and very believable path for them to become incredibly wealthy.'
>
> *Reid Hoffman – Founder of LinkedIn and author of* Blitzscaling

The technical term for this, in 'recruitment speak', is the 'employee value proposition', or, between you and me, 'what's in it for them', and it has to be bigger than a salary. Global recruitment firm Michael Page describes the employee value proposition as 'the unique set of benefits that an employee receives in return for the skills, capabilities and experience they bring to a company', but since nobody other than recruiters and the fun police in human resources speaks like that, we'll leave it there. Focus on the words of Hoffman. He's got it sussed.

Do you have a vision that people can believe in, which is not only appealing because of the difference it can make in the world but because it is destined to make money?

## What's Your Motivation?

You might tell me you want to be rich beyond your wildest dreams, or that you want to save the world, or your motivation may be deeply personal. The point is that we are all motivated by different things.

Let's say you are building an app to solve a problem that you care about. That's great, but it's only important to other people in so far as they can see you are serious and are determined to do what it takes to drive the idea forward. On the other side of the coin, you don't want to look like you're so emotionally driven that you can't see that you're obsessing over a product no one else wants – remember validation?

Forget your motivation. What motivates the people you want to attract? If you can tap into that, you're onto a winner. Maybe, just maybe, money isn't their thing at all. They want the glory. That means awards, publicity, fame and recognition. If you want to headhunt a specific person, it helps if you know a little bit about the things that turn them on. On that note, imagine you wanted that genius of heart-warming Disney soundtracks, Elton John, to compose a song for a feel-good film you had written.

I once heard that if you asked Elton John how much it would cost for him to do the music for a movie, he'd slam the phone down on you. He doesn't need to do anything for money, and the mere suggestion that he would take a project on solely for payment would almost be tantamount to calling him a prostitute. He never has to make another track, do another concert or work in any way for the rest of his life. It would be difficult for him to spend all his money, and he is probably getting richer every second without doing a thing. So, how much will it cost to hire Elton John to create the soundtrack for a movie? A fucking clever idea, that's how much! An idea. That's the currency of creative minds.

Wealth comes in many forms, and sometimes it is not *just* about the money. What are you promising to give to the people you want to hire?

## Let's Start With Money

Let's be honest here. Unless you're already as rich as Elton John, money's going to have to play a big part in the equation. Sure, many of us won't sell our principles for thirty pieces of silver, but we want to make money while we're being superheroes.

The truth is that every entrepreneur who calls themselves 'a founder' and their business 'a startup' dreams of achieving incredible financial freedom through their efforts. There's nothing wrong with that. But it's also true that everyone who works at your startup early on is going to want a piece of that pie. They may not be thinking of buying a yacht and being carried to the office by a carriage drawn by unicorns, but they are thinking, *this could buy me a house, a nice one where the hallways don't smell of cat wee*. Therefore, you have to show them that they can achieve their goals and explain how it's possible. Here's an example:

'Today, we're going to raise $150k at a valuation of $1.5m. This will give us what we need to build an MVP and some early traction, so we can raise a seed of $2m at a valuation of $10m. From there, I plan to sell to X, Y or Z for around $50 to 100m. Your shares at that point, with dilution, should be worth about one million dollars. That's $1 million in three years. Not bad, huh?'

Top tip: get the balance right between exciting and believable. The number of businesses that reach unicorn status (selling for over a billion dollars) is tiny. As the name suggests, it happens very rarely. A $100m exit, on the other hand, although super hard to achieve, is a realistic outcome.

**'The only source of knowledge is experience.'**

*Albert Einstein – Scientist and well-known meme character*

## The Experience of a Lifetime

Nothing beats building it your way.

The opportunity to own the process from start to finish and to be able to say, 'I built that from scratch' is one of the most powerful pills you can offer to a creative professional. The brightest minds will always be attracted to the chance to exercise their creative freedom and build something in the way they believe it should be built.

This kind of promise is my favourite. As an early-stage founder, the one thing that you have, which other companies, later-stage startups and even FAANG[12] businesses don't, is the opportunity to build something from the ground up. Doing it your way means complete ownership. It's

[12] FAANG is an acronym that refers to the stocks of five prominent American technology companies: Facebook (now known as Meta), Amazon, Apple, Netflix and Google (now known as Alphabet).

on you, nothing or nobody else can fuck it up, and you don't have to go through the horrible process of working around or unravelling someone else's mess. Here's what it looks like as a promise:

'You're great at what you do, right? So, you probably get frustrated when you see things done badly that you know you could make better if you were given the freedom to. But, because of legacy systems and processes, you're shackled. Here, you won't be. This is your gig. Your show. Build it the way you think it should be built.'

I promise you, this is the most addiction-inducing thing you can say to great talent. You're inviting them to unleash their greatness, so if the thought of building something from scratch, their way, doesn't get them fired up, don't hire them. They aren't right for this game.

## Grab a Place in the History Books

Let's start with a quiz. Are you ready?
Category: Space travel
Who was the first man on the moon? Correct. It was Neil Armstrong.
Who was the second? Correct, again. Buzz Aldrin. Pat yourself on the back.
Who was the third? No idea? Me, neither.

Next category: Tech startups
Who were the founders of Apple? Correct. Steve Jobs, Steve Wozniak and . . . not so sure who else?
Who was the forty-third employee at Netflix?

You get my point, right? Being the first brings you the coolest kind of notoriety. If your 'wouldn't it be cool if' idea, which started as a scribbled note on a napkin in the middle of a coffee shop, turns into the sensation you think it will, your first few hires will be dining out on that for decades to come. They will be invited onto panels and big-name podcasts, and they'll probably write an averagely successful book. This dream is sexy and real.

You have to sell this as a one-time-only opportunity. They will only get this one shot at being the founding CTO, the first marketing hire, the first operations guy, so you have to ramp up their fear of missing out. Keep pressing that FOMO button, and make sure they know that if they miss out now, that's it.

The thing to remember is that people will work for you if you sell them the dream. Talent is attracted to money, freedom and fame. We're a fickle bunch, humans, aren't we? And that's the bottom line – understanding human nature and using it to your advantage. Give the people you want the path to money, freedom and fame, and they will not only work for you, but they will also deliver outcomes you couldn't have dreamed of.

Now that you know how to hire the top talent, let's take another look at who you're going to hire. Understanding that you need to hire the best people is one thing but finding them is a different matter.

## How Not to Hire the Wrong Fucking People?

When you're in the process of turning your idea into a market-defining monolith, hiring is going to have a major impact. The best teams build the best companies, and the best teams are even better when the players within them are shit-hot, so you want people who are superb as individuals *and* work well with the rest of the team. They say there's no 'I' in 'team', which is fair enough, but strong teamwork will only get you so far if team members are fair to shite.

If I had to sum up the main two characteristics I look for in people, I'd say they are intelligence and a strong work ethic. There's a third factor, however, and this is possibly even more important than the first two: they must not be a dick! Are they going to be a nightmare to work with and make you want to commit violent assaults on a daily basis?

If you even suspect the answer is yes to either of those questions, don't hire. Save yourself the hassle, not only of having to bite your tongue until you are road-raging on your way to work every day but of having to start afresh and find someone to replace them later.

I know because I've been there. Loads of the people I have hired were great, some were okay and a few were horrific (I mean genuinely terrifying)! I don't want you to go through what I went through, so I'm going to let you learn from my fuckups. Let's make sure you hire rockstars, not arseholes.

The startup space is littered with the phrase 'This is [name]. They worked at [big name]' and 'They went to [big name] university', so it's easy to fall into the trap of hiring people based on what they've written in their CVs and résumés. The reason I call that a trap is because people are more than a list of accolades and, besides, those accolades don't always reflect who they truly are, which means that mistakes are often made and those making the hires (you) bear the burden.

## Things You Won't See on a CV

A glance at the world of social media is all you need to see how cheap talk is and how easy it is to paint a false picture from behind a keyboard. Think of all those keyboard warriors for a start. Then there's Chantelle, the office secretary who can barely make eye contact with the office hamster, let alone a living breathing human being, but who posts pictures of herself being the life and soul of the party, after half a fish tank's worth of Stella Artois. Yes, my friend, we cannot believe the fibs people tell us through the lens of social media, and the world of CVs and résumés is no different.

'Was the captain for the school football team' is largely meaningless as it was long enough ago that it's irrelevant today, and it probably wasn't true anyway.

'Thinks outside the box' may mean they've come up with more stories for being late than Agatha Christie wrote whodunnits, and 'works well under pressure' means they don't start until five minutes before the work is due for submission. You get my drift.

What they won't write on the CV is that they take forty-five minutes taking their mid-morning dump, their idea of team building is distracting others in the office by constantly chatting about their relationship problems, and their Olympic gold medal is for flicking freshly picked bogeys (they're dried balls of nasal mucus if you're not British) from one side of the office to the other.

## Some Home Truths

Look, I understand the attraction towards people who have experience, a tier-one education, and more letters after their name than a brain surgeon, but you could find yourself chasing fool's gold. Having experience doesn't mean someone is better at the job; it means they are more expensive. A tier-one education doesn't mean they are more intelligent; it means they are better at academic study and could mean they had a more privileged start in life.

I am not saying people with experience can't be better, especially if it's the right kind of experience and the candidate learned a lot from it, and I'm not saying people with PhDs aren't usually smart, but assuming that someone with experience is better or someone with a PhD is more intelligent is a mistake. Don't assume. They say that to assume makes 'an ass out of u and me', but it can lead to far more serious repercussions than that!

You can never be sure whom you are dealing with until they've signed the dotted line, and they're sitting in your office, but you will get a much better idea by meeting them than anything they've written on their CV or résumé. Interviewing someone is not foolproof, but you'll glean much more insight than you'll ever get from a written document. That is, of course, if you know what to look for and how to ask the right questions. We know what we should be watching out for – intelligence, work ethic and someone we can get on with – so how are we going to go about finding people who have these qualities? Simples: the teacher test, the research test and the feedback test.

Curious? Let's start by checking how smart they are.

## The Teacher Test

**'Wherever smart people work, doors are unlocked.'**

*Steve Wozniak – Co-founder of Apple Incorporated*

The teacher test is a way of finding out whether the person you're interviewing thinks in a way that you don't. Someone who thinks differently from you and isn't afraid to show it could be a major asset. During the interview, have they taught you something you didn't know? If the answer to that question is 'yes', that shows you two things.

Firstly, it means they will add something to the hive mind of your company by dreaming up ideas and solutions that you won't. Secondly, it shows they are happy to raise their head above the parapet, stand up and be counted. When it comes to brainstorming and problem solving, no idea is a bad idea even when it's a thoroughly shit one. Even terrible ideas can be thought-provoking. At the very least, they can be considered and dismissed from an inquiry, as the police would say.

No matter how well you know a subject, there will always be areas you don't know and ways of viewing things you hadn't considered before. Hire people who see things differently from you. Looking at anything from different perspectives creates better outcomes.

That's great, but how do we know if they'll work hard?

## The Research Test

> **'Talent is cheaper than table salt. What separates the talented individual from the successful one is a lot of hard work.'**
>
> *Stephen King – Writer*

I've called this next test 'the research test' because it's a way of checking how much research the candidate bothered to do before coming to the interview. I don't expect them to have read every article I ever wrote in Medium, the name of my pets, or even my hobbies and interests. Sure, in an ideal world, they would hold me on a pedestal and think of me as one of the gods of the tech startup space (tongue well and truly stuck in my cheek), but that's unlikely. No, my friend, I don't ask for much; only that they have bothered to have my company's website. Isn't that fair enough?

Surely, it goes without saying that if someone is serious about working for a company, they will read everything on the website, especially if they are granted an interview? 'What do you know about us already?' is one of those bog-standard questions you expect to get asked at any interview, isn't it?

How do I check how thoroughly they researched my company? I ask them obscure questions that could easily be answered using the information on my website. It's not rocket science, and I don't believe it is too much to expect from a candidate. If they get one wrong, I can put that down to the information not sinking in, my question not being clear enough or a memory lapse; however, if I ask them two or three questions, and they can't get any of them, that tells me they haven't done the most rudimentary research, and that's damning because it suggests they are not interested in the company.

Preparing for an interview can be easy for people who are already in the sector. They can show up and demonstrate that they have the right experience, technical knowledge and a keen attitude. The best candidates will go one step further and put the time and effort into understanding your company. The simplest way to do this is by scouring your website. Test them, see what depths they went to and find out how much work they put in.

This is a great test for finding out how hard someone is willing to work to get results. You want the hardest workers on your team . . . as long as they're not nightmares to work with. That is a biggie. You do not, absolutely do not, want to work with arseholes. Trust me.

## The Feedback Test

> 'We all need feedback. That's how we improve.'
>
> *Bill Gates – Founder of Microsoft, Philanthropist, and Co-Founder of the Bill and Melinda Gates Foundation*

One of the simplest ways of discovering someone's 'arsehole factor' is by giving them feedback during the interview and seeing how they respond. If they take it well, which is to say respectfully and thoughtfully rather than defensively and emotionally, that's a great sign. Ideally, they will ask for more feedback along with suggestions on how they can improve. That's the stuff of dreams, right there: the golden response.

You are going to spend a lot of time with your colleagues, and although their performance and results are important, enjoying working with them is paramount. The people you will find the most difficult to deal with are those who cannot take criticism well. You will spend all your time tiptoeing around discussions and avoiding contact. This is not good. Nip it in the bud. You need to weed this out before it arrives. Apart from wanting to avoid the toxicity of defensiveness and sensitivity, having people who are open to feedback provides the best path to continuous improvement. Find people who strive for this and can embrace criticism maturely.

## Let's Not Forget Culture

Sorry, not sorry, my friend. I know it's become a bit of a buzzword, which conjures up images of an eclectic group sitting on beanbags with iMacs, drinking decaffeinated soya flat whites and laughing at non-offensive jokes; a haven where everyone can be themselves, free from prejudice, and free to share their ideas openly without fear of ridicule or disrespect. Oh, and beers in the office on a Friday afternoon. I'd like to add 'sunny' afternoon, but I live in England, so that can be a bit of an overstretch. I'm playing a bit here, but culture is incredibly important.

You won't always be starting out, and as more people join you, this thing called culture is going to develop all by itself whether you engineer it or not, and it will impact everything from company performance to employee wellbeing. Culture will become an increasingly important feature as your startup grows, so why not recognise that from the beginning, and try to nurture an optimal one?

## Don't Be a Dick! (And Don't Hire Dicks)

Earlier, we mentioned that one of the key qualities I look for in any candidate is that they must not be a dick. I don't want to hire people who are going to drive me or the rest of the team completely bonkers. Isn't it also fair for me to offer the same deal in return? Your company's culture is a reflection of you as the founder, so now it is your turn not to be a dick.

We agreed that you need to find people who are smart, hard-working and agreeable to be around. By the law of karma, we must be the change we want to see, so we should also be smart, hard-working and agreeable to work with. If your company is a toxic place to work, word will soon get around, and no matter how cool your website spiel is, and how much of a great person you may be, you're not going to attract the right people. That means taking responsibility for your actions, your company's actions and your staff's actions. It is all on you because you are the founder.

## What Does Good Culture Look Like?

The foundation of a strong culture is safety. People need to feel safe – safe to be themselves regardless of sexuality, gender identity, race, religious identity, nationality, neurodiversity or disability, to name just a few considerations; and these are just the basics.

They need to be safe to make mistakes without being berated, ridiculed or threatened. They must be protected from mental, physical or emotional abuse from other members of staff, clients, suppliers or you – yes, you, because none of us is perfect, and when everything is going wrong, it's easy to tell someone their work is shit, that they should have stayed at home, or just to fuck off. That's not cool, but it happens, and it's more reason for ensuring you are always bringing your A-game. That's why self-care is so important as well.

The most productive environments promote the free exchange of ideas, which makes sense anyway because sometimes you must kiss a hell of a lot of frogs before you find a prince. Not sure whether anyone's ever used that analogy to express how important it is to brainstorm as many ideas as possible, but I'm a founder, not a professional writer! You get my point. Don't discourage people from sharing their crap ideas. Getting it wrong is often just a stepping stone to getting it right.

A happier workforce is a healthier one. Contented employees are far less likely to shout at each other, suffer breakdowns in communication or play the blame game. Don't think that this is something that your human resources team can take care of. Think of them as the cleaners, there to wipe up the mess after you fuck up. Better not to fuck up in the first place, wouldn't you agree?

If you are the sort of person who thinks anyone who gives a toss about how other people feel is a 'snowflake' or a 'politically correct gone mad' individual or that others should just 'grow a pair' and 'toughen up', this part of the chapter may not be for you. You can come back to it once you've become fed up with the crazy turnover of staff, lack of diversity in your office, bollockings from your HR director (if you have one) or payouts for unfair dismissal. For anyone else, let's look at how to create a culture of success.

From my experience of building a global business, there are five factors that you can control to develop a stronger culture:

- Giving staff a purpose
- Giving staff a voice
- Forging a path
- Sharing success
- Empowering people

Let's explore these ideas further.

## It Starts With Why

If people are going to work their hardest and deliver their best, they have to believe in what they are doing and feel the greater purpose.

> **'People don't buy what you do. They buy why you do it.'**
>
> *Simon Sinek – Author and Inspirational Speaker*

Your first hires, the most important people you employ, might be in it for the financial rewards that will come when the company is sold. They will also want to know they are involved in something magical and a product they can be proud to be remembered for.

What about those who come later; your fifth, tenth or one-hundredth hire? What's in it for them apart from a monthly paycheque? Well, you're looking at a very similar scenario.

Purpose, that's what. If you already have a team, ask them why your company exists: 'What are we trying to achieve, and what's your part in it?' You will be surprised how some people will find this easy while others find it impossible. I know because I've been through this.

I've been in situations where it's tough to answer, and when I reflect on those times, I now recognise they were signs that it was time to move on. You can't have people feeling that way, so work with your management team to make sure the purpose of your organisation is watertight and consistent. It needs to shine through at all points of contact from the website to the job advertisement, at the interview stage when recruiting and during the onboarding process. Another quote from Simon Sinek seems appropriate here:

> **'Great companies don't hire skilled people and motivate them. They hire already motivated people and inspire them.'**
>
> *Simon Sinek – Author and Inspirational Speaker*

## Give People a Voice

The quickest way to ruin a culture is to make people feel irrelevant and like a cog in the machine. Give people a voice. Throughout history, some of the greatest wars and protests have been over people wanting their voices heard. Millions have died for democracy and freedom of speech, so how do you expect staff to feel if they have to forfeit these the moment they step into your office, where they might be spending 75 per cent of their waking lives?

Ask your team. Are you spotting a recurring theme here? Culture is about them. It is about creating the environment for them to thrive, so allow them to drive it. Ask them for their ideas and opinions and make this a core practice. You will be amazed at how such an effortless process positively affects your team's spirit and morale.

When I was starting out, the owner of the company I was working for asked me for my opinion on how we could sell more. Despite a sense of panic at having been put on the spot, I felt empowered. It didn't matter that my suggestion was poor – so rubbish that I erased it from my memory, and even the strongest truth serum will not enable recall. That didn't matter because just being asked and listened to made me feel like a valued part of the team. Thankfully, they never implemented my idea, so there was no harm done. Neither did they belittle me, so my self-esteem was left intact.

Whatever you do, don't just give people a voice. Let them know their voice is being heard.

## Forge a Path

People like roadmaps. It shows them where they are going. Ask any runner how they keep themselves going on a long trot, and they will tell you that they look out for markers that act as milestones. This gives them a sense of progress. It doesn't matter how many runs they did before, or how many times they will put their training shoes back on in the future. What counts is where they are now – passing the church, going under the subway, crossing the bridge, or reaching the top of the hill.

Your staff will have their own goals, which could be money, promotion, more responsibility or simply job security, but it's your job to understand this and identify what individuals want to achieve. Look at how teams operate in the world of sport. They set goals, and this needs to happen in your office as well. We are applying the same principles as we would for the first hires. The roadmap is still important, just slightly different for later hires.

Setting goals is only the beginning. Once you have done that, you must show your team that you are there to support their efforts and to help them achieve them, and encourage your staff to support each other.

This creates a culture of collaboration, where people care about the success of others, where it's about figuring out how we can cross the river rather than how can I.

## Share Success

When a salesperson closes a mega deal with that blue-chip company you've been trying to win over for the last eighteen months, celebrate it. The research and development team find a way to make things quicker? Celebrate. Or maybe the finance team save enough to take the entire team to the Bahamas every month. You guessed right: celebrate it. Shout about it loudly, so those at the back of the room can hear and everyone in the company knows about it. Why? Because the sales team is nothing without a high-quality product that customers want, and because the research and development team will get nowhere without the sales team driving the revenue to support them and telling them what customers want.

Like forging a path, this also feeds into the spirit of collaboration. When you recognise and reward success privately in the one-to-one appraisal or the team briefing, you'll encourage further victories but nowhere near as much as you will by sharing successes with everyone in your company.

Whether it's ringing a bell, going for drinks, giving out doughnuts or run-around high fives, it all counts. If you genuinely believe in the power of sharing, however, go a little further and celebrate success with something more valuable – even if it is just time off work or a bottle of cheap wine.

## Empower People

If your staff are going to fuck up, let them. It's the only way they're going to grow, and if you have gone with rule number one of hiring people who are better than you, they can't fuck it up any more than you would. That would be a problem, but, even then, freaky things can happen. Top tennis players sometimes get beaten by nobodies in the first round. It happens everywhere.

You're not going to like this, especially if you are a bit of a control freak with a tendency to micromanage, but it's the truth. If you want people to feel valued and to create a culture that drives the company forward, you will have to let people make decisions. Forgive the use of a well-used quote, but it belongs here:

> 'It doesn't make sense to hire smart people and tell them what to do; we hire smart people so they can tell us what to do.'
>
> *Steve Jobs – Co-Founder, Former Chairperson and CEO of Apple Incorporated*

Yes, I know . . . *he only went and did it; Tommy boy quoted Steve Jobs in a book about tech startups. That's so clichéd!* Tough. It was a good fit for the point I was making, and he was right, wasn't he? God bless you, Steve. It's the hardest thing to do because founders, by their very nature, tend to think they can do everything better than everyone else. There are going to be times when you'll be encouraged by a recruiter to hire someone with no experience, no relevant skills, and for a salary that's over budget because they're 'a good judge of talent', and you'll agree even though you know you're never getting that 20 per cent recruitment fee back, but if you show people that you trust them and believe in them, and let them make their own mistakes, they will lift you and your company to a place you never expected.

Now you know who the fuck you need to hire, how to make your company into a place that promotes excellence, how to attract the people you want, and how to identify them in interview. You have the product, the investment, the team and some customers.

Now what?

You're going to have to grow this thing, baby, so we're going to explore how to market the shit out of your company without spending an arm and a leg.

# 15.

# HOW THE FUCK AM I GONNA REACH MY MARKET?

You've got a great product. It came to you one day when something in the world simply wasn't good enough and you weren't going to stand for it. *This ends now*, you decided, before sitting down and coming up with a cunning plan. You told your mum about it, and she loved it, of course, and you mentioned it to Billy, Graham and Theresa over a few drinks in the beer garden of The Prince Albert, and they all told you it was a fabulous idea. Even Phil, who has criticised everything you've ever done since you were both five years old, said, 'That's not a bad idea for you, pal!'

Not content to settle for the kind remarks you received from members of your close circle, you spoke to people who were already operating in the industry you want to break into, and you reached out to potential users of your product to find out if they'd see any value in it. They recommended some tweaks to make it better, but it was all good, and you sensed the market validation was there.

What had started as a 'wouldn't it be cool if' (or 'anything's got to be better than this' in your case) was gaining momentum, and you began to realise that you could make this happen. Victory was a long way off but potentially yours, so you put together a core team of co-founders, others who believed in what you were doing and had the experience to add value to your newly founded organisation.

With your heart set on winning investment, you went the extra mile to validate your product and created a mock-up version that could sit on your website. People engaged with it, and you knew you had enough to convince an angel that there is a market for your product and people will pay for it. They gave you the money, and you built an MVP. You're fucking awesome, your idea's a winner, and people will buy it . . .

So, why the fuck aren't you celebrating?

## The Town Crier's Not Gonna Work for You

Once upon a time, in a world that only exists in the history books, old novels and the imaginations of period drama writers, you could have asked the town crier to shout about your product: 'Oye! Oye! The mayor's been fined one shilling for breaking bubonic plague restrictions. He said he was sorry. The Tzar of Russia has declared war on everywhere else. University lecturer arrested for trying to distract students by crossing and uncrossing her legs while moderating an exam. And the new Stakester app means you won't get ripped off in a wager. Let me thank my sponsor, Macbeth Witches' Den Remedies, for funding today's announcements.'

Life in the modern world isn't that simple. If you've taken the advice of the founders who have made it, you already know it's better to dive into as big a market as you can. That's fine, but it leaves you with a massive headache. How the fuck are you going to reach that market? How are you going to grab the attention of the people who need your product and how much is that going to cost?

We are in the middle of a massive revolution – technologically, sociologically and culturally – and change is happening at a mind-blowing pace. Yet, amid all this turbulence, almost in the eye of the storm if you like, the rules of marketing are the same as they've always been. Your market is out there. Your product delivers the kind of value that people in that market are willing to pay for, and your job is to find a way of letting them know that you exist, that you understand and can address their needs and want to make it as easy as possible for them to buy from you. The only thing that's changed is the how. Town criers are out, so let's consider the other options.

## Isn't It Gonna Cost Me an Arm and a Leg?

Well, if you are a bit of a sadomasochist, and you want to sell to a Mexican drug cartel or the Russian mafia. Fortunately, for most of the world, including Mexico and Russia, you can buy and sell things using currency. That said, with the humongous increases in inflation we've been seeing, some may prefer to pay for things with body parts. But seriously, putting aside the sarcasm, yes, marketing can be a costly affair, but it doesn't always have to be.

## How About NO Website and NO Marketing?

Don't forget what Samantha Hornsby and Mae Yip achieved without a website and with no marketing spend. They launched their ERIC festival with nothing more than an Eventbrite page and attracted two thousand sign-ups organically. If that doesn't warm your heart and show you that anything's possible, nothing will.

## Grow Your Startup With a One-Page Website

You might think this is bullshit, something I've made up or read in a marketing playbook, but it's none of those things, my friend. Remember Snag Tights, the birthchild of Brie Read, the entrepreneur who was so frustrated by ill-fitting tights that she launched a brand of her own? Well, she didn't work alone. She co-founded the company with Tom Martin, a charismatic man who likes wearing tights – testing them anyway, or so he said when I interviewed him. If we're going to focus on marketing in this chapter, note that Tom's a techie and Brie used to run a digital marketing agency, so neither of them was a marketing virgin.

Once they had done all the groundwork, scraped together £100,000 from friends and family, set up a supply chain and were ready to take orders, all that was needed was the big launch. The first step was to set up a photo shoot, but procrastination had its way and as the sand slipped away from the top of the egg timer, their end of March deadline crept closer and closer. Until it was staring them so provocatively in the face, almost growling, 'Who the fuck are you looking at, you lazy bastards?' that even a world-class procrastination champion would have had to admit defeat. Action had to be taken. They could procrastinate no longer.

It was the middle of March, and their launch deadline was the end of the month. Within a couple of days, Tom had used Google to source a photographer specialising in shooting plus-sized models, and found a photoshoot director as part of the deal – Jess Guest, the photographer's boss! Jess found the models ('talent' in fashion-speak), sourced a great location, and planned everything.

The clock was ticking . . .

And then it was the last week of March. They did the shoot on a Tuesday and had the processed images by Thursday. Their big launch was just four days away. As they sat together in the Victoria Bar and Grill in Victoria Station, mulling over the photos, Tom suggested that it might, just might, be a good idea to put together a website. Brie agreed before dashing off to deal with a minor home-related chore (founders do have lives, you know). By the time she returned to the restaurant a couple of hours later, Tom had developed the website, written the copy, uploaded the images and it was live!

Do I need to remind you of how rapidly their company grew? They went from zero revenue to almost £2 million a month in the seventeen months from the day they started to when I interviewed them. £2 million! But here's the best bit: when I interviewed them, they were still using the same website that Tom set up in Victoria Bar and Grill four days before their launch deadline!

## How to Build a Website in Two Hours

If you're anything like me, you're wondering how the fuck Tom managed to build a website in two hours. Well, I asked him, and he told me, so I'm going to share his wisdom with you. The short answer is 'ultra-efficiency' – don't put anything on there that isn't required. The fact that someone had told Tom he couldn't build a one-page website also helped. That Tom is a man after this Tom's heart, I can tell you. When someone tells me I can't do something, I feel the same urge as Tom did – to prove them wrong.

Someone had told Brie that it isn't possible to sell from the first page of a website and, therefore, one-page websites don't work. Tom disagreed.

> 'Why am I going to make you look at one page, and then go, "Ooh, would you like to come and see another page? Would you like to click through?"'
>
> *Tom Martin – Co-Founder of Snag Tights*

Tom has a point, doesn't he? Sometimes it pays to question things. Sometimes it pays to be naive enough to think something's possible when everyone else has dismissed it. Why should you have more pages on a website? Why should there be millions of colours? Does there have to be a huge range of products from day one? If so, why? Tom sums it up nicely:

> **'We're a tights company. Here are some pictures of people wearing tights. Here are our products. Would you like to buy some tights?'**
>
> *Tom Martin – Co-Founder of Snag Tights*

When Tom launched the Snag Tights website, they offered four colours and six sizes. He kept it simple. You can apply this strategy to loads of things from dipping your toe in the water before daring to sink your body into a hot bath to asking your friend if it's okay to borrow the lawnmower before launching into a full-on affair with his wife.

Keep it simple. Offer the essentials and then follow a process of monitoring, assessing and tweaking. Some products will not budge, so you can remove them or change them. Once you have a base of products that are all selling, you can add to the range – one or two products at a time – but there's no need to rush things.

## How Did They Attract Traffic to the Site?

Let's face it, even absolute beginners know that traffic won't come to a new website by itself. When you search for something on Google, the first thing the algorithm will do is to look for websites that contain keywords and key phrases that match the search request.

The world wide web is so vast that even for obscure search terms, there will be thousands of matching results. The purpose of Google's algorithm is to ensure you get the most fruitful results for your search, so it will consider a variety of factors: how old is the site (how well established it is), how regularly is it updated (is it active and up to date), how well written is it (clarity), and loads of others. The bottom line is that if you've just launched a site from scratch, I don't care how funky it is, it will get little if any visits without you doing stuff to drive traffic to it. That was Brie's job.

Brie used platforms such as Facebook and Instagram to engage people and generate meaningful discussions. She shared images that her audience could relate to and developed a tone of voice that they liked and understood. By reaching out to people in this way, not only did she generate interest in the website, but she was also able to learn from her growing customer base. What did they want the website to look like? What were their likes and dislikes? More importantly, she paid close attention to every single comment on every platform.

## Don't Fuck Up Your Message

**'These clothes are not for people like you!'**

*The message from many fashion retail outlets, according to Brie Read, co-founder of Snag Tights*

What does sharing images that people can relate to look like? Well, according to Tom, it isn't advertising a gym with pictures of men who look like Adonis and women who look like Greek goddesses. Such images only serve to tell the average Joe and Jo that they are not good enough, and instead of attracting everyday people to book a gym membership, they intimidate them, make them feel shit, and scare them away.

Potential gym members shouldn't be shown supermodels. They need to see average, everyday people, who remind them of themselves. Let's face it; when you join most gyms, that's what you see – mostly ordinary people striving for improvement and a smaller group of people who do, quite frankly, look like they've walked off the set of a Hollywood film. And that's cool because the men with moobs and the women with shapes that don't conform to *Vogue* feel comfortable in their skins and can still aspire to get 'beach bodies', not that that's necessarily mentally healthy. If we are physically fit, we shouldn't be too concerned about our body types, but that's human nature, and I'm not here to preach.

In a similar vein, Brie told me how people often say that sourcing clothes from shops on the high street is a demoralising experience because they can't find clothes to fit them, and others feel bullied by brands that seem to be telling them what they can and can't wear: these clothes are not for people like you; you have to look this way to wear these kinds of clothes.

## What Would You Say About the Brand?

Brie and Tom chose Instagram to ask an important question: 'If you were talking to potential investors of Snag Tights, what would you say about the brand?' One of their brand advocates responded by explaining that she felt as though brands were trying to marginalise and humiliate her. Snag Tights made her feel like someone was trying to make life easier and more comfortable for her. There's a simple takeaway here, which goes right back to the earlier chapter about validation. Understand what your customers are feeling and what their pain point is, and tailor your solution to fit their needs. Choose words and pictures that speak to them directly and personally.

Snag Tights has successfully managed to engage with its target audience emotionally, and that is a key ingredient to winning sales and brand advocates. So, what happened when they launched the website and told the world about it on Facebook and Instagram?

They made their first sale by 11 p.m. that night (one pair of tights at £6.99). Their first £100-day came after around a month. A £10,000-week within three months (WOW!), and five times that amount just three months after that. How do you describe that kind of growth? It's more than two times greater than exponential.

The town crier is not enough in the twenty-first century, but the principles of marketing remain the same, and Tom and Brie have taken advantage of those principles perfectly. You can't use a one-size-fits-all approach to marketing any more than you can apply it to the manufacture and sale of tights. (See what I did there? Perhaps there's a genuinely decent author in me after all.)

When Snag Tights hit Australia, they used an advertising campaign that means something to Australians. 'Snag' is Australian slang for 'sausage dog', so they leveraged this to sell their product.

> **'Tights. Tights. Tights. Sausage Dog – Repeat.'**
>
> *Snag Tights' Australian advertising campaign*

Their sausage dog approach spoke to Australians in a way they could relate to. They've since launched in Germany and other EU countries, and they continue to stride forward from strength to strength.

Snag Tight's marketing strategy isn't just smashing it in terms of growth and customer acquisition, but their customer retention rates are through the roof as well. With 70 per cent of their revenue coming from repeat business, they are doing considerably better than any of their competitors in a market where only around 10 per cent of revenue comes from repeat business.

Brie and Tom almost make it look effortless, but it's easy to get it wrong on social media. What are Brie's top tips for new founders for marketing their startups on social media?

## Don't Fuck Up Your Social Media Campaign

One of the most common mistakes founders make when it comes to using social media is not testing. Brie wanted to maximise the efficacy of every post and every advertisement by comparing responses to different images, colours, text and anything else that could have affected audience reactions. Testing is nothing without thorough measurement, so she checked out every comment, every reaction and other metrics such as click-throughs to the website. She left no stone unturned when it came to monitoring the metrics, and she made sure she was ready to change course where a campaign was not working as well as it should. Be ready to kickstart another.

They don't use hyper-targeted advertisements anymore because they don't believe this approach works well with the current algorithms. Although this was the case when Brie and I discussed it and as I wrote this book, it might not be the case today, as you are reading it, and that's fine. The keyword here is 'test'. Always be aware that the situation could change, and something that worked yesterday might not work today.

### The Algorithm Is Not Your Customer

Besides the fact that the algorithm can and does change, Tom points out that the algorithm doesn't buy anything; people do. Brie creates advertisements that are clear about what they are selling, that show a picture and some simple words to explain what the product is, what it does and why it is better, and she targets women. If your product and/or your website are crap, no one is going to buy whether you post at this time or on this platform or use this targeted advertising campaign. Let your market drive your marketing decisions and pay close attention to what works and what doesn't. The algorithm is not your customer.

Look at what your customers are doing and make data-driven decisions. There's a commonly believed myth that Facebook advertisements can sell anything but, again, it comes down to how good your product is and how easy you make it for people to buy from you once they click through to your site. If you get that wrong, your campaign will be a waste of time.

### Don't Flog Dead Horses

I'd rather you didn't flog any horses at all, but it's a figure of speech, so there you go. Brie points out that it is wrong to think it will take three months to see if a campaign is going to work. Perhaps it depends on the product but, based on her knowledge of digital marketing and experience in selling tights, she believes you will know within twenty-four hours. Whatever you do, you don't want to be throwing money down the drain, but that's what you will be doing if you don't change course when you need to. And when it comes to changing course, that includes establishing whether the fault is with the campaign, the product, or something to do with your website's user journey.

So, don't burn all your capital on campaigns that don't work. On that note, it's time to move away from Tom and Brie's awesome, almost Midas-stroked tale of glory and to shift focus to a startup that ingloriously crashed and burned. Let's look at how the founders of Fast fucked up their tech startup by fucking up their marketing.

## How to Fuck Up Your Startup by Fucking Up Your Marketing

In April 2022, Fast, a startup specialising in online checkout products, announced that it was closing. The announcement followed days of uncertainty after reports that its 2021 revenue growth was modest, and its cash burn rate was high. To make matters worse, it had exhausted most of its fundraising options.

Where had it all gone wrong for Fast? They were selling a one-click payment product, for which there is a massive market and huge opportunities for startups to grab a share and grow it. Was it the quality of their product? Probably not, because they managed to win investment right up to a series-B raise of $102 million led by Stripe. Was it a lack of funds? Read the bit about a $102 million cash injection. If it wasn't a lack of funds and it wasn't a crap product, how did a startup with a great idea, a massive market and tons of potential fail so spectacularly?

### Super-Fast Burn Rate with Very Little Return

Fast reportedly made $600,000 in revenue for the whole of 2021, which amounts to $50,000 a month, while their nearest competitor, Bolt, was bringing in ten times that amount. But Fast's burn rate was off the scale.

They were spending $10 million a month, which is a mind-boggling two-hundred times what they were making! For that to have happened in the first month would be tragic enough – a poor start and an alarming loss of available capital – but for it to go on for a second month and beyond beggars belief. If there's any such thing as the Ostrich of the Year award, co-founders Domm Holland and Allison Barr Allen would be prime candidates for the shortlist.

Sorry, guys, I don't want to rub salt in your wounds, but how did you let that happen? I would put money on it being a marketing fail (if I were a gambling man). Whatever they were doing was not working. Some costs are unavoidable – office space, staff salaries, IT – but whatever they were spending on marketing, whether that was too little, too much, or just right, was not doing its job.

Within weeks of their closure, other tech companies were moving in to snap up their staff, so they can't blame their unfortunate and rapid demise on a poor recruitment strategy. RIP Fast. May your disbanded team find joy and comfort elsewhere.

That's enough negativity for one chapter. Let's look at another quirky success story.

### 'This App's Not Bad, But Our Marketing's Rubbish.'

*One of the advertising messages from George Rawlings and Matt McNeill Love, the co-founders of Thursday*

Thursday, originally Honeypot, was co-founders George Rawlings and Matt McNeill Love's answer to the dating-app boredom that had set in during the pandemic lockdown. What should have been an exciting, fun experience had become tedious, and they wanted to shake things up by creating a new dating app that broke all the rules. The result? Honeypot.

Honeypot was very quickly rebranded to reflect its uniquely unique selling point: the fact that users can only play on this app for twenty-four hours a week – on Thursdays – and Thursday was born. They have almost created a USP from nothing. It is psychological trickery at its finest. On his LinkedIn profile, Rawlings jokes that they couldn't afford the running costs of a server for seven days a week, which highlights the irony. By offering less – an almost fucked-up version of a dating app that people can only access and use one day a week – they have created a buzz, generated loads of interest, and made app-based dating exciting again. In their words, 'It's human nature to want what you can't have.'

### Can't Beat a Bit of FOMO!

There's another point to Thursday – the app, that is – and that is to generate a sense of FOMO, that fear of missing out that crops up time and again. Rawlings and Love wanted to turn everything upside down so whereas, before, singletons often felt left out and envious of their friends who were in relationships, the tables were now turned. Signing up for Thursday gives you membership to an exclusive club.

Fancy seeing one of your single mates on Thursday? You've got no chance because they will be one of the thousands painting the town red with a date they met on the Thursday app, or they will be chilling in the house and looking for dates for the weekend. Rawlings' mission, according to his LinkedIn profile, is 'to make Thursday the most exciting day to be single, every week', and his plan appears to be working.

And this pair of young entrepreneurs have not had to spend a fortune on marketing, thanks to the genius of their marketing strategy. Clubhouse succeeded in growing rapidly using a similar principle – it was only available to iPhone users – but, although it managed to usher in a new type of social media – online rooms – which users could dive in and out of to chat with others, some would say its star has fallen as rapidly as it had risen. Thursday, on the other hand, is showing no signs of going the same way, perhaps because, behind all the hype, it's not that different from the other apps that already work well. The hardest part is recruiting new members, and Thursday has been raking them in. Retaining them should be easy.

### Marmite, Anyone?

Two years ago, in the days when Thursday was known as Honeypot, Rawlings posted a rough-and-ready update on LinkedIn to appeal to investors to take a chance on them. He was determined not to be judged by the same standards as other startups, preferring to do whatever it would take to stand out from the crowd. Rather than dumping money into digital and hoping for the best, a logical move for a dating app, he believed that doing something more unusual would get Honeypot noticed.

Writing a heartfelt, noticeably unedited LinkedIn update is not the slickest or most professional way of asking for investment, but apart from the odd grammatical faux pas, what did Rawlings and Love do that was so risqué?

They included a photo with the update, which showed the pair of them standing outside, somewhere in London, on a rainy day, wearing multicoloured umbrella hats and sandwich boards. Rawling's board featured the words 'Banned from Tinder' as a heading and stated that he and Love had resorted to building their own dating app to find romance or at least a date. Love's pointed out that they'd quit their jobs to launch Honeypot, and while their marketing was rubbish, the app was not bad.

They must have received a lot of enquiries because Rawlings posted a comment to let anyone who had asked for a pitch deck know they would be sending them out in due course and thanking them for their patience.

The comments section is lively, and you don't have to read many of them to realise that the post attracted its fair share of controversy. It's fair to say that Rawlings' post attracted a Marmite response.

For many females, being 'banned from Tinder' was a red flag because dating apps had been (and still are) in the firing line for some time for not being seen to do enough to protect users, particularly women and girls. Many others were curious enough to ask the question directly: why had they been banned from Tinder?

The pair had been banned for setting up an app to compete, but many people read the placard messages as meaning they had been banned from Tinder because of their behaviour and had set up an app where they could do what they want. When they gave their explanation, even that got them in hot water from some quarters; 'false advertising', somebody quipped.

The name of the app also came under fire. One man suggested that 'Honeypot' has connotations of honeytraps and strip clubs, and that this could deter women from using the app; however, a click on the reactions for the post shows it gained just as much support from women as men, if not more. They also had plenty of positive feedback from females in the comments, and one woman expressed an interest in investing in them.

**People Love Marmite!**

Nobody but Rawlings and Love can know whether this piece of LinkedIn marketing was the result of a very cynical and well-thought-out marketing strategy or a true reflection of their marketing shitness that just happened to work for them. Lottie Unwin, a marketing expert whom I interviewed for my podcast, reckons that as raw as Rawlings and Love's campaign may have been in execution, a highly paid marketing agency had come up with it. Either way, the update has done remarkably well: 3,907 reactions, 286 comments, and ninety-two shares! The fact that they've since re-branded leads me to suspect they had enough sense to know they had to make some noise, stand out, not be afraid of generating controversy and be happy with taking risks, but also knew they were winging it.

The thing about Marmite is that some people love it. Another thing about Marmite is that when those who hate it make a noise about it, all the people who love it come out of the shadows to jump to its defence. I don't think Marmite cares about the people who don't like it or even hate it. It has plenty of fans, and they will sing its praises from the rooftops forever.

The fact that some people either didn't like Rawlings' message or even hated it only went to help the post get more traction and attention from the people it was aimed at – potential customers and investors. The current zeitgeist is for people to stand up for what they believe in with pride, conviction and courage, and attract others from the same tribe. That's all well and good, but you don't have to be like Marmite to build a community, and this is something the co-founders of food-sharing app OLIO demonstrated with style.

## How to Build and Leverage a Community

Growing up on her parent's farm in North Yorkshire, and having to pull her weight with feeding cows, mucking out, moving stock and all the other tasks that needed to be done gave Tessa Clarke a deeper understanding of how much effort goes into producing every morsel of food we eat. Consequently, she hates the thought of food going to waste, but unlike most people who complain about stuff they don't like, she decided to do something about it. Tessa became interested in creating an app to help people share their unwanted food instead of chucking it away.

What began as a seed of an idea in her mind grew into a passion that she'd speak about to anyone who would listen. Who else would join her in her mission?

It didn't take long for her to find a kindred spirit in the form of Saasha Celestial-One, and the pair of them were determined to do their bit to transform what they saw as a 'throw-away society' into a 'give-away society', by encouraging like-minded people to share more and waste less. This eventually led to the launch of the OLIO app, which enables people from all around the world to build hyper-local sharing communities in their areas.

Tessa's community-building journey began when she recruited Saasha to join her as a co-founder. OLIO was founded in 2015. By the time I interviewed her for my podcast six years later, they'd built a community of around two million, and now that's grown to more than five million. They also have over thirty thousand trained volunteers ('Food Waste Heroes') who give up their time to collect surplus food from big-name supermarkets, caterers and other organisations where food is often wasted and distribute it within their communities, and they've attracted fifty thousand ambassadors who are fervently spreading the word about OLIO.

Just to be crystal clear about this, that's effectively fifty thousand free recruits who want to help Tessa and Saasha propagate their message around the world and get more people to sign up for the app. While many founders struggle to find people who have the right skills, experience and attitude, who are aligned with their mission and whom they can afford, Tessa and Saasha get the privilege of a huge queue of people who are fanatical about what they are doing and would almost pay to work for them. That shit's priceless. Please go back to the last chapter, which was focused on recruitment, tear every page out and throw them on the fire.

Okay, I'm kidding. Don't do that. You'll need that chapter. But *do* read on to find out how Tessa did it, because we can all learn from her experience. Even though this chapter is all about marketing, I must congratulate Tessa and Saasha on absolutely not fucking up their startup at any stage of the process. Let's walk through it.

## Start with the Homework

They both recognised that waste was not cool, but they didn't know how damaging it was until they began researching the subject. This led to some pretty damning discoveries. As our world is steadily becoming hotter, scientists are becoming increasingly determined to slow down or even reverse the process by reducing the emission of greenhouse gases. Food waste contributes to this. To put it another way, if food waste were a country, it would be the third-largest source of greenhouse gases in the world, after China and the US.

Speaking of China, the amount of food wasted is the equivalent to the annual produce of a landmass larger than China being thrown away every year. Worse still, we're struggling to feed a global population that is rapidly moving towards ten billion, so the last thing we should be doing is wasting food. Finding out stuff like this just made Tessa and Saasha even more determined to do something about the problem.

## Move Quickly to Validation

Once they'd realised how huge the problem was, they wondered whether others cared about it as much as they did. They both felt passionate about reducing food waste and helping to build communities based on the principle of giving and sharing, but how much of a shit would anyone else give? Enough to want to download an app and get involved?

They put together a questionnaire using SurveyMonkey, which they shared with every relevant group they could think of on Facebook. They asked very simple questions. For example, one question asked people to describe how they felt about food waste by picking a rating between one and ten, where one signified not giving a fuck and ten related to feeling 'physically pained' at the thought of throwing away food. They deliberately chose such highly emotive words because that's how strongly they felt about it, and they wanted to find out who felt the same way. Incredibly, out of almost four hundred respondents, one-third of them admitted to feeling physically pained at the thought of wasting food.

Bingo! That was far more validation than they had expected, and it encouraged them to go a step further. They contacted everyone who had scored a ten and asked them if they'd be willing to take part in an experiment. All participants needed to do was to join a WhatsApp group where they could meet like-minded individuals and share food among themselves. Would they share food with strangers?

## Next Stop: Proof of Concept

They managed to get twelve people, who lived in North London and didn't know each other, to agree to take part in a two-week experiment. The group was launched on a Saturday, and by Monday morning someone had posted half a bag of shallots. They were snapped up within twenty-three minutes. A meet was quickly organised in a local coffee shop near Finsbury Park, and that was the start of many similar sharing experiences.

At the end of the two-week experiment, they had solid proof of concept, but they also asked their volunteers how they had found the experience – what they had liked, what could be improved, and what they would expect from an app. The responses were enlightening, to say the least. When they had originally dreamed up the idea, they had loads of preconceptions about how the app would operate – users would have to set up an account (after all, it was bringing strangers together), they'd have to create a profile, and the app would enable user ratings and reviews – but what they learned from their early testers was that the app didn't need to be much more sophisticated than the WhatsApp group. The next step was screaming at them:

> 'We must build this.'
>
> *Tessa Clarke – Co-Founder of OLIO*

## Building a Minimum Viable Product (MVP)

They went back to the drawing board and questioned every feature they had originally envisioned. Through this process, they were able to strip back the app's functionality, discarding unnecessary features and focusing on what they needed to build a minimum viable product. What features would be required to enable two people who live near to each other to share food?

> 'Someone needs to be able to create a listing and add a photo and a description and an approximate location and add it to the app. Someone else needs to be able to see that, and they need to be able to message and request it, and then the person who's added the listing needs to be able to take it down.'
>
> *Tessa Clarke – Co-Founder of OLIO*

They incorporated the company in February 2015, and the app was built, tested and launched on the app store exactly five months to the day later. Now they needed to figure out how to get people to use the app as quickly as possible. They had no users, and their budget was so tight that any expenditure of a tenner or more had to be discussed.

How did they do it? How did they go from having no money and no app users to successfully raising £42 million in series B funding and growing their membership base to over five million? The short answer from Tessa was 'Blood, sweat, tears, rinse, wash, repeat!' because it didn't happen overnight.

## 'How Can We Help?'

One of the first things they learned in the early days was that people tended to fall into one of three camps: those who were passionate about the concept and couldn't get enough of it, a second group who got it intellectually and saw the value but were slow to act, and a third group who were never going to get involved with food sharing no matter what they were told about the benefits.

There was no point chasing the third group, so they ignored them. They also spent very little energy thinking about the second and focused all their attention on the first group, the early adopters, who were fanatical to the point of being obsessed with OLIO.

People in the first group didn't just want to use the app and actively give and receive food, they also wanted to know how they could help. It wasn't simply a matter of having an app that allowed them to be helped and to help others. They wanted to get behind the project and encourage others to use it. They frequently reached out to Tessa and Saasha and asked how they could help.

Tessa and Saasha used this to their advantage by calling people to discuss how they could collaborate to propagate the message. Between them, they made hundreds of calls, listening carefully to what they were being told and seeking to understand what made their customers tick, what their drivers and motivators were, and to find out their skills, capabilities, what they did, and where they lived.

They were building a two-sided marketplace, so one of the most obvious ways people could help was by clearing out their shelves, identifying the stuff they weren't going to use and being on standby to post these items on the launch date. Ensuring there were offers in the app at launch would kickstart activity by encouraging interaction. On that note, since its launch, the average time it takes for an item to be requested within the app is just twenty-one minutes, which is two minutes quicker than it took for the first offer to be grabbed in the WhatsApp experiment.

## Building an Army of Ambassadors

Understanding what motivates people is one of the cornerstones of knowing how to collaborate with them. Tessa and Saasha identified two key motivators: on the one hand, early adopters wanted to attract others from their neighbourhoods, so there'd be more food to go around. There's no point having a party without guests. Secondly, they were also keen to encourage others to get involved because they believed in the mission, and they wanted to make the world a better place. Understanding that enabled Tessa and Saasha to build a community extremely quickly.

Those early adopters who reached out to Tessa and Saasha were brand advocates in the making. The willingness was already there from an army of people who were prepared to commit time and effort to further the cause, but they didn't have the tools or a plan. All they needed was leadership, and OLIO's founders were happy to oblige. The pair set to work creating ambassador packs, which contained flyers, posters, letters and anything else that could help to spread the word.

Ambassadors could order these for their own hyper-local guerrilla marketing campaigns. Orders came in thick and fast, and they still are – they send out hundreds of these packs every year. They provided templates for press releases for reaching out to their local town criers – ahem, I mean local news outlets – and presentations that they could share to empower others. They settled on a format for a 'Community Potluck' event and gave guidance to ambassadors on how they could run these in their local areas.

Within three weeks of launching, they had open-sourced a comprehensive playbook on how to grow OLIO and run it anywhere. When they began their mission, even though they knew they were addressing a global problem, they had only thought about making a big difference in a small area of the world, London, but word spread much quicker and further afield than they had ever imagined it would. Loads of people reached out to them from London, but it wasn't long before they were being contacted by people from across the nation and internationally. Today, more than half of their community is based outside the UK.

OLIO's success boils down to the ability of its founders to grow a strong community of active members and provide them with the tools to self-service and reach out to others; however, from ideation to validation to proof of concept, and so on, its founders used a solid approach at every stage.

### A Community is Only as Strong as its Weakest Members

> **'Community strength is very much determined by its norms and its rules, and you need to be really, really strict on identifying up-front what your norms and rules are for your community and then kindly asking volunteers and ambassadors and community members who do not conform to those norms and rules to step down.'**
>
> *Tessa Clarke – Co-Founder of OLIO*

Building a community is one thing but nurturing it and keeping it healthy is another. Tessa and Saasha were keen to listen to and collaborate with their community members. By learning what made their ambassadors tick, they were able to achieve more by enabling a simple quid pro quo: ambassadors could get their fix of feel-good neurochemicals by knowing they were doing their bit to save the planet, while OLIO had a highly charged and empowered team of eager beavers who were ready and willing to do whatever it would take to help. With that quid pro quo in mind, Tessa realised very early on that OLIO's ambassadors appreciated feedback. By letting them know what kind of difference they were making in terms of new members, new groups, meals saved, etc., she was acknowledging them, making them feel valued and letting them know their efforts were important.

On the other side of the coin, Tessa recognised that not every member was a good member, and a bad egg could do a lot more harm than good. Ambassadors must behave in a way that reflects the values, norms and rules of the organisation. If they don't, they can damage its brand and affect the morale of their colleagues, so they must be removed. This may seem counterintuitive where volunteers are concerned, but whether they are paid or not makes no difference because they are still representatives of OLIO. Tessa told me that sometimes members would become very angry when they were asked to leave, but if something must be done, it must be done. That goes with the territory of leadership.

## Key Considerations for Community Building

OLIO presents a perfect example of how building a community and leveraging it can help to grow a startup, but how rapidly you can attract people depends on several factors:

- Does anyone else care about what you care about?
- Do they care enough about it to take action?
- Do you know how to reach those that do?
- Do you know how to deliver your message in a way that resonates with them?

These questions and considerations can be summed up with one word, 'brand', and that's a topic we'll be coming back to in more detail later on.

In a moment, I'm going to introduce you to someone else whose fantastic community is the product that her startup sells. She is addressing a need that many founders have. Founders are experts in their field. That doesn't make them marketing gurus.

## I'm Not a Trailblazer

I've highlighted some of the excellent ways that other founders have found a route to market. Their stories are far better than mine. As I've pointed out several times in this book, I have never had any intention of pretending to be an authority on startups or innovative ideas. The truth is that I am someone who gave it a go, winged it, fucked up, learned lessons, carried on some more, fucked up more, and managed to stagger to where I now stand – and it's still damned hard. What's my point?

You don't have to be a marketing genius. You don't need the expertise of any of the founders I've mentioned in this book. Others have been there first, and you can learn from them just as I have. Better still, if you're not a trailblazer, perhaps some of your mates are! And if they're not?

## Become a Copycat Marketer!

Lottie Unwin, one of my podcast guests, set up a company called The Copy Club, which has fuck all to do with copywriting. Unfortunately, she launched her startup long before I had a chance to publish this book, so she never got to read the bit on how not to fuck up a name. Never mind. It hasn't stopped her business from thriving, and although she admits that a rebrand may be on the cards at some point, it's not an urgent matter.

> 'Now, I have to explain on a daily basis that we're not just copywriters and live with the inordinate regret that I went with a stupid name.'
>
> *Lottie Unwin – Founder of The Copy Club*

I respect your honesty, Lottie, but your startup is still killing it, so hats off to you!

## The Power of Cross-Pollination

The Copy Club is a network of senior marketers who get together to share ideas and experiences over a glass of wine or coffee. What's special, however, is that its members come from a wide range of industries and are actively encouraged to beg, borrow and steal each other's marketing tactics. One of the club's slogans is 'Steal with pride'.

Think about it. If you're talking to another senior marketer or an export from an industry that has no relationship to yours, you can be open. They pose the same threat to you as you pose to them – no threat at all.

> 'Imagine a world where we all sit in silos, and the travel business-people go out for dinner and talk about travel business marketing, and the fizzy drinks people go and talk about fizzy drinks marketing. The result of that kind of cross-pollination is going to be incredibly boring and incredibly identikit.'
>
> *Lottie Unwin – Founder of The Copy Club*

As Lottie points out, believing that a hive mind of marketers from the same industry is going to lead to new ideas is a mistake. Okay, it will. Of course, two brains are better than one. The more brains the better, but if they are all from the same industry, they are also likely to hold the same attitudes and beliefs, and they will have the same blind spots.

Looking at other industries creates an opportunity for lateral thinking without blind spots – lightbulb moments. According to Lottie, 'innovation is just borrowing and reapplying an idea', and she has a point, doesn't she?

## Do It Like PROPERCORN

An excellent example of cross-pollination in action comes from a PROPERCORN campaign that Lottie launched for the popcorn brand. Their approach to making PROPERCORN fashionable was to sponsor London Fashion Show and have the catwalk models proudly wearing the brand as fashion accessories.

Hugo Cornejo made banking fashionable as a key player in the launch of Monzo, a bank that doesn't sound like a bank, look like a bank or act like a bank! More on Monzo later.

Another example is the dating app Thursday. Lottie pointed out that they are not doing anything new, and that's not intended as a dig or an insult. Bumble was using very similar tactics several years ago. Some founders look at Thursday and believe that its marketing tactics were dreamed up by an unpaid marketing intern, which is yet another illustration of the campaign's genius. But as we've seen, this is highly unlikely to be the case, according to Lottie, who believes a highly paid marketing agency probably came up with the strategy.

So what? It's worked for them. It can also work for you. Leaning on someone else's budget is a great hack. Copy with pride.

> 'Why not ride on the coattails of someone else's media spend, someone else's expensive work? Startup marketing, fundamentally, is about pulling rabbits out of hats; that you have to make the impossible happen with no resources.'
>
> *Lottie Unwin – Founder of The Copy Club*

So, what other campaigns does our copycat champion think we can learn from? She mentioned a couple of great products.

Little Moons launched a line of mochi ball ice creams. They leveraged TikTok when the platform was still very new, and threw everything into a campaign to promote their product. Notably, they weren't precious about it and created a very down-to-earth, engaging campaign. The proof of the mochi is in the eating, and Little Moons Mochi Ice Cream sold out in all the UK's main groceries. The best ideas are the simplest. Don't go for complicated ideas unless you have to.

Dr Will's ketchup is sweetened with dates rather than sugar, which means a much healthier product. Compared to other well-known brands, which were using more than a few sugar cubes for a typical bottle of their sauce, Dr Will's was using two dates. They used a radical approach to promote their product.

For the 'Save our sauce' campaign, they approached shoppers on their way into the supermarket and asked them to buy Dr Will's sauce, explaining why it was important to do so. You can't beat a bit of blunt honesty. Again, sometimes simple is better. Why complicate matters? They spoke about the sauce on LinkedIn, in their newsletters, on Instagram and wherever they could, talking openly about how many units they needed to sell. It was a bold move but one that paid off.

Speaking of food, I hope this chapter has given you a lot of food for thought on how you're going to reach your market. Even if you don't take anything else away from this chapter, take this: if you can't come up with a genius idea of your own, look around at other campaigns, and look beyond your own industry. Talk to other people. You never know what inspiration you will find.

Now, did I say there were no town criers anymore? Scrap that. It was a harmless lie that I came up with to make a point, and in the next chapter you'll find out why.

# 16.
# THE RISE OF THE NOUVEAU TOWN CRIERS

What a chapter that was! We covered a lot of ground on identifying and engaging with a target market, and we looked at some excellent examples of how to get it right and how to fuck it up. Brie Read and Tom Martin, co-founders of Snag Tights, showed us how to engage with customers online in a genuine way, learn from them and make it easy for them to buy from a simple website.

George Rawlings and Matt McNeill Love, co-founders of the online dating app, Thursday, demonstrated creative bravery and innovative thinking by not being afraid to stand out from the crowd, not only regarding their product but how they shouted about it. They chose a Marmite approach to getting their name out there and, fortunately for them, more than enough singletons loved what they were about to make their idea a hit.

Tessa Clarke and Saasha Celestial-One provided us with a masterclass on building and leveraging a community to launch and grow a brand. They had a mission, and they knew how to find others to join them. The result? OLIO.

And for those who were stuck on their marketing approach and couldn't see a way to boost sales, Lottie Unwin launched The Copy Club network where senior marketers and founders from different industries can hear about each other's winning ideas. If you can't beat them, borrow their ideas!

But at the start of the last chapter, I referred to the town crier as a thing from the past, a cultural relic and a lost gem from the world of marketing. So, the burning question is this:

## Who Are Today's Town Criers?

Town criers are still alive and kicking, but they go by a different name.

These days, they are known as 'influencers'. The internet is full of them – Kim Kardashian, Logan Paul and Beyoncé, to name a few.

Influencers are people who have grown massive followings on social media platforms, often because of what they've achieved, such as Beyoncé or football's living legend Cristiano Ronaldo. Sometimes, they have set out to become influencers from the start, as YouTubers, such as Logan Paul. Kardashian was unknown, working as an assistant to 'it girl' Paris Hilton until a 'sex tape' scandal catapulted her into the public eye. A television show followed shortly after, and *The Kardashians* became a thing.

> **'Over four billion people use social media globally. We're spending more time on social media on our phones than watching traditional TV.'**
>
> *Jennifer Quigley-Jones – CEO and founder of Digital Voices*

Before you make any judgements about any of these influencers – questioning why people follow them, whether they ought to be followed, or whether they are decent role models – just know this: these people have tremendous influence. They only have to fart loudly, and someone will be writing about it on the other side of the globe within minutes. With that kind of pulling power, they can easily make or break a brand's credibility with one sentence.

Jennifer Quigley-Jones is an expert at leveraging the power of influencers, and she generously shared her knowledge with me on the *Back Yourself Show*. The name of this hyper-modern art of tapping into the pulling power of today's town criers is 'influencer marketing', and if you haven't considered it as a route to market before, you need to pay attention to what follows.

## Why Is Influencer Marketing So Important?

According to Jennifer, the CEO and founder of global influencer marketing agency Digital Voices, social media is where the markets of most startups are to be found, and the best way to connect with those prospects and customers is through the individuals who already have their attention.

> **'Brands need to find a way to connect with their customers, and the best way to do it is through individuals online who have followings.'**
>
> *Jennifer Quigley-Jones – CEO and founder of Digital Voices*

Most individuals don't want to engage with a brand. Ask yourself how many brands you follow on Instagram or other platforms. I don't follow any brands . . . apart from Duolingo on Tiktok because their channel is fucking mental. They've managed to appeal to my sense of humour, but, generally speaking, Jennifer's right; people don't want to follow brands. For further evidence, notice how LinkedIn is home to plenty of brand pages, but most people pay little attention to them, preferring to connect and interact with other humans.

Our customers want to follow people they can trust, they want to be entertained and they want to learn things. Many startups make the mistake of spending a lot of time and money trying to grow a massive online presence and a huge following. There's nothing wrong with having a brand channel on YouTube, TikTok, or whatever, but it's unlikely to become as popular as the YouTubers and other influencers who are already killing it.

We expect to be able to find brands online, but your brand will probably never be funny, entertaining or informative enough to have people visiting your channels regularly. Why would they? You're probably not a comedian or entertaining to anyone else but your partner, the kids and your dog, most of the time.

If you've launched a dating app, and you're posting useful tips and articles about finding love, people may land on your blog when they're looking for answers to specific questions. *10 Ways to Know Whether He's Into You* and *3 Reasons Why You Keep Getting Ghosted* may be getting loads of traffic, but no one wants to spend ages reading about dating or revisiting such a site every lunchtime. They will dip in when the topic comes to mind. Then, they will bounce from your channel to get on with life and seek thrills, spills and entertainment.

Something else that many of us forget is that while our startups are offering something new, original and wanted, we may not be the wisest choice as the face of our brand. If you are a founder, but you don't match the profile of your ideal customer, shouldn't you find someone who does?

Unfortunately, being an innovative, gutsy and intelligent person doesn't guarantee that you have the charisma necessary to be the front person for your brand.

> 'Startups should be using influencers to test their messaging, to get their content out there to drive a passionate community so that they can prove the value proposition, raise more money, and raise more sales.'
>
> *Jennifer Quigley-Jones – CEO and founder of Digital Voices*

Trying to get people to follow a brand can be a major distraction. Finding the right influencer to partner with can save you a lot of time, energy and money.

## Who Is the Best Influencer for My Brand?

For a start, you want to be sure that the influencer you choose is talking to your perfect customers. To suss that, you will have to consider what they talk about and what kind of content they create. An influencer that produces fantastic videos that show aspirational people how to make their pads look like show homes will be a good bet if you sell a product that blends in with their mission.

Think about it. A revolutionary adhesive, polychromatic wallpaper, a singing mirror . . . it could be anything as long as it is something that an aspirational person might buy to make their home look better. But remember, it's going to have to suit your influencer's agenda as well. If they think it's a tacky idea that might turn off their viewers, they probably won't (or shouldn't) be interested, so for the second time in this book, forget about the singing mirror. It's a shit idea.

The adhesive may be a good fit because it is not intended to be seen or shown off. It is purely functional, so your influencer will still have the freedom to talk about the wonderfully creative décor ideas they've been thinking about for that episode, and they can throw in the fact that 'Fairey's Solid Stick Adhesive' will work perfectly when it comes to attaching new skirting board to the base of the walls.

## Don't Partner with a Tosser!

It's probably worth mentioning that you and your influencer need to reflect well on each other. If you want your brand to be seen as risqué, and you fancy yourself as a bit of a disruptor and a provocateur, you may decide to pick an influencer who oozes these qualities. But you have to get it right, because picking someone who is the epitome of everything that your brand isn't, whose values seem to contradict yours, will benefit neither of you.

Don't pick a tosser unless they have a huge following of ideal customers, and you don't care how your brand looks to everyone else. Before you scratch your head for too long, thinking about that, just don't. It's a very dodgy path to choose, and most people would fuck it up. It's better to stick with someone safe, popular and relevant.

## But What About Data?

You've found the perfect influencer partner for your startup. They're wholesome, niche, highly relevant to your brand, and they have seventeen gazillion followers. Perhaps they can also assure you that their weekly YouTube show gets a regular and consistent audience of forty-eight million viewers. But will any of those followers make a purchase or even give a shit?

In 2019, an influencer on Instagram with well over two million followers hit the headlines after she was unable to sell thirty-six T-shirts. Arianna Renee, who was just eighteen at the time, posted to say that she was launching a clothing line but needed to place a minimum order of thirty-six items with the company that was producing them. Her mission failed, and she was left having to explain why she wouldn't be able to deliver to the few people who had placed orders.

It was embarrassing all round, and Arianna did herself no favours by posting a lengthy Tweet about how she had been let down by the people she had expected to support her. She faced a backlash from the public, and the incident sparked a discussion about how effective influencer marketing is. Experts at the time put her monumental failure down to the fact that her flagship brand didn't match the image she had created and was poorly planned and executed. This is further evidence that you must match the product with the influencer carefully.

Apart from not fucking up the planning and execution of a campaign and ensuring we've got the right influencer for the product, how can we be sure that it will lead to new enquiries? This is where Jennifer's experience and expertise come in very useful. Her agency collects meaningful data every time it launches an influencer campaign for any of its clients. So, her team can provide historical conversion data on how well an influencer has performed with other brands. They can match an Instagrammer or YouTuber with a startup based on evidence, so viewings are more likely to lead to sales.

> 'This person has viewers who match your target customer, but they don't actually drive sales. Whereas that person has viewers who match your target customer and drives sales at a much higher rate so spend your money with them.'
>
> *Jennifer Quigley-Jones – CEO and founder of Digital Voices*

## Is It Going to Cost a Fortune?

The short answer is it depends on who you use. People tend to only think of the super celebrities as influencers, but there's a whole ecosystem out there – from those with much smaller but highly relevant and super loyal followings to medium-sized, right up to globally recognised names. Jennifer recommends starting with smaller influencers, or even running an in-house campaign, before shelling out a ton of money on a big hitter.

If you've built up a decent following of your own, nothing that would qualify you as an influencer but enough to justify your channel's existence, you can offer your subscribers a free product or similar special offer to see how they respond. If it works, scale up by partnering with a D-list influencer that is not going to charge you a huge fee, because, yes, the Kim Kardashians of the world will likely charge a few million dollars just to mention your company's name once in passing.

Better still, once you've tested the water with an in-house experiment, hire someone like Jennifer to find you an influencer to work with. You know that throwing money at the right campaign will yield results, because you've already tried with your own tiny following. That means it's worth ploughing more in, but if you're serious about amplifying your success, use a professional to get the best results.

## What's the Best Way to Reach Out to an Influencer?

We looked at this several chapters ago when we considered how to approach potential investors, and again when we looked at sales automation. How would you like to be approached? You want to be treated as a human being, don't you, and you don't want to feel as though your email's been stuck in a mailshot. Make it personal. Never copy and paste or do anything that suggests you are mass-messaging. Direct messaging them is a personal way in, or you can use any contact details they have shared on their profile page.

A basic template may be:

'Hey, I'm Stacey, and I'm the founder of Stacey's Skateboards. We manufacture cutting-edge skateboards that look as cool as they ride, and I'm looking for feedback from content creators who really understand our brand.

I would love to hear your thoughts.

And we have a budget for this!'

According to Jennifer, mentioning that you have a budget for the campaign is a must, and she advises that you mention that it's a 'paid brand opportunity' in the subject line. Influencers are constantly being asked to do stuff in return for goods. They have offers coming out of their ears. Show them that you will pay them from the very first message, and you will, at least, have their attention.

Your opening message is not intended to close a deal. At that stage, you should be trying to get them on a call, so they can see that you're human. That will give you a chance to connect, to explain more about what your product is and what outcomes you are looking for. Discuss what they will do and, whatever you do, make sure you get a contract together. Too many people miss this bit out, but getting an agreement on paper ensures you can withhold payment if the services you were promised are not provided in the way you expected.

## She Said, 'Yes!', Now What?

Now, we need to consider how not to fuck up our influencer campaign! One of the most common ways that big brands fuck up their influencer campaigns is by asking their partners to read a script. Trying to script an influencer doesn't usually end well. Sometimes, they don't like the script, so they will up their fee. But more than that, they might not be very good at reading the script in a way that is engaging, natural or convincing.

For a simple reminder of why not to try scripting an influencer, picture (or look up) the scenes where Sylvester Stallone's hero in one of the *Rocky* sequels is being paid to feature in a television advertising campaign. He has to do one take after another and still sounds as though he is struggling to read, and all that raw charisma that the boxer had was lost. Brilliant acting by Stallone, I must add.

> **'Is there something you've always wanted to do but didn't have the money for that would fit in with what we're trying to do?'**
>
> *Jennifer Quigley-Jones – CEO and founder of Digital Voices*

You're hiring an influencer because they know how to attract the eyeballs that you want. Why fuck that up by getting them to do something shit and unnatural that makes them sound like a robot or worse? Don't be a control freak. Sure, you have to consider the guidelines of the Advertising Standards Authority, but it's better that you ensure your influencer understands these and allow them the freedom to integrate your message in a way that suits their style. Does this mean giving them a blank slate to say anything they want? Absolutely not, and that's what the onboarding call is for.

Discuss what you want, and find out how they want to approach it: 'Is there something you've always wanted to do but didn't have the money for that would fit in with what we're trying to do?' is a good opener, but don't expect them to know what works or how to sell your product. Respect their creativity, and offer specific guidance based on what you know. Jennifer suggests phrases such as 'When you use this call to action, it works better', and 'Legally, we have to say this'.

## Can Influencer Marketing Work with B2B?

It is logical to assume that because influencers are so effective at reaching out to individuals, they are only useful for selling to the consumer. When I asked Jennifer straight out, she said, 'The brands for doing influencer marketing, the clients that we see scale the quickest are D2C [direct to consumer] brands with a hardcore e-commerce objective.'

So, yes, without a shadow of a doubt, you can use influencer marketing to sell your dating app or your new kind of tablet, but is this all that influencers are good for? Not according to Jennifer.

Jennifer referred to a campaign that her agency ran with Meta to convince entrepreneurs of the power of personalised ads. The campaign, which ran on Instagram, LinkedIn and Facebook, used influencers with entrepreneurial authority, such as Steven Bartlett, to speak to other entrepreneurs. What you have to remember is that founders and other business decision-makers are human beings. We respond to people we like, trust, and can relate to. Can I believe something that Steven Bartlett says about growing a startup? Fuck, yeah, because I know he's been through the same kind of shit that I have.

## I Want to Be an Influencer. How Large Does My Following Need to Be?

While Jennifer doesn't recommend that you focus too much time and energy on becoming an influencer, some of us have large followings of our own. At what point does someone with a following become an influencer? Are you an influencer? Am I?

The land of social media is full of 'nano influencers', and these typically have upwards of five thousand followers. That's the point at which, provided you have built your following with a smart content strategy that has attracted the right people, a direct promotional post may convert interest into orders. Don't become another Arianna Renee!

The ten-thousand-follower mark used to be an important milestone for members of the Instagram community, because it would open up access to the platform's swipe-up feature. While the swipe-up feature is still only available to accounts with at least ten thousand followers, anyone can use the link sticker feature, which is equally powerful. Users can use Instagram to drive traffic to specific landing pages now, using a sticker link on a promotional story.

TikTok offers people the chance to go viral with almost no followers. The focus is on content rather than creators. If you post something that ticks (don't excuse the pun) the right boxes, you could be all over the world within hours, even as a newbie.

## Remember to Not Fuck Up Your Brand

If the numbers become more important to you than the quality of your content, you're going to fuck up your brand by looking like a sell-out. Make sure that the content you create and the people you associate with reflect accurately, relevantly and kindly on your brand. If you need to up the viewing figures, focus on creating better content rather than jumping on the next bandwagon you see.

The figures that count aren't the ones that stroke your ego. Views, likes, claps, comments, reactions and retweets don't pay the bills. Focus on bums on seats, orders, average order value and revenue growth. If these are all going in the right direction, you're doing something right.

## A Lesson for Big Brands

There's a natural tendency for smaller brands to look to the more established, larger companies for insight, but big brands can learn a lot from startups where branding is concerned. Startups are more likely to exude authenticity because they have no choice. Big brands often approach stuff from a traditional marketing perspective and treat influencers as brand ambassadors. They use polished celebrities.

Founders of startups are unlikely to have the budget for a polished celebrity and will be themselves on social media. They are real people who fuck up, and provided they don't do anything too damning, their audience will love them for it. Pay attention to the metrics that count and focus on performance and scaling. As you grow, you can carry out brand awareness activities at key moments during the year.

## Jennifer's Top Tips for Raising Your Profile

Jennifer worked on YouTube for a long time, and her experience on the platform taught her some solid lessons, which can be applied to other platforms. She has five top tips for founders who want to raise their profile and, who knows, maybe become influencers.

1. Be consistent – if you can't post multiple times a day, post something great every week. People appreciate consistency. It makes it easier for them to tune in and pay attention to the content they like.
2. Experiment – don't be afraid to try different approaches. If something doesn't work, forget about it. Do more of the stuff that works.
3. Use a content calendar – find out the important dates for your product or sector. Plan content that ties in with key events.
4. Don't be a perfectionist – perfectionism is the enemy of innovation. There is a place for fine-tuning things, but it's better to do things that are 95 per cent perfect and work than sticking with one task.
5. Delegate – just because you run the company doesn't make you the

best person to run the social media campaigns or front your brand's YouTube channel. Get someone better to do it. Find someone in-house if you haven't got the budget for an agency.

These takeaways will serve you well no matter how large or small your startup is.

**'If you work harder and smarter, you will succeed.'**

*Jennifer Quigley-Jones – CEO and founder of Digital Voices*

One word that has come up repeatedly during our journey today is 'brand'. In the next chapter, we're going to zoom into the topic of branding, why it is important, and how not to fuck it up.

17.

# HOW NOT TO FUCK UP YOUR BRAND

Well done for coming this far. You're a rockstar and you've successfully launched a great product and found a way to reach your market. Sales are growing, your team is expanding, and you can even afford a few new pieces of artwork for the walls of your office's reception area.

Don't count your chickens just yet, not without at least considering your brand.

## Your Brand Will Make or Break You

Even when we've done everything right from the get-go – a great idea, validation, proof of concept, MVP, etc. – the more successful we become, the more important our brand becomes, and the more potential there is for it all to go wrong. Yep, some would say branding is everything.

We looked at how not to fuck up your product name a few chapters ago, but that's only one way to get the branding right. There are many other pitfalls to watch out for. Before we look at some contemporary branding fuckups, I think it's only fair that we delve into the annals of history and revive some classics. One, which has since become the stuff of legend, is the story of how the CEO of a high-street jeweller almost destroyed his brand in seconds with one gaff.

Let's go back to 23 April 1991. Gerald Ratner, the then CEO of Ratners, a company he had inherited and built into a multi-million-pound business, was addressing a room full of businesspeople at an Institute of Directors conference in the Royal Albert Hall. In the middle of his speech, while talking about how Ratners was able to sell its cut-glass sherry decanter set, which included six glasses and a silver-plated tray, for just £4.95, he dropped the clanger of the twentieth century:

> 'People say, "How can you sell this for such a low price?" I say, "Because it's total crap."'
>
> *Gerald Ratner, former CEO of Ratners*

What the absolute fuck! Had he been drinking the sherry – perhaps from one of his cheap decanters – or had someone spiked his water with sodium pentothal, the truth serum? Telling the world that he was selling people total crap wasn't enough. To make matters worse, he went on to say that one of the sets of earrings his company was selling was cheaper than a Marks & Spencer's prawn sandwich, adding that 'the sandwich will probably last longer than the earrings'.

## Don't Do a Ratner!

It didn't take long for the press to find out what he had said, and the value of the company dropped by half a billion pounds quicker than a fool could down a litre of sherry and decide to chat shit at a conference. I know this might seem like common sense, but if a highly successful businessperson like Ratner could get it so terribly wrong, it's probably worth reminding ourselves that people don't want to be told that what we're selling them is crap. Sure, it's fair to say that Ratners was not a brand people associated with class and high quality, but their products were selling well. Why insult the customer base?

Incredibly, the brand survived, but Ratner was fired from his own company the next year. The Ratner story will forever be remembered as a cautionary tale to remind others of the importance of brand over quality. There's nothing wrong with selling low-priced goods that everyone can afford, and even if they don't last that long or the quality is lacking, that's fine because people know what they are paying for – but don't rub their noses in it. Don't let it happen to you. Don't 'do a Ratner'! One of the simplest ways to fuck up a brand is to say the wrong thing to the wrong people at the wrong time. Had Ratner been chatting to one or two people in a private dinner, his offence may have been deniable, but there are plenty of tales of people being caught out by ambitious journalists looking for the next big scoop. With that in mind, it is probably better to go with the principle of never saying anything about your brand that you wouldn't feel comfortable about splashing all over the news.

## And Don't – UNDER ANY CIRCUMSTANCES – Do What Calvin Klein Did!

There's no one-size-fits-all solution to branding because every product's different. What would be acceptable for a lingerie brand wouldn't go down well in a marketing campaign for children's pyjamas, but the marketing department at Calvin Klein came close to making that mistake with a television advertising campaign in 1995. Even though they did nothing legally wrong, they made an error of judgement that made the advertisements memorable for all the wrong reasons.

The video featured young-looking male and female models being interviewed in a basement in a way that sounded quite sleazy a lot of the time, giving the advertisement the kind of vibe you'd expect for a porn film, not a commercial for jeans. The fact that some of the models looked so young caused even greater concern; so much so, that the advertisement was banned, and the US Justice Department launched an investigation.

**'Have you ever made love in a film?'**

*One of the questions posed to a model in Calvin Klein's infamous video advertisement*

No offences had been committed in the making of the film, but the damage to the brand's image was so damning that the company took out a full-page advertisement in the *New York Times* to say how taken aback it was by the public's reaction and that it was shutting down the campaign.

The original Calvin Klein video advertisement is easy to find on the internet, so feel free to take a look and judge for yourself but be prepared to be disturbed; people generally describe it as creepy. If you had to write a rule to avoid making the same mistake, you could call it the 'Rule of Association'. Don't do anything that risks associating your brand with something negative unless your product's job is to fix the problem.

## Women Belong in the Kitchen

Before you slam closed this book, swearing never to pay attention to another word I ever say or write, give me a chance to explain that I am not putting in an entry for the Darwin Award for Brand Fails, and I do NOT believe that women belong in the kitchen. Believe it or not, neither does the company that adopted this as the headline for a disastrous advertising campaign; at least, not in the sense that most people would associate the statement. And this was a big fucking brand, not a bunch of amateurs, which is what makes its marketing team's faux pas even more remarkable.

It was early 2021, and Burger King, yes, Burger King, was running a recruitment campaign. What was it thinking when it ran its 'Women Belong in the Kitchen' campaign? Was it trying to bring back a bygone era where men were men and women stayed at home and did what they were told or else? No, they were actually trying to redress inequality.

> 'We're on a mission to change the gender ratio in the restaurant industry . . .'
>
> *A line taken from Burger King's 'Women belong in the kitchen' advertisement*

Burger King's researchers had discovered that only 20 per cent of chefs were women, so they went on 'a mission to change the gender ratio in the restaurant industry by empowering female employees with the opportunity to pursue a culinary career'. I've taken that text from one of its tweets, but it also ran a full-page advertisement in the *New York Times*. Here's the full text from that ad.

'Women belong in the kitchen.

Fine dining kitchens, food truck kitchens, award-winning kitchens, casual dining kitchens, ghost kitchens, Burger King kitchens. If there's a professional kitchen, women belong there.

But you can guess who's leading those kitchens these days? Exactly. Only 24 per cent of chef positions in America are occupied by women. Want to talk head chefs? The number drops to fewer than 7 per cent.

This is where the new Burger King H.E.R. (Helping Equalize Restaurants) Scholarship comes in. It's a commitment from one of the biggest restaurants in the world to help their aspiring female chefs. Because every woman with a passion deserves the chance to advance, whether it's in culinary school, a Burger King kitchen, or any other kitchen in the world.'

Did I mention that they ran this advertisement on International Women's Day?!

Clearly, Burger King's heart was in the right place, but you know what they say about good intentions. They got it wrong. Very seriously wrong. But it gets worse. Their tweets were the stuff of branding nightmares. I mean, writing that women belong in the kitchen is dangerous enough, even when the play on words is explained in the rest of the text of the advertisement, but for some reason that nobody could fathom, they posted a tweet saying 'Women belong in the kitchen' and posted the explanation on a separate tweet. Utter madness.

The text in the follow-up tweet read, 'If they want to, of course. Yet only 20 per cent of chefs are women. We're on a mission to change the gender ratio in the restaurant industry by empowering female employees with the opportunity to pursue a culinary career. #IWD'

That was followed by 'We are proud to be launching our new scholarship programme which will help female Burger King employees pursue their culinary dreams!'

If Burger King had any doubts that it had fucked up its brand, other helpful Twitter users were willing to offer suitable guidance in the inimitable style of, well, Twitter users – no punches pulled. To be fair to its marketing department, Burger King published an unreserved apology, explaining that it had made a mistake by posting the initial tweet without a full explanation of its intention, and it attempted to redirect focus toward what it was trying to achieve.

## Women Belong in Your Marketing Department

How did Burger King fuck up its branding so much? Anyone wanting to be generous to the company could try to shift most of the blame onto whoever was managing its social media for proving that common sense is not so common. Perhaps they'd be better off in the kitchen than running a Twitter account, but let's not forget that the full-page advertisement, which did carry an explanation of the headline, failed to hit the mark as well.

Given how terribly the brand's 'women belong in the kitchen' campaign went down, you've got to wonder whether there were any women in the team that produced the concept; and, if there were any women on that team, whether they voiced their true opinions or whether they were heard. Either way, the people who dreamed up the campaign were out of touch with those they wanted to reach. Perhaps the chiefs in Burger King's marketing department weren't practising what they were preaching, and the public's message to them is 'Women belong in your marketing department.'

If the rest of us want to avoid making a similar fuckup, the best thing we can do is to go back to the basics of validation – check your marketing and branding ideas with as many people as you can, especially the ones you are trying to target.

Burger King was trying to do the right thing. It wanted to score a goal for gender equality but fucked up its messaging. Imagine if they'd been bang on with their copywriting approach. Could have been a fantastic campaign, right? Wrong! Or, at least, not necessarily. It is possible to champion a cause, strike the right chords with branding, and still fuck things up. How's that possible? One word – hypocrisy!

## Be the Change You Want to See

When brands jump on bandwagons to show support for causes that they are not fully aligning with, they are likely to be outed for it. As social media continues to evolve at an incredible rate and its position as the front line of public discussion and movements for change is consolidated, brands have to ensure they are doing more than paying lip service to campaigns for civil rights and social progress.

For example, before brands post a black square or talk about how Black lives matter, they ought to reflect on whether Black people are represented in their workforce. Likewise, if a company wants to shout about LGBTQ rights and adopt a rainbow version of its logo for Pride Month, it would do well to make sure it isn't operating in countries where same-sex couples can be put away for life or even executed by the state – at least not without doing something to protest or change things while they are there.

Those people who are directly affected by racism, homophobia, gender inequality, disability discrimination or prejudice because of their religion for example – and those who genuinely care about preventing discrimination in all its forms – do not take kindly to people or organisations pretending to give a damn just so they can look good.

The power of the internet means it is easier for prying eyes to observe big brands and catch them out when they don't practise the values they claim to support. The answer is simple: either be the change you want to see or don't shout about how much you care. Nobody likes a hypocrite, and companies, especially large multinationals, are being scrutinised more than ever before.

I'm not here to tell anybody what to do, and I think it's commendable that brands want to use their popularity and reach to make the world a better place; however, they must be mindful that as soon as they start playing politics, they leave themselves wide open to criticism.

By now, you're probably feeling more brain freeze than a ninety-year-old wearer of dentures who's just planted their teeth into a fresh-from-the-freezer scoop of minus-five-degrees ice cream. Enough of these branding horror stories. Let's see what clever branding looks like.

## It Takes Two . . .

The marketers at Argentinian condom manufacturers Tulipán must have felt very smart when they published a video to show off a new kind of packaging that could only be opened with four hands – two pairs. The principle behind Tulipán's 'Placer Consentido' (or 'consent') condom was that both parties would have to consent before the packet could be opened. Tulipán wanted to make a positive statement about consent, but its plan almost backfired for several reasons.

Firstly, some accused the brand of not fully grasping what consent means, and there were concerns that a Tulipán condom packet may turn up in the courts as evidence that consent had been given in sexual assault cases. Putting on a condom does not equate to consent to all sexual activity.

Twitter user Julia Pugachevsky tweeted that the 'consent condom' dumbed down the idea of healthy communication regarding sex 'in a harmful way' and was the 'condom equivalent of dudes asking for recorded videos of consent'.

The brand was accused of being ableist because some disabled people, such as amputees, for example, would not be able to open the packaging, which is a valid criticism, while those who liked to engage in, let's say, polyamorous activities felt the branding was excluding them.

So, why am I holding up Placer Consentido condoms as a branding success? Well, those criticisms may be valid if Tulipán was selling its consent condoms in the shops; however, as its executive creative director, Joaquin Campinas, pointed out at the time, Placer Consentidos were never intended to be taken seriously as a product that could be purchased. The sole purpose of the video advertising campaign was to draw attention to the issue of consent, and as far as they got people talking, they succeeded in their mission.

## The Building Blocks of Learning Braille

Danish children's toy brand Lego did something beautiful to help visually impaired children to learn Braille through play. The studs that are moulded onto the top surface of Lego pieces are perfect for configuring into Braille patterns to match letters and numbers, so Lego produced a Braille set of bricks.

The sets have been inclusively designed for use by sighted people as well, so parents, teachers and classmates can also learn Braille. The Braille Bricks collection was officially launched in 2020 and distributed for free to select institutions. Here's an excerpt from Lego's website:

'"With these Braille Bricks, the LEGO Foundation has created a totally new and engaging way for children with vision impairment to learn to read and write," says David Clarke, Director of Services at the Royal National Institute of Blind People, which worked with the LEGO Foundation to develop and test the bricks in the UK. "Braille is an important tool, particularly for young people with vision impairment, and these cleverly designed bricks enable children to learn braille creatively while also engaging with their classmates in a fun and interactive way."'[1]

Lego got its brand name from the Danish phrase 'leg godt', which means 'play well'. You don't need to be a marketing guru to see that in this case, the brand played very well indeed. It's no wonder that the name has been going strong for over three-quarters of a century! Who didn't play with Lego as a kid? I know I did, my parents did, and possibly even my grandparents did!

## Brewery Does Its Bit to Prevent Drinking and Driving

In 2019, the World Health Organisation (WHO) had recently reported that São Paulo had the highest number of road traffic deaths in the world, with drunk driving being listed as the second-most-common cause of these deaths. A report from the Federal Highway Police showed a significant spike in the number of drivers who were charged with drunk driving or refused to take a breathalyser test during the fifteen-day Carnival Festival. They also noticed that the frequency of serious drink-related accidents was much greater in areas where there was a higher concentration of bars, such as the areas in São Paulo where the Carnival Festival takes place.

Scottish brewery and pub chain BrewDog, which brews ales and beers for distribution all over the world, wanted to do its bit to help prevent drinking and driving, so it collaborated with the Waze navigation app to launch a safety message to coincide with Brazil's Carnival Festival.

Fifty fatal crashes, which had occurred over the previous years, were mapped into the Waze app, so drivers could see where they had happened. By clicking on an incident, drivers could see genuine media coverage of the accident along with a message reading 'Don't let it happen again. Don't drink and drive.'

BrewDog used the hashtag #THROWBACKCRASH to promote the hard-hitting campaign, and although I haven't seen any figures for 2019 to 2020, I feel confident that it will have prompted many drivers to think twice before drinking and driving. While what BrewDog did was great, they had a little help from Leo Burnett Tailor Made, the advertising agency.

While I can throw out some powerful examples of the good, bad and ugly brand campaigns, I am not qualified to tell you what works and what doesn't, but we can learn a lot from the successes and failures of others. Here's what we can learn from the brands we'd looked at in this chapter:

First, the Don'ts:

- Don't do a Ratner: never talk down the quality of your product
- Be clear
    - – steer clear of negativity (remember Calvin Klein's dodgy basement videos)
    - – don't joke around with sensitive subjects (women *don't* belong in the kitchen, Burger King)
    - – don't leave room for ambiguity (talking to you, Burger King), so don't post something that makes you look like a first-class tosser and then try to explain it later!
- Don't be a fucking hypocrite! If you care about an issue, try to do something about it and shout as loudly as you want. If you're not putting your money where your mouth is, you might be better off shutting the fuck up.

And now for the Dos:

- Be the change you want to see (the flip side of not being a hypocrite)

- Be creative (Tulipán showed a lot of imagination with their consent campaign)
- Be part of the solution
  - BrewDog's campaign won't eliminate drink-driving, but it will have made a difference in São Paulo
  - Lego has made learning Braille fun for the visually impaired and others who care about them
- Align yourself with good causes (Tulipán with consent, BrewDog with helping prevent drink-driving, Lego with helping the visually impaired and, yes, even Burger King gave it a go with gender equality, even if they did fuck it up).

But there are two more very important dos and don'ts that even a branding dunce like me can understand.

DON'T mess with your branding if you don't know what you're doing!

DO hire experts, either by

Employing staff who are much smarter than you, or
Hiring an outside consultant or agency as BrewDog did!

That's where knowing Nick Braund, the founder of Words and Pixels PR, comes in very handy. I interviewed Nick for my *Back Yourself Show*, and he shared a lot of useful insight about branding, what it is, and how we can use it to strengthen our startups.

## What the Fuck is PR?

Nick describes himself as a 'brand whore'. His passion for brands started at a young age when he was naturally drawn toward brands such as Abercrombie and Nike and wanted to wear their gear because he loved their logos. He was drawn to brands and had no idea why.

Logos, like any other work of art, have that inexplicable pulling power. Why do some people prefer the work of Escher over Picasso, Da Vinci over Van Gogh, The Simpsons over Shakespeare, or Kylie Minogue over Beethoven?! Logos are where art and values come together. Think of some of your favourites.

Such was the strength of Braund's fascination with all things brand related, he went on to study branding at Southampton University and came away with a first-class honours degree. Since then, he has thrived in the industry for well over a decade and successfully launched a highly innovative branding agency that helps other similar disruptive startups.

*OK, great*, you may be thinking. *It's good to read that Nick knows what he's talking about, but I'm still waiting for an answer – what the fuck is PR?*

> 'PR, as a practice, is not rocket science. It's understanding a story and a narrative and how you communicate that to the right audience.'
>
> *Nick Braund – Founder of Words and Pixels PR*

When you put it like that, Nick, I guess we should all be a lot better at it than we are.

If you're one of the few who is wondering what 'PR' stands for, it's the commonly used abbreviation for 'public relations', so you might say Nick's speciality is managing the relationship between his clients and their ideal customers – at least in so far as how brands relate to their audience. When you look at it that way, it is easy to see how the brands we looked at earlier in the chapter either managed their relationship with their customers well – by effectively communicating a positive narrative that was aligned with their brand – or fucked it up entirely.

Nick can't stop founders from doing or saying things that make them look like dicks, but he can make sure they are gaining exposure through appropriate press channels for the right reasons. Having a heart of gold, good intentions and being a genuinely great bunch of founders with an earth-shattering, revolutionary product that's going to save the planet is not enough. You have to make sure that people know it. If they don't, you may as well be the anti-Christ, and it is very easy to come across almost as negatively as that if you fuck up your PR and branding.

They say all PR is good PR, but who wants to be known for a sexist remark or their association with a dictator or their ties with the Russian mafia or for watching the Turkish version of Teletubbies surrounded by pink pillowcases on Wednesday evenings (don't ask – I made it up)?

## What Do You Want to Be Remembered For?

A notable example of the effectiveness of PR is the comparison between

Umbro and Nike. According to Nick, what makes Nike the clear winner between the two is Nike's heritage – its previous ad campaigns, which have dropped deep and positively into the psyche of the brand's fanbase, and the sportspeople, teams and values with which it is associated.

That makes sense, doesn't it? When you think about a movie franchise such as the James Bond films, what makes the brand so strong is its history and the great actors associated with it – Sean Connery, Roger Moore and, more recently, Daniel Craig. Then there are the leading ladies, the 'Bond girls', who include the likes of Jane Seymour, Grace Jones and Halle Berry. Bond has become a national institution, something the British people are proud of.

The question is this: what do you want your brand to be known for, remembered for and associated with? Are you achieving that already? If you know how to do it, what are you waiting for? If not, perhaps you should be speaking to someone like Nick Braund.

> 'The bit that I get most excited about, that genuinely gets me out of bed in the morning – which sounds really clichéd, saying it out loud on a podcast, but it's true – is working with companies and founders and entrepreneurs who have come up with something that they think is incredible.'
>
> *Nick Braund – Founder of Words and Pixels PR*

Nick makes it sound easy, but if PR is understanding a story and a narrative and communicating that to the right audience, how do we go about doing that? According to Nick, we need to know who our ideal customers are, where they hang out, what media they consume – and we must ensure that we are there as well.

Putting ourselves in front of the right audience, however, is only part of the solution. When Gerald Ratner stood in front of an audience of directors, having the microphone proved to be a liability. Why? Because even if he understood the story, he fucked up his messaging. So, once we have the attention of the people we want to sell to, we must deliver our message effectively.

> 'PR is the practice of taking things about a company or a person and communicating that through the press – simple as that – and what a PR agency, a PR consultant, a freelancer, an internal PR

> person does is take that information and frame that in a way that is digestible and interesting to the press.'
>
> *Nick Braund – Founder of Words and Pixels PR*

There are parallels between reaching out to the press and the process of validating your fabulous new products and services. When it comes to PR, while your target is the person who is consuming the content on a platform, you have to persuade the gatekeeper – the editor, owner or content manager – of that website or other press outlet that you have something of value to share with their audience. Why should they pay any attention to anything you have to say, let alone offer you a platform? What's in it for them? More importantly, what's in it for the reader, the listener or the viewer? What value are you bringing to the table?

## What's in it for the Reader?

One of the many benefits of PR is that you don't have to pay for it – if you pay for it, it ceases to be editorial – which is appealing in its own right, but not paying for it also makes it more effective. Anyone can pay for an advertisement to say how great they are, and if they pay for editorial, also known as 'advertorial', publishers have to be transparent, so their content will be highlighted as 'Sponsored' or similar. Besides, copy that says that your product is the best thing since the invention of Tinder and that you have the charisma of Muhammad Ali, Tom Cruise and Oprah Winfrey rolled into one magnanimous, legendary person is bound to give the game away. That kind of write-up's rarely true of anybody, not even me (he typed, smirking, trying to kid the reader that he wrote it with his tongue in his cheek when he knows he is a demigod)!

> 'It can't be promotional. It can't be like "X company is the most amazing thing ever," says its boss. No, because no one's gonna read that, and no one wants to read that this company has launched, they raised some money, and now they're a huge success. The end. You want to hear about the troubles, the strife, and all the challenges they dealt with on a day-by-day basis.'
>
> *Nick Braund – Founder of Words and Pixels PR*

PR, then, is a subtle art. The message you want to share slips in through the back door, hidden behind a story about how a founder dealt with mental health problems in the middle of the pandemic, why it's so important that business leaders empower their staff, or why Joey Public needs to read about the new changes in legislation (that your company just happens to address).

## What's Your Angle Going to Be?

The harder it is for your target audience to see you coming, the better. Being included in a discussion about local traffic calming measures as the founder of a company that manufactures stab-proof vests or one that sells an app for clocking how many calories you're putting in your shopping basket is not going to help you to sell stuff, but it will positively raise your profile. That's an example of how PR can be used to put forward a more personal value proposition – that you're a good person, who takes an interest in community issues and, by extension, is probably running a highly ethical company.

Meanwhile, if your new app helps to keep vulnerable people safe when they have to travel at night, giving an expert perspective in a discussion about violent crime or the flaws in new government regulations on how violent offenders will be handled will win you kudos. That's probably as in-your-face as your messaging can get.

Other angles include job-generation, but that kind of story might not appear on as specific a platform as you'd like. Media outlets need to make money as well, which is done increasingly through advertising, so if they suspect that your message sounds more like a recruitment drive than a piece of news, you'll be directed to their advertising personnel.

## Make Life Easier for the Journalist

According to Braund, you have to look at PR as a two-way street.

> **'It's a very careful balancing act. On one part, we are in the middle because the journalist wants to get information from the company, and the company wants to get information to the journalist.'**
>
> *Nick Braund – Founder of Words and Pixels PR*

Putting aside the editor, who may have other ideas, the journalist is the gatekeeper that stands between you and a double-page feature in the *Financial Times*, *Forbes* or *Crunchbase*. They have a job to do, and it can be overwhelming. Put yourself in their shoes for a moment.

On the surface, they've got it made because everyone is trying to provide them with stories about themselves and their organisations, but there lies the rub: how to split the wheat from the chaff from the hundred emails and hard copy press releases that have landed on their desk. They want to present their readers with the most relevant, exclusive and engaging content. If you can make that job easier for them, you're creating a mutually beneficial scenario.

## Know the Gatekeeper!

How do we go about doing that? The best approach, says Nick, is to take time getting to know the journalist you want to approach. What is their writing style, what do they tend to write about, what are they keen on, and what don't they like? That shouldn't be rocket science. Back in 1936 Dale Carnegie was telling us all that the key to winning friends and influencing people is to show an interest in them, with his classic book, *How to Win Friends and Influence People*!

## Journos Are Not Exactly Shrinking Violets

It's much easier to get to know these things about a journalist than, say, an accountant or a chiropodist. You only need to find the content they've produced, and that will tell you almost everything you need to know.

Obviously, you will have to do a bit more digging if you want to know what their dog's called, how many toyboys they have on the side, and how often they get a Brazilian, but you probably don't need to know that just to get them to publish an article about your everlasting bubble bath mixture – unless you're planning on blackmailing them (don't do that!). On a serious note, however, if you know just one small detail about them that is not common knowledge – their favourite soccer team, for example – it might help you to build a rapport with them later.

## Building Trust and Credibility

People and organisations look for press coverage for many reasons. In Chapter 12, we looked at how not to fuck up your personal profile. Sharing thought leadership and insight will help to establish credibility for you and your brand, and that's what it's all about according to Nick Braund.

> 'You're looking to build credibility. Rather than just saying, "My startup is amazing," you want someone else to say, "Hey, check these guys out." It's that external validation.'
>
> *Nick Braund – Founder of Words and Pixels PR*

## What Else Can PR Help You to Achieve?

We don't treat PR as another way of advertising. If you want to tell people how magnificent your product is and ask them to make a purchase, there are other ways of doing that. That approach won't win you PR, but neither would you want it to. PR can do so much more than putting bums on seats or shifting stock. Your sales are only as good as today's figures. Branding, on the other hand, is an investment; when it's done properly, it's the hen that keeps laying golden eggs.

> 'PR can create that external trust.'
>
> *Nick Braund – Founder of Words and Pixels PR*

You can use PR to raise your profile positively, show what a great person you are, how ethical your brand is, everything you're doing to save the Tapanuli orangutans of Sumatra, and share your organisation's story of triumph over adversity. And more than all of that, it creates trust. But who do you want to share your message with?

> '[PR] can . . . get you in front of new customers or new partners or new investors or anyone who might be interested; and so, by doing successful PR, you could grow, you could scale, you could diversify, you could hire because people might think "I really like what you're doing."'
>
> *Nick Braund – Founder of Words and Pixels PR*

PR is not just a mechanism for putting your brand in front of customers. It can help you win investment, partners and even talent. Rather than seeing it as a selling tool, we should look at it as one part of the marketing mix – how to get others to like who you are, what you do and what you stand for.

## What's Your Strategy?

With so many applications to choose from, it's easy to go out there with a scatter-gun approach, but this would be a big mistake. During my interview with Nick, he said that one of the most common things people struggle to grasp is how important it is to have a PR strategy. What do they want to achieve, and how are they going to go for it? If you want to hit a particular market, you won't get very far if nobody has heard of you. Therefore, one of your goals may be no more than to gain enough exposure for your potential customers to have heard of you and not for the wrong reasons.

This resonates with me. We were trying to get one of my earlier startups, which was tiny, into banks, and we knew we'd have no chance if nobody had heard of us. By working strategically with Nick's PR agency (you can pay me later for the plug, Nick), once we got into the room with the key decision-makers, they had already heard of us. Being recognised was a game-changer without a shadow of a doubt.

But as Nick pointed out to me in our podcast interview, we didn't get coverage in the *Financial Times* because they wanted to do us a favour – oh, let's help out this startup; no, they gave us the coverage because we gave them a story that they believed their readers would be interested in.

## What Journos Want

I've mentioned that journalists have the tough task of having to sieve their way through hundreds of press releases to find the best content for their audience. What criteria do they look for? What will make your press release stand out from the rest?

> '. . . they want a good story that is relevant to their readers, whether it's in fintech, whether it's in startups, whether it's broad consumer, a journalist will include something in an article or an interview because they think it's interesting and there's value.'
>
> *Nick Braund – Founder of Words and Pixels PR*

Nick's attitude is to give journalists the content they are looking for, and that's what you need to do as well. If you have developed a new banking app, you should be looking for platforms that are relevant to banking and fintech but consider other factors such as age ranges, socio-economic status and geographical location.

You are less likely to be selected for inclusion in an international publication if only people in Swansea can use your app – unless your product is particularly sexy, and you've persuaded the journalist that it's one to watch because it's going to go global very quickly (appealing to their FOMO). Likewise, there's no point being seen in *El Pais* if your product is only on sale in the UK. Even if they give you coverage, how's it going to benefit your brand?

> 'If your business doesn't sell in Timbuktu, there is no point trying to get coverage in The Timbuktu Times because it is not relevant to the readers of The Timbuktu Times because you are not targeting Timbuktu. The point is that it has to be relevant to the reader.'
>
> *Nick Braund – Founder of Words and Pixels PR*

Nick puts it beautifully with his Timbuktu analogy, but is there a kind of PR acid test for checking how likely it is that your press release will be welcomed? Yes, my friend. There is!

## 'So What?'

If you want to know how attractive your news piece is to journalists and editors, ask yourself this one question: So what? This is the ultimate litmus test to check out the sexiness of your content. Nick regularly challenges his staff with this question when they approach him with PR stories they have put together for their clients. This not only helps to keep everyone on their toes – including Nick himself – and promotes a process of growth and continual improvement, but it ensures the best results for their clients.

If you can't answer the 'so what' question with something impactful, chuck it away. 'We'll have fifty-six staff members instead of fifty-two' is not news. Neither is 'Well, our new logo is a lighter shade of blue.' You have to do better than that. On the flip side, 'This is the first factory to open in the area for fifty years, and it's going to generate 150 new jobs' has a lot more oomph – it's groundbreaking, good for the region, and promises better things to come. If you can answer the 'so what' question with something solid, you're onto something.

## Hire an Agency or Keep It in House?

If you have your own in-house spin doctor, that's excellent. They will save you a lot of money, but what if you don't? What should you look for in a PR consultant or agency?

Nick suggests that you consider several factors:

1. **Relevance** – Hire writers who have the relevant experience, particularly if your market is more specialist. Look for alignment.
2. **Size** – Some PR agencies charge a fortune, and they are worth the money because they are fantastic, but they're better for larger organisations that can afford to lose ten grand over three months because it's going to take six months for the strategy to bring results. Don't risk bankruptcy for a strategy that might not work quickly enough.
3. **Do they care about you?** – Sometimes, larger firms will neglect smaller clients while focusing their attention and resources on bigger accounts that they perceive as more lucrative.
4. **Discuss expectations** – Make sure you know how you are going to work with someone and that your expectations are going to be met.

> 'We've won a number of clients where they worked with an agency that either over-promised and under-delivered or they have become less important to the agency 'cause they're a small company and they're not paying the same as some of their larger clients, and they don't get the attention they deserve.'
>
> *Nick Braund – Founder of Words and Pixels PR*

Now, you know how not to fuck up your branding. If you don't have the right people within your organisation to come up with the winning words and pixels to get you press coverage, you know how to find someone who can.

The main focus of this chapter has been on how the words and deeds of founders will impact brands and how to effectively share your brand's message with the people who need to hear it.

In the next chapter, we are going to look at how the look and feel of your product speak volumes about your brand and how careful consideration of these elements can almost help your product to sell itself.

18.

# WHAT THE FUCK IS PRODUCT MARKETING?

In the last chapter, we were able to learn from other people's branding fuckups while looking at how to use the press effectively to strengthen our personal and business brands. Some of it *should* be common sense but is often overlooked when people become complacent. A few sherries can do that to anyone, and even the most teetotal among us can become intoxicated with success. If everything we are doing is working, we may start to feel invincible. I'm not, you're not, no one is, so stay on your guard – always – where your brand is concerned.

Earlier in this book, which I hope you're enjoying, we looked at how not to fuck up your product name. Even a great product can fail to do well if its name happens to be the Greek word for a sphincter or the French for disastrous. If you're late to the party, I made these two examples up: they're not real examples but perfectly plausible as branding fuckups.

## You've Come Too Far

When you've given up yonks of your time, spent every last penny, done half of your mates' heads in – like one of those multi-level marketing people who only ever speak about the product they're selling – and gone as deep as you could with your due diligence; when you've bounced back from rejection and the feeling that there's no finishing line; when you've gone through all of that, you don't want to fuck it up by sticking your product in the worst packaging imaginable or creating a logo that's hard to look at without getting a headache.

Branding is a multi-dimensional affair. You have to consider everything because everything you can imagine and some things that you haven't thought of will impact what people think of your brand: the courier rings the bell and leaves the product on the step before anyone's come to the door, you haven't written a Hindi version of the instructions, your product is only available in three colours, and you haven't created one in Hawaiian turquoise!

## It's On You Even When It's Not

It doesn't matter that you don't own the courier company and didn't employ the driver; and, yes, you didn't include Hindi instructions because 90 per cent of your market is in the UK, 8 per cent is in the US, 1.75 per cent is in Australia, and the other quarter of a per cent could be anywhere from an Afghan prison cell to a Tibetan monastery.

None of these matter, though, because as far as the customers are concerned, you didn't care if their Fluffy Pinky Poodle that they bought for their three-year-old daughter was stolen at the doorstep, that the man in Mumbai couldn't understand the setup instructions for his new tablet, and – fuck me – what kind of a psycho doesn't appreciate Hawaiian turquoise?

## Change Threats Into Opportunity

The point here is not that you can control what happens to a product once it leaves your warehouse, that you can include every single language of the world on the instructions – there are over three hundred in Nigeria alone – or that you can cater for everyone's taste in colour.

You can't control everything, but you must understand that whatever the customer experiences when purchasing your product will be associated with your brand in some way. We have to be mindful of this, but it cuts both ways. We can consider it as a threat or an opportunity.

When we look at everything that we can control as an opportunity to improve customer experience, to encourage our customers to love our brand more, to be so cool that people want to shout about us and become brand ambassadors – remember OLIO? – we can take our marketing to a whole new level.

From the packaging to the note inside that thanks a customer for making the purchase, there are many moments of truth that we can exploit to wow people. This is one area where another guest from my podcast, Hugo Cornejo, stands out majestically.

## Meet Hugo Cornejo – A True Master in the Art of Standing Out in a Good Way

Back in his native Spain, Hugo was in engineering and computer science, working as a developer, but he went on to play a pivotal role in the design of the Monzo card and has since founded the London-based delivery service, Packfleet.

As a developer, Hugo left no stone unturned when mapping out the perfect user journey, and he saw no reason to change his methodology when working in other areas of design, such as the look and feel of a product – a principle which has enabled him to excel in the art of product marketing. Let's start with the hot coral, which is instantly recognisable everywhere, the Monzo card. It's rare for products to become as iconic as the Monzo card, and it's even more incredible that Hugo has pulled this off in the otherwise unsexy, stiff industry of banking.

Young people have been snapping up digital accounts with Monzo simply to get their hands on the card, which has almost become a status symbol. With its bright pink coral colouring, it is the plastic equivalent of a bright red Ferrari in the middle of the High Street and stands out magnificently wherever it is flashed. If you haven't seen one, I can only assume you are living in a cash-only commune somewhere in the Outer Hebrides. Look it up on Google!

If you don't spend any time in London, you've probably never seen a Packfleet van but, believe me, they are something wonderful to behold. These are unlike any other vans you've ever seen. *What? Are they also coral pink?* I hear you thinking. Nope. Better than that. They're not white. They're not green. They're not even chequered. Packfleet vans are iridescent! Their colour changes depending on the angle you view them from so, no, they're not coral pink; they go from green to blueish to purple. Now, if that isn't cool, what is?

## Product Marketing Rule Number 1 – Develop an Aesthetically Pleasing Product That Stands Out

Does the colour of the Monzo card have any bearing on how ethical, efficient or useful Monzo bank is? Does an iridescent van mean Packfleet offer a better service? No, but let's assume you subscribe to the view that all bankers are wankers and financial institutions only exist to provide the bare minimum level of service while screwing people over; let's also say that one delivery service is as crap as any other – the drivers are overworked, underpaid and can't be arsed waiting for someone to answer the door because they've got a quota to reach. That's a pretty bleak perspective and not one I share, but let's say it is, just for now.

Would you rather have a bank card that looks cool, that you couldn't possibly leave lying around and would be difficult to lose or a bog-standard, dark-coloured one? What brings you more joy – a white, grey, or dark blue delivery van or one that looks like a piece of the future that's dropped into our world through a wormhole?

Look, if a product looks and feels great, it adds to the user experience and gives people another reason to want to identify with your brand. But there's another angle here. When a product stands out from the crowd because of the way it looks, there's an unspoken suggestion – that it's substantially different in how it performs and the value it delivers.

Does Monzo deliver a radically different service? How about Packfleet?

## Product Marketing Rule Number 2 – Back Your Brand Up with Substance

A fancy card and some flashy copywriting only get a foot in the door. If all you're offering is another run-of-the-mill financial service that people will moan about, they'll soon see right through a beautiful piece of plastic.

Multi-coloured vans will always attract attention, but who would want to draw attention to noisy trucks burning diesel and kicking out air-polluting toxins? And if your driver's so pissed off with the job they throw a fragile package into the garden and stick up a finger at the customer, an eye-catching van with your brand name all over it will only make the negative experience even more memorable.

You have to offer substance. Back your brand with quality.

### A New Way of Banking

Hugo believes that most banks treat their customers unfairly with hidden charges, and he hates them for it. He wanted to be part of a bank that was on the side of the customer – one that would make money fairly and transparently without profiting from people's misfortune or allowing them to lose money through poor decision-making.

Monzo's founders have worked hard to develop a brand that delivers on its promise by providing customers with more accurate, up-to-date information about their accounts, more control over their money and more effective safeguards.

## A Greener Delivery Service

As far as Hugo's concerned, considering the environment isn't an optional extra or a marketing gimmick. He believes going green should be taken as a given when developing any new product or when providing a service, and he cannot foresee a future where society is still using petrol and diesel vans, so Packfleet vans are electric. Many of its competitors are too big to make the switch to electric vehicles overnight. They have huge fleets of vehicles, so it is going to take time to adapt. This is one way that being small gives Packfleet a competitive advantage.

By building a zero-emissions company from scratch, Hugo is securing his position in tomorrow's world, contributing to a healthier environment, and giving his business clients another reason to shout about using Packfleet. Customers in London love Packfleet's environmentally friendly approach.

Hugo's perspective on how staff should be treated is also forward-thinking. For a start, he does deliveries like everyone else, although he admits that the electric vans are fun to drive, and it allows him to talk to customers directly. Working side by side with other drivers says a lot about his (and therefore, the company's) attitude to employees.

## Treat Staff as You'd Like to Be Treated

Hiring inclusively and treating staff well is important to Hugo, but it also makes good business sense. When someone orders an item online, and the thing they've bought arrives at their doorstep delivered by a courier, that experience is the product. The delivery driver is a key part of that experience, so it's important they take pride in their work and bring their best selves to the doorstep.

An unhappy, undervalued, underpaid driver is less likely to be in the mood to cheerfully greet the people they are delivering to. They may feel rushed, overwhelmed or exhausted. 'Delivery was great. A scruffy van parked wonkily in front of my house, blocking the road and pissing off my neighbours, who needed to get to work. Then, the driver, with a half-burnt cigarette sticking out of his mouth, stepped out of the vehicle, shouted my surname and threw the parcel straight at my head from thirty feet away' doesn't look great on any customer review page.

Hugo believes in valuing employees by taking them as staff members with fair contracts – rather than picking them up and putting them down on zero-hour contracts or treating them as self-employed – and making their job as easy as possible.

Packfleet drivers are fully employed and provided with company iPhones that come with an app that makes life easier for them by planning their route for the shift. They are paid a fair wage for their work and made to feel valued. Hugo's vision is to reach the point where prospective drivers can download the app from the App Store, sign up and apply for work through the app; however, unlike Amazon, which offers people the chance to work for them on a self-employed basis, using their own, personal vehicles, Packfleet drivers would be taken on as staff and given company vehicles.

Hugo left no stone unturned with this empathic approach to managing employees. He applied the same analytical way of thinking to the warehouse processes, and it makes sense. If the system is more efficient and easier to use, not only will the pickers and packers be happier and better at their jobs, but the operation will be more profitable, and customers will be happier with the service.

### Build a Product That Will Sell Itself

A well-thought-out product that looks good and delivers genuine value will almost sell itself once it gets into the hands of its customers. One that doesn't do both will need a lot more marketing work and energy just to stand still.

How did Hugo and the rest of the team at Monzo go about ensuring they had a product that was as exciting and different as its coral pink branding? And how did Hugo know what people wanted from their delivery drivers?

## Product Marketing Rule Number 3 – Talk to Your Customers

A crucial step for any startup is validation. There's only one way to find out whether anyone else will give a fuck about the product or service that's keeping you up at night. You have to speak to people. More importantly, you have to listen to what they say and take it seriously.

### Why Coral Pink?

Monzo's founders wanted to produce a prototype for a few hundred people to use, a kind of alpha test. With that in mind, Hugo wanted to make something that would stand out, create a buzz and a sense that this was a limited edition – a taste of tomorrow's world.

Hugo discovered that he could choose a fluorescent colour by accident. Initially, he wanted to create something flashy to get attention and revert to something more traditional later. When he realised how popular the card's design was – customers regularly commented on it – he made the smart decision to move forward with it. We need to listen to our customers.

According to Hugo, the most important thing is to talk to people, very openly, about their problems and how they do things. He recommends open, genuine conversations about the product rather than a structured approach such as a questionnaire. Allow the discussion to flow and learn from it.

When Monzo was first launching, Hugo and others on the team interviewed around 150 people, asking simple, open questions such as:

- How do you manage your money?
- Do you know how much money you have right now?
- How do you know if you can afford something?

They wanted to get to the heart of the issue and know customer preferences at every step of their journey from opening an account to managing their money and, yes, how they wanted their card to look. Hugo got so into this process that he was recording the interviews and leaving no stone unturned in identifying lessons they could learn from them.

The interview process uncovered customer likes, dislikes and frustrations. When people log on to their bank account or access it through an app, things such as how accurate the balance is and whether a purchase they made two hours earlier has been accounted for are important.

### Have the Guts to Risk Rejection

It takes courage to talk to our customers because they may piss on our great idea. There's also a risk that we will sell a crap idea to a potential customer who agrees with us and lets us think a rubbish idea is better than it is. The second option is the scariest. I'd rather get told to go back to the drawing board until I get it right than sell something that's shit – that's a brand killer.

Remember what scientists do – when they design an experiment to test a theory, they try to disprove it by proving that any effect happened by chance (null hypothesis). It pays to be just as vigorous over product design. Do everything you can to find faults with it.

But the conversation doesn't stop at the pre-launch stage . . .

## Product Marketing Rule Number 4 – Keep Talking

When Hugo and his colleagues were first interviewing people, they weren't speaking to customers. No one had taken out a Monzo account at that stage. They were finding out how people felt about the products that were already out there – discovering their likes, dislikes and frustrations and putting together a 'wouldn't it be cool if' list.

Once people signed up for Monzo, the conversation continued but it changed. Once we've acquired customers, we can learn from them and adapt accordingly.

> **'Now, they can talk about problems that, actually, your product has created, or your product hasn't solved. Or they might tell you the things they would like to do that, actually, your product solves, and they don't know because it is just too complex, or they haven't found the right button or done the right experiment.'**
>
> *Hugo Cornejo – Founder of Packfleet*

## Product Marketing Rule Number 5 – Keep Listening

Conversations without action are pointless. The best bits are the bits we don't want to hear. They're the bits that we can learn from. Of course, it's great to hear that we're doing something right. Take note, and keep doing what works, but listen carefully for those subtle and not-so-subtle hints that you could be doing some things better. We listen to learn.

## Product Marketing Rule Number 6 – Focus on What Customers Want and Need, and Then Reiterate

Hugo applies this to every area of his business. Learning that Monzo customers loved the colour of the card didn't mean the design process was finished. He spent a lot of time making small tweaks here and there to make sure the cards were just right. The time and money spent fine-tuning the look and feel of the card was a wise investment – a good bet – because the end product is a valuable asset and a key part of the Monzo brand.

> 'This is one of the things I learned very early on: to constantly ship things that maybe you're a little uncomfortable with because you think they are not polished enough or good enough, but to be OK with it, and to learn from it.'
>
> *Hugo Cornejo – Founder of Packfleet*

Listening to, learning from and acting upon customer feedback on Monzo's banking service allowed Hugo and his team to evolve their offering and deliver more value.

Hugo's hands-on approach at Packfleet has helped him to improve the experience for the drivers he employs, ensuring that he is treating them as well as he would want to be treated – and making sure they are working as efficiently and comfortably as possible. Listening to, learning from and acting upon the feedback he has received from customers at the doorstep has helped him to ensure Packfleet's service is as notable as its vans.

When you develop a product that stands out, that's constantly evolving to match the wants and needs of your customers, so that the value it delivers is just as sexy as its logo and sales pitch, you achieve something else . . .

## Product Marketing Rule Number 7 – Develop a Product That Is in a Category of Its Own

> 'We just looked at everything that was out there from UPS to Royal Mail to DHL to all the players and said, "OK, what is it that we can create here that is unique, and it can create a new category."'
>
> *Hugo Cornejo – Founder of Packfleet*

Although Hugo uses the word 'category', another way of putting this would be to create something so out there, so ambitious, so adventurous, so unlike everything else that has come before, it is in a league of its own. It's its own class and cannot be compared to the other products that try to do the same thing. He puts it another way when he talks about Monzo.

> 'Whoever has a Monzo card, they don't have a bank account with Monzo. They have a Monzo. It's kind of like in its own category. That's what we are trying to do with Packfleet, that when you get a delivery with us, it just lives in a slightly different category. In your mind, it's not like Hermes, or like DHL, or like any of these players. It's like a slightly different thing.'
>
> *Hugo Cornejo – Founder of Packfleet*

## Product Marketing Rule Number 8 – Be Memorable for the Right Reasons

Make sure you are standing out for the right reasons. Don't rest on your laurels, don't settle for mediocrity, and don't be afraid to take chances. Hugo's taken his developer's mindset and applied the same process to branding and physical product development.

### Hugo's Top Tip – Try Anything That Is Not Too Expensive to Reverse

He allows his vision and imagination to show him what's possible but takes baby steps in any given direction while paying close attention to how those small changes are received by the people who count most – customers. Just like the discovery that he could produce a fluorescent bank card in hot coral, many things happen through luck, but we can build the conditions for luck to go our way. An agile approach facilitates that process and makes good luck more likely.

## Product Marketing Rule Number 9 – It's Okay to Get It Wrong

None of us wants to own up to this, but who likes to admit they've got it wrong? As a former developer, Hugo could feel as precious about his work as anyone. Let's face it, we all get a little attached to a project, an idea, or a plan of action. Things do go wrong, however, and that's part of the process of building anything great. Mistakes are there to learn from. Embrace them, learn from them, and take action to undo them. It's counterintuitive at first but a fantastic habit to develop.

Now, you know what product marketing is and how not to fuck it up. Assuming we've developed an excellent product, launched it, listened to our customers (and employees), and are growing as a company, what else can we do to accelerate that growth?

Yes, in the next chapter, we are going to look at that most important of skills, the art of business development and how not to fuck it up!

19.

# HOW NOT TO FUCK UP YOUR BUSINESS DEVELOPMENT

It doesn't matter how great your idea is, how thorough your validation process is, or the technical development of your product – and you can have the most eye-catching, dazzling logo and smart slogan – if no one is buying it, you haven't got a business.

Not running at a profit – for years, even – is forgivable. Not being the market leader is forgivable. Fucking up is forgivable. Growing slowly is forgivable. All these things are forgivable, provided someone (or preferably *people*) values your product enough to pay for it. If that's not happening, you haven't got a product and you haven't got a business, and the more that continues, the more unforgivable it gets.

But, hey, you're on the nineteenth chapter of a book about not fucking up your business. If you've read it rather than pulling the pages out to make paper aeroplanes, you've brutally assessed your idea, ensured it offers value, built something great, and branded it beautifully, so there's no reason people won't be buying it. Fuck, if you've come this far and taken all the advice from all these great minds that I've shared with you, and still don't have customers, get a job in Tesco, and take up gardening.

None of that means that business development is easy. In Chapter 15, *How the Fuck Am I Gonna Reach My Market?*, we considered some fantastic examples of how startups took off with a one-page website or by using the power of community, and we saw how the Marmite effect can be used to attract people who love us. We also looked at what not to do – don't burn all your money chasing business development avenues that aren't working.

## We've Already Taken a Peek into the World of Business Development

The story of Snag Tights, more than anything, illustrates that when you solve a problem that people want you to solve, all you need to do is show up in front of them and point them to a website, and they will flock to it. I shared that story because it is also a great example of how a startup can jump from nothing to thousands of pounds of weekly revenue within months.

Co-founder Brie Read happens to be a bit of a whizz with paid ads on digital platforms, and she has shared some useful gems of knowledge, but what I think was most special about what she and Tom Martin achieved was that they understood their market, developed a product that the market was screaming for, and brought in shitloads of revenue with a one-page website.

Tessa Clarke and Saasha Celestial-One rapidly built a community of people who were at least as keen about their mission as they were. Once they had got the ball rolling, the business almost grew by itself through the power of the community they'd built. Brand ambassadors appeared organically and with a bit of encouragement became the driving force for growth.

## And We've Nailed Branding

Over the last couple of chapters, we have learnt how important it is to leave no stone unturned in the development of your product and how to talk about your brand in the press. We looked at how those with the tact and diplomacy of Donald Trump and Boris Johnson on a bender can hire an agency or freelancer to handle their press for them.

Every word that comes out of your mouth, is printed on the box, or is uttered by your employees will reflect on you and your brand. How you treat your staff will affect how they represent you to your customers. You must pay as much attention to – and exercise due diligence in the development of –your brand's look and feel as you do to its functionality.

These things – a solid product, a mechanism for selling, a good-looking brand that your customers relate to, effective PR to raise your profile in front of the right audience, and an existing customer base – are the foundations you need to go from up-and-running to magnificent. How are you going to maintain momentum? How are you going to supercharge your revenue from there?

## Let's Take Business Development to Another Level

In this chapter, we're going to explore other methods for generating leads and business, including an area that's been growing rapidly in recent years – sales automation. But first, let's look at how to grow your brand with zero budget. What the fuck did I just say? Zero budget? Yes, I did, but don't take my word for it. I'd rather you listen to my Italian friend, the co-founder and CEO of Digital Oracles, Sara Simeone.

## How to Grow With Zero Budget

Long before launching Digital Oracles, an online platform that helps bring together startups and investors, Sara had a passion for digital marketing. She spent seventeen years as a digital nomad, working in five different countries, for the likes of international communications giant WPP, before finally landing at Manchester University to do a master's in digital marketing strategy – one of her lifelong ambitions.

While at university, she was researching the impact that blockchain will have on the future of digital marketing. That led to opportunities to speak at various events, which got her noticed by representatives from Crypto Valley Labs (CV Labs) in Zug, who asked her to mentor for their blockchain and crypto accelerator programme, the first of its kind in Europe. It was through this work that she found her passion for startups, particularly helping them with their digital strategies, and that experience drove her to launch Digital Oracles as she was finishing her master's.

## Don't Be Afraid to Experiment

I asked Sara what she felt she had learnt from her master's degree that she may not have got from her hands-on experiences. On the one hand, she felt that the course gave her a more holistic understanding of digital marketing strategies and encouraged her to look at things from different angles and question everything. On the other hand, that process stifled her creativity because whatever ideas were put forward would have been considered, analysed and criticised by someone before, and that led almost to a feeling of constantly second-guessing her ideas.

**'One thing I know for sure is that no one is right, and no one is wrong.'**

*Sara Simeone – Co-Founder of Digital Oracles*

As Hugo Cornejo pointed out in the last chapter, whenever you try anything, you will learn something. If something you do works, throw more energy into it. If it doesn't, scrap it, but always make sure you can reverse whatever you have done, so no long-term or significant harm is done.

Sara says that when it comes to digital marketing strategy, no one knows the answer for sure. The world of academia is great at knocking every idea, but ultimately no one is right and no one is wrong. Be creative, be brave and give it a go.

Although many of the companies that Sara worked with had budgets for marketing, sometimes huge budgets, she has always enjoyed looking for ways to grow businesses with zero budget. How does that work?

We saw how building a community worked for the founders of OLIO, but how can it work for you? Sara has broken down the process generically, so anyone can find a way of building and leveraging the power of community.

## A Step-by-Step Approach to Building a Community

> 'Building your community doesn't cost anything – if not your time. If you show them your passion, what drives you, the values that you've got as an entrepreneur and as a company, then people will buy into that.'
>
> *Sara Simeone – Co-Founder of Digital Oracles*

Here are the six key steps that Sara recommends:

- **Know yourself**. As simple as it sounds, you have to know who you are, what you are passionate about, why you are passionate about it and what you want to achieve.
- **Build a profile**. Decide how you are going to put yourself forward.
- **Choose your platforms**. Where do your tribe live?
- **Show up as you are**. Use the power of authenticity to attract the people who are most likely to support you.
- **Give stuff away**. Give your followers a good reason to stick around.
- **Build trust**. People won't recommend you, buy from you, or collaborate with you unless they trust you.

### Who Are You?

Make no mistake about it, this is one of the most neglected superpowers around, and a lack of self-awareness is one of the most common afflictions. I'm not here to be your spiritual guru (or any guru), but if you can nail self-awareness or at least start working on it, the growth potential is enormous. You'll notice huge improvements in every area of your life as a result, but it comes in particularly handy for entrepreneurs.

Let's loop right back to the beginning of this book. Why do you want to be an entrepreneur? What experience helped you to identify a 'wouldn't it be cool if' idea? Why does it mean so much to you? Be honest! If you've devised something that saves time, admit that you're impatient and you can't stand waiting for things. The chances are your ideal customers will be the same.

You probably don't need to worry so much about what your favourite meal is or whether you prefer action movies to romantic comedies, and nobody needs to know about your love life – unless any of these things is relevant to your product and the value it provides. But if this is the first time you've ever tried an exercise such as this, I recommend throwing it all at the wall, including the kitchen sink. You can get rid of the irrelevant stuff later.

If you can identify the things that matter, and that are relevant to your product, you have the juice for building a community.

### How Are You Going to Show Up?

Once you've identified who you are, decide how you are going to express yourself and where. Would a YouTube channel work for you? Perhaps you should consider a TikTok channel. TikTok has proven itself to be much more than just a channel for kids to show dance moves. It depends on your product, but some brands are making the platform work for them.

Where does your tribe live, and what's the best way to relate to the people that belong there – written articles (Medium), video content (YouTube, Vimeo, or using the native apps of the various social media platforms), multimedia updates (text plus photo, link, video or montage). Clubhouse worked for Sara.

Your strategy will probably incorporate a bit of everything, so you might be killing it on LinkedIn with posts two or three times a week or even every day. You could be Tweeting when you feel like it, and perhaps you will create a Facebook page for bringing like-minds together where you can engage with them, learn from them and potentially sell to them. Mix it up.

Whatever you do, don't fuck it up. In Chapter 12, we looked at how not to fuck up your personal brand and to consider what potential investors would want to see. Now, we're considering your customers, but don't let that confuse you. If you are presenting the best front for your customers, that's going to work wonders for your investors too.

Showing up is a long-term game. A strategically planned social media post can win immediate orders and even offers for investment, but if your overall posting strategy is sound, the effectiveness of your posts will grow over time as your network grows and as the audience you want to reach gravitates towards you.

If you are clever about it, using a variety of tactics from storytelling to exploring themes, from how you interact with other discussions to the kinds of conversations you start on various platforms, you can draw attention to the different value propositions you have in your toolbox – without saying, 'I can do this for you. Do you want to hire me?'

You're building a solid profile – that's your focus – and it may sometimes feel as though you are spending time and energy for nothing in return because the results don't come overnight.

### Keep It Real

Bring the real you to every situation. If you don't at least do that much, you're wasting your time. You don't want to be like that guy at parties, who has carefully crafted a new identity – adopted a new accent, started going to the opera and taken to eating in places where they serve portions of nouveau cuisine that wouldn't even feed a pet gerbil – because they don't want to be 'found out' as working-class; or the girl from Kensington who's doing her best to sound like an Eastender.

Firstly, no one gives a fuck where you're from or your background (or they shouldn't). They want to know who you are and what you bring to the table. More than that, the façade usually falls apart after a few drinks or when they get emotional, so it's easier to throw the mask away at the beginning.

Don't be naive about it. Prejudice does exist. It's real. But for every person who will judge you because you were born in a rough place or because you went to Cambridge University or because your parents were mega-rich (take your pick), there are many more who will see you for who you are and love you for it. Some people are arseholes and will not like you for things you cannot change – racists, misogynists, homophobes and the list goes on. Never shy away from being you. Haters gonna hate and all that jazz.

Wear your authentic self with pride. Listen to the music you want to listen to, wear the clothes you want to wear, and don't do anything with your accent unless people can't understand you (then you can tone it down for clarity rather than pretending to be someone you are not).

How about swearing? In case you haven't noticed, I'm a bit fucking sweary. I probably wouldn't do it in a pitch meeting, to be honest, although I have no qualms about swearing on my social media posts. Swearing has as much to do with context as anything else. Would I swear to a vicar? Probably not. Would I tell someone they are a wanker, a twat or an arsehole? The cap would probably fit them so fucking well that I wouldn't have to. They'd know it already. And to be clear, no, I don't swear at people – swearing at people and throwing in the odd f-bomb are not the same.

Remember that for every person you turn off by being yourself, you will attract many others who see you as a kindred spirit. Bringing yourself to the table is much more than choosing whether to swear, show your tattoos, come suited and booted or opt for smart casual. It's about showing what you care about, sharing your values, expressing your passion, and being open about your mission, your drives and the difference you want to make. Show up!

> 'I am Sara. I am a very determined Italian entrepreneur based in the UK with an international background, with a passion for blockchain, crypto and startups; and that's who I am! And people buy into who I am. I do that with the Tweets I send, with the LinkedIn posts that I write, with the articles that I write for a lot of digital magazines, both in Italian and other languages; and the communication that I have got with other people on channels such as Telegram and Clubhouse, which is a huge channel for me.'
>
> *Sara Simeone – Co-Founder of Digital Oracles*

I've heard people say, 'Be yourself, but if you can be a unicorn, be a unicorn.' Fuck that shit! Being yourself wins every time. You don't need to worry about letting your guard slip and facing the humiliation of being found out for who you are, and the people who like you (and who you gel with) will be the ones you form the closest relationships with. Let your business become a unicorn. You stick to being the best version of your natural self and let that shine through everything you do and say. Show up majestically on all the platforms upon which you should be seen.

#### Offer Value

Sara's fourth tip for leveraging the community you are building is to give them value. You don't have to give them products. Value could simply mean sharing useful insights or tools that help them enormously without making your services redundant. Don't forget that the people in your community might end up buying from you, so they make great guinea pigs for you to share ideas with and for checking the validity of your product or services.

You don't have to be an expert in a topic to deliver value. For example, Sara talks about blockchain and NFTs (non-fungible tokens) but doesn't put herself out there as an expert. Instead, she shares her experiences since starting to learn about them in 2016, as she struggled to find the right exchange, the right tools or the right communities to learn from. She almost had to teach herself how to trade, buy cryptocurrencies and understand the ins and outs of wallets.

By sharing her experiences with cryptocurrency, openly and honestly, she can educate her community and show them how they can discover useful information for themselves. This exposes her vulnerability to an extent – we naturally want to appear as experts who are in control of everything – and this helps her to win trust.

### Are There Any Scalable Methods for Building a Community?

It takes hard work and lots of it is the short answer. There are no short cuts to building a community, but there are techniques for speeding things up. For example, during the crypto 'gold rush' of 2017, when there were loads of initial coin offerings (ICOs), a lot of people wanted to cash in and get rich quick, and they were working hard to build communities on the cross-platform, encrypted messenger Telegram. It was obvious that some of them were using techniques to build those communities quicker. What kind of techniques?

One tactic that Sara mentioned was the use of 'airdrops' as incentives to encourage people to join a channel, subscribe to a blog on a specific website or a waiting list for something. An 'airdrop' is the term used for dropping cryptocurrency into someone's wallet, so using that approach involves paying people, but it doesn't have to be a lot, and you should see it as an investment.

## Differentiate Yourself

When I asked Sara how to get noticed as a founder, she spoke about the importance of standing out from the crowd. This is especially useful for getting noticed by potential funders or investors, but it is an effective way of attracting customers, brand ambassadors and potential partners. It's about raising your profile.

## Partnerships and Collaboration

Forming commercial alliances can lead to rapid growth. Sara is a mentor for Crypto Valley Labs, which is an endorsement for her. She gets the logo on her website and all the credibility that goes with that. In return, she helps their startups get more deals. How did that partnership come about? She approached the founder on LinkedIn and ended up becoming one of their UK ambassadors. Again, she is not paying anything, but she gives back by offering Crypto Valley Labs her time, experience and expertise. Not only does she gain more kudos because of her alliance with them, but she also gets to form new relationships with some exciting startups. Some of those will go on to join Digital Oracles.

Digital Oracles is a startup that is built on the principles of community. It demonstrates the power of community, helping investors to find the seeds to tomorrow's success stories, and helping startups with massive potential to win investment. Sara wins as well, so it's good on all counts.

## What's the Dirtiest Word in Business?

Some will say 'advertising'. What was once considered a very powerful tool for generating business and enquiries has taken a bit of a hammering in recent years. Everyone, yes, *everyone* hates pop-up advertising on the internet. That's why we all enjoy browsers that prevent them – so we can jump down those ridiculous rabbit holes that show up in our feeds ('One Hundred Things You Didn't Know About These Well-Known Celebrities' – with a photo of an A-list actor dressed as a veterinary surgeon) without having to jump to a new page of mostly advertisements every two paragraphs. Now, those pointless click-bait articles only take thirty minutes to read instead of potentially half a day (if you lasted that long).

Advertising is not the bad guy in marketing, however. Poor advertising is. Unimaginative, repetitive, intrusive, boring – otherwise known as 'shit' – advertising is. But ask anyone who's invested in Google AdWords what they think about advertising. Ask anyone who's been smart with Facebook advertising how it's worked for them. No. Advertising is not a bad thing, but terribly designed, poorly targeted advertising is.

Everyone hates advertising until they spot something that they want and need and have been thinking about. They suddenly become all feline and curious, open-minded and explorative, and they click more to find out whether there's a cure for their rash, a method for losing weight that's going to work for them, or the next big productivity tool to help them work more smartly and efficiently.

> **'Never write an advertisement which you wouldn't want your own family to read. You wouldn't tell lies to your own wife. Don't tell them to mine. Do as you would be done by. If you tell lies about a product, you will be found out.'**
>
> *David Ogilvy CBE (1911–1999) – British advertising tycoon and the founder of Ogilvy and Mather*

One of the reasons advertising has a dirty reputation is because some subscribers to the art have been economical with the truth at best and blown even the most dishonest politicians out of the water when it comes to telling outright porkies. Cheats never prosper, as they say, and the man known as 'the father of advertising', David Ogilvy CBE, put it well when he said that liars always get found out. Why lie to the people who are going to be most important to your brand, your customers and potential customers? If you lose them, you've lost everything.

**'A good advertisement is one which sells the product without drawing attention to itself.'**

*David Ogilvy CBE (1911–1999) – British advertising tycoon and the founder of Ogilvy and Mather*

Another complaint about advertising comes when the way the message has been delivered distracts from the value of the product. When brands annoy us by bombarding us with advertisements, ruining an otherwise good song that's been changed into a jingle, or because the television or radio companies that host them bump the volume up by three notches for commercial breaks, or because their message is hidden behind an obscure concept, they make us less likely to buy into their products.

Advertising experts might disagree with everything I've just said. I'm not an expert and don't claim any authority on the subject, but I know that stupid, uninteresting, noisy advertisements that are repeated everywhere I look and listen threaten to drive me insane. I fucking hate them. How about you? Maybe the industry experts have some stats that prove that kind of approach works – or drives people into submission – but that's not how I want to sell my products. And it's not how I want to make people feel about my brand.

This leads me to the most sensible advice I can give you on the subject . . .

## Find an Expert

As is the case with PR, you can give it your best shot, but whereas fucking up your attempts to get free coverage won't cost you anything (apart from potentially having all your future emails automatically binned by an editor), fucking up your advertising could leave you bankrupt.

I'm writing a book about not fucking up your startup, and I want it to be as inspirational and useful as I can. There was no way I was going to bring up the subject of advertising without throwing in any opinions of my own or the odd quote from David Ogilvy. But take note – I am not qualified to preach about advertising, and you won't become an expert by listening to quotes from the gods of that topic either. Hire an expert.

## How Does Free Advertising Grab You?

It may not be a dirty word, but most people would agree on one thing – advertising can be costly and, if you don't know what you're doing, it can be as useful as burning money to keep warm. That's where someone like Hannah Redgewell can be invaluable for a startup.

Hannah is the Investment Principal at Channel 4 Ventures, which offers an unusual and interesting service – media for equity. This is particularly useful for companies that have spent their initial seed funding but haven't yet grown large enough to attract large venture capitalists. Instead of spending your limited cash on business development campaigns that will deliver variable results, you can keep your capital and gain access to free advertising . . . sort of. It's not free, but you don't have to pay anything upfront for it. Channel 4 Ventures doesn't ask for money. It asks for equity in your company.

It's not quite the same as a 'no win, no fee' arrangement because they will own a slice of your company whether the advertising campaign helps your startup to grow or not; however, the more successful the campaign is, the more valuable their stake in your business becomes, so they are incentivised to generate growth.

Channel 4 Ventures is not *selling* advertising either, strictly speaking. It is an investor, which means that companies need to prove they are investible just as they would for any other investment vehicle.

> **'What we're doing instead of providing that cash; we're providing a million pounds' advertising budget with Channel 4, so that can be used across Channel 4 suites – the channels. It can be used on our VoD (video on demand) platform, All 4, and we basically help companies to run really great marketing campaigns that maybe otherwise they wouldn't have been able to do.'**
>
> *Hannah Redgewell – Investment Principal at Channel 4 Ventures*

There are several reasons why this kind of deal might suit a startup. It might have reached a point where its digital marketing costs are starting to soar, and its founders need to explore other avenues to hit the growth metrics they are looking for. Perhaps the founder is aiming to supercharge their personal brand and become famous, and television advertising is an excellent and effective way to do this in the UK – according to Hannah, Channel 4 reaches 75 per cent of the population every month.

So, if you want to have your name and face splashed all over Channel 4 during the commercial breaks of the next season of *Celebrity Bake Off*, what can you do to excite Hannah enough to invest in you?

## What Does Hannah Look For in a Startup?

> 'There are just some companies where you go onto the website, and you're just excited to be on there; they've really thought about the look and feel of the brand, the logo, the tone of voice with which they write. Anything distinctive, unusual, and modern, there, gets us really excited because it's not necessarily a given that most companies have that.'
>
> *Hannah Redgewell – Investment Principal at Channel 4 Ventures*

This is a reminder to us all that you can't pick and choose what to care about when it comes to how your startup shows up in its market. You have to be on the ball with everything – the quality of your product, your branding, the look and feel of your website, and any other points where your company interacts with your customers (and potential investors).

If you put yourself in Hannah's shoes, she has to decide whether a brand is going to appeal to Channel 4's audience. She has to go with her gut to some extent, so if a brand resonates with her and her colleagues, it's probably going to go down well with Channel 4's audience, and she will have a feel for where to place it.

There are several other factors you need to consider if you want to go down the television advertising route. Hannah needs to know these criteria are met before she can invest in you.

- Your product must be scalable. If you are hand-knitting socks, you're not going to be able to meet demand.
- Your product must be suitable for the mass market. If it's too niche, you need a more targeted vehicle.
- You need the right marketing funnel. Will your system cope with a large influx of orders?
- Your website must be able to cope. Is your website robust enough to handle thousands of visits at once?

At the end of the day, people are not always prepared for success. Had you ever wondered what it would take to crash your website, how many orders you could process at once, or what level of demand your startup could meet?

If you are serious about growing your business, you must be strategic about how you're going to make that happen, and all the operations of your business must be configured for success. Put faith in your plan and prepare your business for a flood of enquiries.

Before we park television advertising, let's ponder another inspirational quote from the world of advertising.

> **'I don't know how to speak to everybody, only to somebody.'**
>
> *Howard Luck Gossage (1917–1969) – an innovator in the world of advertising and copywriting, often referred to as 'The Socrates of San Francisco'*

The final word on advertising is to make sure you know who you are talking to and align every word, phrase, sentence and image with them. If you get a chance to research more about Howard Gossage, get stuck in because he won a fearsome reputation as a copywriting ninja. Speaking of martial arts analogies, the next person I want to introduce you to is a black belt in the art of sales automation.

## How to Grow Rapidly With a Sales Force of One

Let's assume you are open for business and fully prepared to take over the world. Your product is scalable, you know that shitloads of people will buy it, and your website is powerful enough to handle a gazillion orders at once. But you haven't got the money for television advertising, you can't gain investment from Channel 4 Ventures, and your sales force consists of one person – you. Hmm, did you miss the chapter on building a team? Never mind if you didn't. There's no point in crying over spilt milk. A better option would be to learn from Anthony Collias, who co-founded Stasher, the world's first luggage storage network that 'connects you with hotels and stores that can keep your luggage safe while you enjoy your time in a city' (according to its website).

Anthony Collias is also the CEO of Treepoints, which he co-founded to make it easier for everyday people to live more sustainably by helping them to offset their carbon footprints and rewarding them for doing so.

Unsurprisingly, given their passion for fighting climate change, Anthony and his co-founder Jacob Wedderburn-Day run a tight ship when it comes to reducing their own carbon footprints and ensuring Treepoints is as green as possible.

Anthony has a passion for efficiency, and it is this drive for gaining maximum results for the minimum effort that led him down the path to sales automation. Why have a sales team of twenty people when you can leverage the power of technology to automate your sales process?

When it's done wrong, sales automation is a pain in the arse for everyone. No one wants to receive spam from bots; and annoying, easy-to-spot, poorly written, impersonal messages can fuck up the brands of the sender (if human) and the company they represent.

When sales automation is done properly, it can boost growth exponentially, so let's look at how not to fuck it up.

## What's So Special About Sales Automation

When you look at how processes can be automated and how much time can be saved, traditional methods such as cold calling, sending bespoke emails to people individually, and knocking on doors don't compare and can't compete. Believe me, I know how time-consuming and tedious sales can be.

When I interviewed him for my podcast, Anthony said the first thing that pops into most people's minds when they think of sales is someone with bags of energy, standing up, with a phone glued to their ear, and getting increasingly excited as they steer the person on the other end of the wire to a close. I was that guy, working in a boiler room!

> **'You kind of realise increasingly it's just so much more efficient to find processes to reach people at scale rather than have an excellent salesperson make a ton of calls.'**
>
> *Anthony Collias – Co-Founder of Treepoints*

Anthony knows the feeling as well because, in the pre-Covid era, he was using door-to-door sales teams to generate business. When pandemic restrictions meant they couldn't do that, they discovered sales automation by accident; and when they realised the power of automation, they were not interested in going back to knocking on doors.

> 'One person who can find an effective way to reach a thousand people all over the world in a couple of weeks is way better return than sending people to find ten different locations around the world or trying to find contractors and manage them.'
>
> *Anthony Collias – Co-Founder of Treepoints*

## Sales as an Afterthought

One of the problems with founders, and this applies just as much to me as to anyone, is that we tend to focus on building the product and we forget all about sales in the beginning. We assume that generating sales is going to be an effortless process that we can nail by hiring a sales team, organising some great PR, or paying for Google AdWords.

All those things are excellent, but you should have a strategy in place long before you need the sales to come in, and if you intended to use the more well-trodden routes to bring in orders, it tends to take a while for momentum to build up.

## Some Automation Dos and Don'ts

Sales automation can speed up the process dramatically, but make sure you avoid the most common fuckups:

- **Don't piss people off.** This comes down to targeting and messaging more than anything else. You can't blame automation for a negative reaction to a shit piece of copywriting.
- **Don't send mailshots from your main email account**. Don't fuck things up by sending too many emails at once and getting email addresses from your domain block-listed as SPAM.
- **Don't launch into a full-on SPAM assault from scratch.** You'll be asking for your domain to be flagged as SPAM.
- **Don't write shit, boring, lengthy subject lines.** 'An introduction to psycholinguistics and how you can use the power of words to get people to like you' is not going to get you many reads, even though most people probably would be interested in knowing how to become more likeable and influential.
- **Don't sound like a fucking droid.** A shit salesperson can sound like a droid on the phone if they are reading from a script or are so

bored with the job that they reel off the same deadpan spiel repeatedly.

Whatever approach to sales you use, it is always going to be a numbers game, and that's part of the problem. It takes so much fucking time. And just because you are hand-crafting every email, or only messaging people you have warmed up with a call, or taking prospects for dinner to close them, don't think you're not still going to get rejected or told to piss off. Some people are just shitty. Others will have an issue just because you are selling something, so don't dismiss the possibility of automation just because you are frightened of pissing people off.

> 'The truth with a lot of sales stuff is that you have to take a lot of swings to get a hit.'
>
> *Anthony Collias – Co-Founder of Treepoints*

Automation allows you to take a lot of swings very quickly, so you can boost the number of hits you get. You can mitigate the risks of annoying people by making sure you are targeting the people who need your product and approaching them with well-written copywriting.

## Don't Be Embarrassed About Pitching or Offering to Connect

Provided you are targeting the people who need your validated product or service, there's no reason for you to approach from a position of inferiority, embarrassment or to feel as though you're Oliver Twist asking for more. You're doing them a fucking favour. Many will ignore you; a few might think you're a tosser but scroll on, and some might tell you to fuck off – because of the horror that someone on a social media NETWORKING site has had the gall to ask them to connect even though they hadn't met in the real world. So what? What do they have that's so sacred that they won't connect with you? If you are polite and write something that doesn't make you sound like a fucking droid, most people will connect with you.

## Don't Overlook the Power of LinkedIn

Sales automation is not just about scaling up your power to pitch. We don't have to ditch relationships. Anthony points out that we can use automation software, such as PhantomBuster, that works well with LinkedIn by allowing you to make new connections at scale by working at a rate that won't alert the platform's anti-spam algorithms. PhantomBuster's search facility lets you target the people who are most likely to be interested in your product, so you can grow your network rapidly into a large community of potential customers. No aggressive emails are necessary.

More connections mean greater reach, which means more chance of productive interaction and sales further down the line. There is no reason not to use this technology.

Why LinkedIn? This is *the* platform to be on whether you're looking for investment, talent, clients or collaborators.

> **'LinkedIn is such an interesting space. Because it's for business-people [who] tend not to be trolls.'**
>
> *Anthony Collias – Co-Founder of Treepoints*

Let's say you are going to use automation software to let people know about your products, services and special offers. That's fine, but you have to be careful not to fuck it up. Here are some more tips from Anthony.

## Set Up a Side Domain

There are plenty of ways to reduce the risk of getting your domain block-listed, but you can play it safer by using an alternative domain for sending out mailshots. If it goes wrong, and that domain is flagged as SPAM because someone complains, it's not the end of the world. Just set up another one.

## Don't Forget to Warm Up Your Domain

It is better to use a smaller list to start with, sending out a few hundred emails at once rather than going all in from the off with a mega list of thousands. That's just asking for trouble. Start small and build up slowly from there.

## Don't Look Like a Robot

Not looking like a droid isn't just a case of writing some cool, natural-sounding, engaging copy. Avoid using software that makes it obvious you are using software. Don't make it look like a newsletter either because that would make it impersonal. It must look like it has been manually sent by an individual for someone's specific attention.

The best software will automate your sales process without giving the game away that you're automating. You want every recipient to feel special. Use software and copywriting that makes them think you have just reached out to them. Anthony recommends Apollo.io and points out that even the free version is very powerful. Apollo lets you send loads of weekly emails, create lists, perform searches and import LinkedIn contacts.

## Think Smart – Set Up Flows

At some point, you might need to respond to an enquiry personally, but the aim is to automate as much as possible. If you are smart in the way you construct your emails, you should be able to predict (or encourage) key responses from recipients. Apollo allows you to set up simple flows, so you can respond automatically. You can also use software such as Zapier for tying things together; for example, you can link your email shot with a customer relationship management (CRM) platform such as HubSpot.

Remember this: automation software is only as smart as your strategy. If you have no game plan, no target market, no idea how to write decent copy, and no sense of a funnel, sales automation is only going to amplify your potential to fuck things up. You can't blame automation for that. Let's not forget that I once raised half-a-million dollars from a GMass mailer. That's not to be scoffed at.

## Apply Some Common Sense

If you are looking for an outcome from your mailer, and you should be, some of the people on your mail list will be hotter than others. These may need more careful attention. Send a manually typed – and carefully proofread – email to the top twenty-five people on the list. For the next seventy-five, you might use a semi-automated email. Then, the rest of the list can be fully automated.

## Become a Process Architect

The keyword here is 'test'. You should be seeking to constantly fine-tune your approach to mailers. You should always use brief subject lines, but you can test to see what types of headings get more engagement – questions or statements, for example. Test your subject line, email length and the effect that including images will have – emails with images are more likely to be flagged as SPAM.

## Where Do You Get Good Data?

When I was on the hunt for investment, I hired someone to manually search for people on LinkedIn. The cost per contact was just thirty-five cents. However, there are other ways of getting data. Anthony points out that automation software such as Apollo offers access to lists from its database. You can also use products such as ZoomInfo for detailed data, but these are very expensive for what most people are trying to achieve. For the more technically gifted, you can use software to scrape data from relevant websites. For many, exporting from LinkedIn is a great start.

## Three Things That Must Happen in Any Email

Earlier in the book, I shared my approach to putting together an email for an investor, but what about emails designed for other purposes? What if I have an offer to share? What if I am trying to get people to sign up for something?

In my experience, there are three elements that you must include in any email, and this is even more important if you are planning to send out mailers. The more strategic you are about how to construct your email, the better your outcomes will be.

### Gain Interest

You must capture their attention from the subject line and keep their interest with every word you type. That's why the subject line is so important. If you don't get that right, they won't even open the message up. Once they've opened it, don't fuck it up by writing a shit message. Grab them by the short and curlies with the first sentence. You have to gain their interest.

### Add Credibility

Imagine you've just received an email from someone. They've managed to grab your attention with the subject line, and they've gained your interest. Do you believe them? Do you believe that they can deliver on the promise?

Credibility is everything. When you think about it, it's been the elephant in the room throughout the whole startup process. Only ideas that address issues that other people care about, by providing credible solutions that offer value, evolve into successful products. Only teams that look as though they can deliver on promises are likely to win investment. Credibility is the key.

So, once you have the attention of your reader, stick something into the text to show why the reader should listen to you.' It could be a statistic, a piece of research, or a factual statement about your credentials in the field.

### Include a Call to Action

There's no need for any aggressive sales tactics here, but you must give your reader a clear suggestion on how to act. You must know what you want them to do. Do you want them to click on a link, subscribe to something or download a freebie from your site?

> 'Are you the right person or can you point me in the direction of the right person? With a question like that, and it's non-aggressive – you know, a lot of people will be like, say they don't want to deal with it, but they think it is kind of interesting, they will actually point you to the right person.'
>
> *Anthony Collias – Co-Founder of Treepoints*

By offering them the chance to be helpful even if they are not interested in you or your brand, you invite them to show how important they are. Everyone likes to feel valued. We all like to feel as though we are useful.

## Keep an Open Mind and Explore

It's the middle of 2022 as I type, and we are living in one of the most fast-paced technological revolutions the world has ever seen. I can only provide you with a freeze-frame glimpse of what's out there today. That's all anyone can do. Some of the software and platforms I've mentioned today may become a thing of the past by the end of the decade. Anything's possible.

What would you do without LinkedIn or any other platform you are using? Will Apollo, GMass or PhantomBuster still be around in five years?

All we can do is keep an open mind. The spirit is more important than the letter, and the spirit to adopt for business development is one of curiosity. Be open to things like sales automation, contra deals (whether that's gaining advertising for equity or some other mechanism) or hiring someone on Fiverr to compile a list.

If I were going to give you a comprehensive guide to business development, I'd probably need to speak to another few dozen specialists in the area, and that would be another book. If you've learnt anything about not fucking up your business development, it should be to explore all avenues.

## Wondering What Comes Next?

In the next chapter, I'm going to assume that you've made it. You have nailed everything up to this point, including business development. Your startup is growing at a healthy rate and, fuck me, you might have splashed out on a new Jag or whatever takes your fancy. But if that's the case, we both know that 'made it' makes it sound cushier than it is.

What the fuck are you going to do now? Keep growing forever? Sell up? Start another business? In the next chapter, we will consider these questions and others to make sure you don't fuck up your startup.

# 20.
# DON'T FUCK UP BY BEING COMPLACENT

It's time to break into a new bottle of champagne. I've almost finished my debut book! Tom Fairey, author – how the fuck did that happen? Who cares? It's done now. I'm going to chill out in the jacuzzi of my Bentley, surrounded by honeys, listening to loud hip-hop music, cruising through London's Knightsbridge, and figuring out what to say in my acceptance speech for when I win my first award for *How Not To F*ck Up Your Startup*.

Seriously, though, if I wanted to do that, you might call me deluded, but there'd be no harm in indulging myself apart from the cost of the champagne, flash car hire, a chauffeur – hmm . . . these costs are stacking up. There's no reason I can't relax and pat myself on the back for accomplishing the mission. But we're talking about a book. Launching and growing a startup is a different kettle of fish.

## Have You Looked Down Yet?

If you're anything like me, you're not there yet. There's still loads to do, even if you don't realise it. Sure, the sales are rolling in, user growth is exponential, you're mates with Sir Richard Branson and Lord Sugar, Sir Lewis Hamilton has spoken publicly about using your product, and it feels as though you're in pole position (see what I did there? *That's terrible, Tom!*). All that is great, and if you fancy a quick getaway to Monaco, feel free – you've earned it – but you cannot rest on your laurels at this stage, not for too long anyway.

Launching a successful startup is like walking a tightrope across the Grand Canyon. Let's assume you can do that. One thing you're not, absolutely not, going to do is to look down. Even though the business is booming, so are the customer support tickets and the server bills, and if you want to see something terrifying, check out your payroll bill! It's time to start taking the boring stuff seriously.

## Keep Your Eye on the Ball

Being an entrepreneur is one of the most exciting things you can do, but the reason it is such a roller-coaster ride is that it is not easy and not without risk. Even highly successful founders encounter self-doubt, anxiety, sleepless nights, highly stressful situations and plenty of hard choices. What would happen if, for whatever reason, you couldn't find the cash to pay your staff at the end of the month?

Do you think that's not going to happen? Plenty of founders have had to whip cash from every direction to meet their payroll commitment when the shit's hit the fan. You know those forecasts that you make – you *are* forecasting, aren't you? – yes, those. They don't always come true. Sales can and do slow down, and sometimes turnover shrinks! Scary as fuck, I know, but no amount of trembling, sweating buckets or crying for your mum is going to help when things don't go the way you want them to. It's best to bear in mind the adage 'the bigger they are, the harder they fall'. Just because your company's valued at £300 million, doesn't make it bulletproof.

## Firing People

One of the most difficult things any founder will have to do is to let people go. Earlier in the book, we looked at strategies for recruiting the best people. Hopefully, if you took every step to ensure you were hiring top talent, you shouldn't have to fire them. That said, there are no guarantees. You won't know until you've hired them, and even the most talented, enthusiastic, loyal employees can fall out of love with you, their job or your company.

Either way, even if your recruitment strategy was crap, it is fair to say you started out liking your staff. Nobody wants to hire a dickhead but occasionally, and this happens to everyone, you might hire someone who turns out to be as superb at the job as you'd suspected but is an arsehole. It's easy to fire an arsehole – well, easier – but when the person is a hard worker who is trying their best, and you like them, the task becomes more challenging.

Even good people, whom you like, can become toxic to your organisation, and they might end up holding you back or dragging you, your company or other team members down. When that happens, you don't have a choice, not if you want your startup to thrive. You must remove them from your company.

Sometimes it's not about them, their attitude or the quality of their work. The sad truth is that companies fail, and if that starts to happen, founders find themselves in a position where they have to shed considerable weight to stay afloat. That means letting good people go.

Even when things are going well, running a startup can be a lonely pursuit but, if the ship starts sinking, the situation can be even more frightening and the weight of keeping it afloat will bear down heavily on the soul. What's more, it's difficult to find anyone to talk to. As CEO, if you say the wrong thing, your brand could turn into toast overnight. Remember Ratner.

As I type, the CEO of a US-based sales and marketing startup has just been hammered by public opinion for speaking out about his heartbreak at having to lay off staff. His post went viral for all the wrong reasons, attracting tens of thousands of reactions, thousands of comments, and hitting headlines away from LinkedIn, the platform on which he had posted.

While some people thought what he did was gutsy, the majority view was that being a leader means having to take the rough with the smooth and make difficult decisions. Most commentators had little sympathy for the 'Crying CEO' and felt as though his post should have been more about the people he laid off rather than himself. People are brutal.

## How to Fire an Employee

Well, firstly, you should be very careful what you announce on social media and in other public places, but the main thing is to be honest with anyone you have to fire. That's the least you can do, isn't it, especially as they are probably hard-working, decent people whom you like. Even the ones you have come to consider as twats will have their good qualities. Just because they're not your cup of tea, and you might not be theirs, it doesn't make them bad people. Anyone you employ deserves honesty.

Let's look at some Dos and Don'ts, then:

### Dos

**Do be honest.**

They deserve to know why you're firing them.

**Do be as direct as you can without throwing tact out of the window.**
'Have a seat. I just wanted to thank you for all your hard work to date and to let you know I'm firing you because you're shit at your job' is not the best way for the conversation to go down.

**Do let them know how they have not lived up to expectations.**
Constructive criticism will help them to process things while giving them something to work on for their next role.

**Do be kind.**
You can tell them their productivity was too low without calling them a lazy bastard. You can let them know that you needed a higher sales conversion rate without making your business development manager feel like shit.

### Don'ts

**Don't be dishonest.**
If they were poor performers, they were poor performers. That's not your fault. Yes, you want to be kind, but kindness isn't wrapping them up in cotton wool and leaving them in the dark. If you can't bring yourself to tell them they were unreliable or their products didn't work, you might as well tell them you don't like them or just tell them they were shit. They will be wondering what they've done to deserve to be fired, and that's going to eat away at them. It's demoralising. Don't let them make up a narrative that may be worse than the truth. Spit it out.

**Don't use wishy-washy language.**
You can say it as it is without insulting them, but they need to know the truth. Blurring the truth with vagueness is just another way of being dishonest. There's no point trying to protect them from the truth. Besides, if their performance is poor, they will probably be expecting to hear you say it.

**Don't leave it too long.**
I go with the 'fire fast, hire slow' philosophy when it comes to employing people, and I'd encourage you to do the same. If you hired efficiently,

every pair of hands is important and there to fulfil a need. When an employee is not living up to expectations, or not meeting their goals, the cut must be swift and clean. Once they've gone, you have the more time-consuming and trickier task of finding someone to replace them.

**Don't assume they'll be devastated.**

Poor performance can sometimes be a sign that someone wants to leave. They may even be looking for other jobs on your time. Telling them that you're letting them go might be the best news they've had in ages. You could be doing them a favour. Many people want to leave their jobs but find it difficult to make the jump.

**Don't show the world your dirty laundry.**

Unless you're shedding loads of jobs, you don't have to announce that you're losing people, and that's probably for the best. Being overly transparent about stuff like that can end in disaster.

## Bankruptcy Sucks

The second most horrible thing to deal with is laying off staff. The most horrible thing to deal with is bankruptcy. Having to go bankrupt will make you feel like a failure. Let's not mince our words here. You must avoid it if possible. Not only does it mean having to put your dreams on hold and serious personal financial stress, but it will also likely mean having to lay off all your staff. And we thought laying them off one at a time was bad enough.

But do you know what? It is not the end of the world. It's shit! Let's be clear about that. It's a major setback, but it's not the end of you as an entrepreneur. Founding a startup is stressful, so you must be prepared for that. Bankruptcy is just one of many stressful events that you might have to face. Know what you are getting into from the start.

Failure is common in the business of startups. I'm not going to hit you with a load of stats – it's not that kind of book – but let's just say most businesses fail, and that tends to happen within the first twelve months. Don't expect your business to fail. Fuck no. That's the last thing I want you to do, but you do everything you can to succeed, and if it doesn't work out, know you're in good company and it happens to the best of us.

So, now that you've been reminded of the possibility of failure, let's look at how to avoid it.

## How to Avoid Bankruptcy

The quickest way to lose control of a startup is by not keeping an eye on incomings and outgoings. By now, I'm assuming that you have a finance director to ensure your company is financially healthy.

Things go wrong for several reasons. If your startup is losing more than it is making for too long, it can run out of money. Many startups are loss-making for many years, but there has to be cash flow. Money has to come from somewhere. By this stage, you've either bootstrapped your business or you've gone through several rounds of funding, and you are expected to be standing on your own two feet.

What should you do if you are haemorrhaging money and not bringing enough in?

## Don't Try to Save Your Way Out of Bankruptcy

Trying to cut costs might seem like the intuitive answer to having a cash-flow problem, but it will only make matters worse. Sure, if you can see areas of inefficiency that you can easily tighten up, go for it, but that is unlikely to be enough to save your startup from bankruptcy. The temptation for many founders is to scrimp, save and even cut corners. You don't have a leakage problem. You have an income problem. How are scrimping and saving going to help you earn more?

This is another reason you can't afford to take your foot off the gas. There's no such thing as cruising in business. Don't kid yourself that you haven't got competition; assume that new competitors are popping up all the time. The longer you sit still, stop looking over your shoulder, and lose your hunger for growth, the more time you are giving others to steal orders that you should be winning or, worse, steal customers that you're already serving.

## Aim for Growth, Growth and More Growth

Sales are the answer to your cash-flow crisis. Go back to basics. What can you do to increase the numbers that count? If sales are down, get to the bottom of the cause as quickly as you can. Are you targeting the wrong people? Is there an issue with your product?

No two days are the same, which is why we always need to be on top of our game. That's why founders need to forecast. If a massive wave is about to hit you, you want to at least be ready for it. Various factors can make the waves choppy: seasonal trends, major local and global events, and changes in the markets that you are swimming in.

Whether you are meeting your forecast or not, be aware of it, and try to understand why. If you are exceeding it, something is going in your favour; and if that's something you are doing, you want to identify it, so you can do more of it. On the other side of the coin, if you're doing worse than you expected, is this because of a temporary blip, a specific event, or is it a sign of things to come?

Either way, whatever you can do to increase revenue is going to make it less likely that your ship will capsize.

## Reconsider Your KPIs

Key performance indicators provide a helpful form of tracking work progress, but they tend to stifle creativity and initiative. Even at the best of times, KPIs are only as useful as they are relevant to meaningful performance. If a KPI has no bearing on sales, the quality of the product, customer satisfaction or other valuable goals, what's the point in monitoring it?

The pandemic turned the world upside down and changed the way businesses were run. Working from home quickly went from being the exception to the rule to becoming the norm. Many companies failed to adapt their KPIs to take the new conditions into account, and this led to increased stress among staff. The last thing you want to be doing is pissing off decent staff by asking them to jump through hoops for the sake of it, so assess what you are measuring to make sure it is useful and meaningful.

Productivity and staff happiness are essential ingredients for growth. On the flip side, these are key factors for employee retention, and that's vital because every time you lose someone you didn't want to fire, you are losing experience and knowledge from the business.

## Let Staff Set Their Goals

At my startup, Stakester, we experimented with a new approach. Instead of giving new joiners job descriptions, we asked them to scope out what they were going to achieve and to propose targets on KPIs on which we would agree. They were the driving force, not us. Provided they were working within the field we took them on for – there's no point getting a developer to do the copywriting and vice versa – we were happy to give them the freedom to produce a strategy and a plan.

Never underestimate the power of team morale. If your team are working on a plan that they have devised, they are more likely to throw themselves into it. They are the experts at what they do, so put your trust in them. Let them do what they do best. No matter how thorough your recruitment process is, you can't possibly know your staff's strengths and weaknesses from day one. Let them settle in, see how they get on and adapt from there. Staying agile is key.

By encouraging every employee to grow and adapt, you will have a more agile team and your startup will be better equipped to handle adversity. Forcing a model on people with highly detailed and prescriptive job descriptions – that's so twentieth century! – will limit their productivity and creativity. Let them do what they do best and take ownership of it.

## Mental Health, Equality, Diversity and Inclusion

Although the pandemic seems to be almost behind us, it has left its mark, and some things have changed for the better. Many employers now offer their staff the option of working from home or a hybrid setup. Mental health has never been higher on the list of priorities, although companies still have a long way to go. Along with much more awareness of and a change in attitudes towards mental health, issues such as equality, diversity and inclusion are now being considered more than ever before.

By ensuring you are employing the best people you can, leaving no stone unturned to find them – sourcing them from every community – and creating a working environment that promotes mental health, well-being and the freedom to be creative, you are setting your company up for growth.

## Crossing the Ts and Dotting the Is

You're not an amateur. You're running a multi-million-pound business, so make sure you have the legal stuff in place. From corporate governance to employment law, from intellectual property rights to trading standards, there are loads of ways to fuck up legally. You have worked too hard and come too far to watch it all fall apart because someone was sloppy.

The larger your startup becomes, the greater the risk of a fuckup. When you founded the company and built the core team, you knew everyone by their first name, how they liked their tea, and you may have visited each other's homes. Now, you're walking past people who may not have been interviewed by you and don't know who you are – or they do, but they never speak to you because you're the boss.

You are relying on the tightness of the ship, the slickness of the operation and the management skills of other team members. When you are employing over one hundred staff, it is impossible to know what everyone is doing. It is all on you, but you have to trust them to do what they are supposed to do.

If you are laughing because this all sounds like common sense, you'd be surprised how many founders go with the flow and end up winging things; right up until the point when they can't sell their business because it can't function without them, or they end up with hefty fines because they are using dodgy, cracked software to save on licence fees.

## Don't Forget Culture

People make a meal out of this and write books on it, but it shouldn't be rocket science. Your company's culture is a product of several factors. It starts with you. Nobody is perfect, so I guess I must be Nobody. The old ones are the best. Seriously, though, nobody is perfect, and some of our weaknesses are so ingrained or hard-wired that it's hard to iron them out. Values, however, are something we can reflect on and seek to become more aware of.

For example, if you're the sort of person who thinks that other people's feelings are none of your business, and if they get offended because of something you've said, that's their problem, you may well come a cropper in today's rapidly evolving society.

This isn't about being 'woke' or banging the drum for 'freedom of speech'. Put down the polarised positions. It is about realising that as the leader of your startup, what you do and say carries weight and shows others how you expect them to behave. We all have a perspective on things, but be mindful that your personal perspective may not be the best perspective for your startup where tens or hundreds of other personalities are working together.

It starts with you, but you could say it finishes with your staff because if you're employing one hundred people, you are outnumbered by one hundred to one. You may be a living saint, but you make up less than 1 per cent of the workforce. There are one hundred other people who could fuck things up for your company.

Therefore, your company's culture will be greatly affected by the people you employ, and that boils down to how you recruit. Just because they get on with you and don't seem to be dicks does not guarantee that they will get on with everyone else.

Again, if you are not checking yourself and how you come across, you could end up employing clones of yourself – hence missing out on the top talent, making your company less diverse, and creating a culture accidentally. Look, I believe I'm a good person, but for some people I will be the biggest twat they've ever met. Some people are like chalk and cheese, aren't they? So, on balance, maybe I am 90 per cent great guy and 10 per cent twat. Just as I want to hire people who have the skills that I haven't, I want their personalities to complement mine – not be a direct reflection of it. Where I fall short, they can lead the way.

## The Cost of a Toxic Culture

If your startup's culture is toxic because team morale is low, everyone is out for themselves, communication is poor, friction is rife and there is a lack of harmony, it's going to hit performance. Whether it's productivity, errors or fewer great ideas because creative thinking is in short supply, a toxic environment is going to cost you dearly.

You can add to that the extra costs and hassle of a greater turnover of staff, time spent dealing with disputes between the company and employees, and between team members who have clashed. You don't need any of that aggravation. Unhappy workers are bad for business, on and off your premises. If they feel as though their voice is not being heard at work, they may take to social media.

Sure, you can fire them if you covered yourself for such an event in their contract, but having an employee telling their LinkedIn network that you're a shit boss and your products are second-rate is not good for business. Firing them is not going to undo the damage. This is another reason you need to pay attention to the culture you are creating. The way your employees show up on social media may be seen as a reflection of your startup, particularly if your logo is splattered all over their profile page.

## Learn From Your Mistakes

You are going to make mistakes. The people you hire will make mistakes. Your startup will take knocks because of those mistakes. Learn from them. That's all you can do. If you're making loads of mistakes, it means you're learning a lot, unless the same ones are cropping up time and again – that means you're stuck on repeat and learning fuck all!

Patrick Ryan is no stranger to mistakes. When I interviewed him for my podcast, he happily admitted to having made loads of mistakes throughout his career as an entrepreneur.

> **'I made a ton of mistakes. I made a ton of stupid assumptions.'**
>
> *Patrick Ryan – Co-Founder of Odin*

Patrick, or 'Paddy' as he prefers to be called, is the co-founder of Odin, an investment platform and community for 'people building the future'. The Odin platform has been built to make it simpler to launch and invest in syndicates, special purpose vehicles (SPVs) and funds. Paddy shared one of his fuckups with me, so you don't have to make the same mistake.

The Russian rouble had collapsed, which created an opportunity to buy premium products in Russia at rock-bottom prices, for sale elsewhere where their value would be greater. Paddy has a degree in Russian and French, so he is fluent in both languages, and headed for Russia.

Paddy spotted the opportunity to arbitrage a product, and the first thing that came to mind for Russia was vodka. He wanted to create an artisanal brand of vodka for export, so he did loads of blind tasting, trying many different brands of vodka until he found one that he loved.

Having found a vodka that he felt people would like, he contacted the distillery that made it, based in Vladimir, and discussed plans for them to brew two thousand bottles of the stuff. He had used a local designer to create a design, the labelling, etc., and he was all ready to go, but he wanted to know there was a demand for it.

## Always Read the Small Print

He set up a crowdfunding campaign on the Indiegogo platform to raise the funds to make it happen. The brand name he chose was Ishka, Irish for 'water', and he launched the campaign with a photo of the Ishka bottle, which ironically was filled with water because he didn't have a product at that stage.

The Indiegogo campaign raised £11,000. Fantastic! What a great start! Wrong. He'd fucked up by breaking Indiegogo's rules. Although the rules allowed funds to be raised for an alcoholic drinks manufacturer, alcoholic products cannot be given to people as a reward. What Paddy was supposed to do was offer people vouchers, not the drink itself. Indiegogo took the money back and refunded it to all the investors.

Moral of the story: always read the small print.

Paddy had to brush himself down and find another way to launch his business.

While Paddy's fuckup happened before his brand had even launched, it illustrates how important it is to dot the I's and cross the T's. Being vigilant never stops, no matter how successful you become.

## Don't Have Nightmares

If the thought of fucking up and going bankrupt has scared the shit out of you, get over it now. Fear is the enemy of creativity. Let's say your company folds, and you are declared bankrupt. This may come as a surprise to you, but who cares?

Almost every entrepreneur has failed, and many have failed many times. It happens, but get this: your angel investors and your venture capital backers have probably already written off the loans they made to you. At least 80 per cent of all investments fail. It sucks, but it is a part of life, and investors recognise that.

As long as you have done the best you can, no one will hate you and it is highly likely that many of those who invested in you before will invest in you again when you launch your next startup.

Whatever happens, keep learning from your mistakes. You will not only learn how to run a business more proficiently, but you will also discover things about yourself along the way, and you will grow from the experience. The bigger the fuckup, the more valuable the lesson.

What's next?

## Stick or Twist?

Is the next step to consider whether to exit your startup – to sell up and ride off into the sunset or even start a new one? Possibly, and if that's what you want to do, I wish you the best of luck with it, but that topic is outside the scope of this book. It is not something that I can speak about authentically, and I don't even believe I have enough second-hand knowledge at this stage to write a chapter called *How Not to Fuck Up the Sale of Your Business.* Nor do I think that a subject of that magnitude can be covered with a chapter. That's another book. Did I just sow a not-so-subtle marketing seed for my next book? That's for me to know (or not, as the case may be) and others to find out. It doesn't matter today, because what matters now is that we haven't quite finished looking at how not to fuck up your startup.

The next chapter is the most important chapter of this book. You must read it. Not reading it and not absorbing the final lesson is a sure-fire way of fucking up your startup.

21.

# YOU HAVEN'T MADE IT

You haven't made it!

That's a sobering thought, isn't it?

*But Tom*, you may be thinking, *my idea was exactly what my customers needed, I was streets ahead of other people in the field, and the fact that I am now turning over three million a year speaks for itself. I'm a fucking winner.*

Woah! Hold on. When did I say you weren't a winner? I've said you haven't made it, and that's the truth. Furthermore, until your startup's journey comes to an end, whether that's because you sell it, it collapses (and it could) or you have to wind it down for any reason at all, you haven't made it, and the struggle isn't over.

Never forget that.

## There Are No Guarantees

If it all goes belly up, forget the blame game. It could be your fault. It might not be. As I write, BrewDog, mentioned earlier in the book, has announced that it may have to close six pubs because of the upward spiralling cost of energy, and the tabloid press is reporting that the cost of a pint could rise to as high as £20. With little faith in the incumbent government to effectively intervene amid the crisis, they believe they need to close businesses down to save the overall business.

You can't guarantee anything. The universe is the master curveball thrower. You can't guarantee that your most valuable team member won't fuck off and leave you without so much as a week's notice. No, you can't, because they're human, and life puts a variety of interesting pressures on us all that sometimes force us to act out of character. You can't predict what another person will do.

That goes for customers too. You can't guarantee that the people you are serving today will still be loyal customers tomorrow. *But I've got a signed contract*, I can hear you thinking. So fucking what? I bet your chief engineer was supposed to give you three months' notice as well. The same rule applies. You can enshrine agreements into written contracts. You can set up contingency plans to soften the blow. Shit hitting the fan will still lead to very messy walls.

There are no guarantees, except for this one: You are going to encounter problems. Every. Single. Day!

## What is the Ultimate Fuckup?

The ultimate fuckup is not fucking up your ideation, your validation, your MVP, your investment pitch, your marketing or any of those other essential issues that we have discussed in this book. The biggest fuckup you can make is to take your eye off the ball. And that happens when people get too comfortable, think they've made it, and think they've won the game.

## You're Right to Celebrate Success

I don't want to piss on your fire or dampen your enthusiasm. That's the last thing I want to do. I am not telling you that you are not a winner. I am telling you that you haven't made it and not to think you have. There's a difference between believing in yourself and celebrating your victories, and thinking that the journey has ended.

Celebrate every single piece of success that you achieve. When someone other than your mum and your best mate tells you your idea is great. Plucking up the courage to email a potential investor is worthy of celebration. Countless others don't have the guts. Celebrate every millimetre of progress on your entrepreneurial journey and don't beat yourself up when things go tits up.

## How Did You Get Here?

I invite you to reflect on that question, but here's my two pennies' worth. You got here by solving problems, unlocking doors and taking risks. Layer after layer of challenges, like one of those old computer games where you have to beat up the minions and defeat the baddy to get through to the next level. You fucking did that. Of course you're a fucking winner.

It's who you are. Just to complete any one of those layers tells me (and I sure hope it tells you) who you are.

And nobody or nothing can take that away from you. You will never be someone else. You are an entrepreneur. You are a founder. You did something with your idea. You created a product. You built a team. You hired people. You got investors to believe in you and give you their cash.

Winner.

Not because of the fortunes of your startup. If your startup fails tomorrow, you are still a winner. If you are deep in the shit right now, you're still a winner. And if a previous venture has already become past tense and you're licking your wounds, all it takes is time. Winning is in your blood. You can't escape your destiny. Another startup is inevitable.

## Don't Take Your Eye Off the Ball

Again, don't think you've made it, because you haven't. You have made it this far. You have made it to this level. Game over could happen any time, but it's more likely to happen if you take your eye off the ball.

Go back through the book, take notes (if you haven't already), and remind yourself of how not to fuck up your culture, your recruitment strategy, your product development or your sales automation.

You must keep working, and you have to keep practising.

## Don't Believe Your Own Hype and Train Like a Beginner

The world is constantly changing, and so is technology. The things that attracted people to your startup yesterday may not work today. The marketing tactics you use today to generate exponential growth might become redundant by the end of the year. Stuff that you are planning to do on TikTok next week might not be interesting to anyone before the end of this week!

To come this far, you've proved you have the aptitude, determination and resilience to keep going, pay attention to what's going on and adapt to a changing world. The thing is, though, that no matter how much of an expert you are on understanding yesterday, you are an absolute beginner at understanding tomorrow. Because everything that happens from this moment – now – is new.

Nobody knows the future.

Not even you!

Companies fail. Not founders. You're a winner already. It's who you are. Never stop being you. Just be the best version of you that you can be.

Good luck.

# EPILOGUE

Thanks a lot for reading *How Not to Fuck Up Your Startup*. If you can't tell, I'm passionate about startups, and I am keen to help others who are on the journey. I sincerely hope that what I have shared in the pages of this book comes in useful, and believe me when I say that I want you to succeed.

As well as being in the thick of it with my own startups, we're all part of a community. We've come this far, let's continue together. Find me on LinkedIn and feel free to drop me a line.

# INDEX


accelerator programmes 34, 119, 131
advertising 240–5
  advertorials 213
  fails 203–6
  'free' television advertising 243–5
  poor or dishonest 241–2
  pop-up 240–1
  professional help 242
Affinity Capital 6–7
Airbnb 35, 122
airdrops 240
algorithms 171, 174
Allen, Paul 44
Angel Invest 80
angel investors 66, 70, 75, 131, 132
Apollo.io 250, 251
Ashley Madison 87–8
Aviary 77

*Back Yourself Show* 16
bank loans 106
bankruptcy 258–9, 265
Barker, Ronnie 86
Barr Allen, Allison 176
Bartlett, Steven 197–8
BASIC 44
Betamax video 40
Beyoncé 191
blockchain 234, 239
Bolt, Usain 2
BookMyNight 31–2
bootstrapping 69, 70, 83, 104
brainstorming 33, 158, 162
branding 201–20, 233
  alliance with good causes 208–9, 210
  bandwagons 206–7, 209
  brand ambassadors 173, 180, 184, 185–6, 222, 233
  brand consistency 121
  brand names 45, 52–7
  Dos and Don'ts 209–10
  expert help 210–11
  face of the brand 192
  fails 201–6, 209
  imaginative 210
  influencers 191–9
  negative/ambiguous messages 201–6, 209
  public relations (PR) *see* public relations
  threats and opportunities 221–3
  *see also* product marketing
Branson, Richard 23
Braund, Nick 210–11, 212–13, 214, 215, 216, 217, 218, 219
BrewDog 209, 210, 267
Bumble 188
Burger King 204–6, 209, 210
business books 2
business development 232–53
  advertising 240–5
  commercial alliances 240
  contra deals 243–5, 253
  experimentation 234–5
  going for growth 98–9, 117, 146, 259–60
  leveraging the power of community 235–40
  partnerships and collaboration 240
  sales automation 234, 245–53
  scalability 64, 117, 244
  social media 235–40
business plans 94

# INDEX


Calvin Klein 203
Campinas, Joaquin 207
car, as a product 90–2
Carey, Eamonn 35, 51, 68, 73, 79, 96
Carnegie, Dale 215
Carson, Frank 52
cash flow 69, 84, 259
  crisis 255, 259–60
Celestial-One, Saasha 180–6, 190, 233
Channel 4 Ventures 243–5
chief finance officers (CFOs) 82
chief marketing officers (CMOs) 141
chief technical officers (CTOs) 81–2, 141
Chumby 52, 53
Clarke, David 208
Clarke, Tessa 179–86, 190, 233
Clubhouse 177, 236
co-founders 10–11, 70–82
  chief finance officers (CFOs) 82
  chief technical officers (CTOs) 81–2, 141
  co-operative working 64, 76, 77, 79–80
  complementary skills 34, 74, 78–9
  disagreements 78
  friends 24, 75, 76–9, 80
  getting on together 80, 81
  leadership 79
  married couples 79
  reasons for bringing in 64, 72–5
  shared sense of purpose 76
  team dynamics 79–80, 80–1
Coca-Cola 55
Collias, Anthony 245–7, 248, 249, 250, 251, 252
commercial alliances 240
community
  building 179–86, 193, 233, 235–40
  cross-pollination 147, 187–9
  leveraging the power of 235–40
  networking 41–2, 82, 129–31
  offering value to 239
complacency, avoiding 254–5
computing requirements 94–5
  software 95, 101–2
computing startups 37–8, 44
confidence 18, 61, 63, 140
Consilience Ventures 113
consultancy work 69
Convergys Corporation 87
Cookson, Oliver 70
The Copy Club 187–8, 190
Corbett, Ronnie 86
Cornejo, Hugo 188, 222–30, 235
cost calculations 94–105
  computer essentials 94–5
  hidden costs 101
  marketing costs 103–4, 168–9, 176
  networking expenses 102
  office space 97–8
  personal living costs 96–7
  staffing costs 99
Covid-19 pandemic 48, 246, 260, 261
Crane Venture Partners 34
creativity 19–20
Cremades, Alejandro 122
Crypto Valley Labs 240
cryptocurrency 41, 234, 239, 240
culture, company 160–6, 262–3
  collaboration 165
  empowering 164, 165–6
  free exchange of ideas 162
  giving people a purpose 163
  giving people a voice 163–4
  mental health, equality, diversity and inclusion 261, 263
  road maps and goal setting 164–5
  safety 161–2
  sharing success 165
  toxic 263
  *see also* staff
customer relationship management (CRM) platforms 250
customers
  feedback 229
  reaching *see* marketing
  talking and listening to 226–8

D-Box 52, 53
dating apps 192
  *see also* Honeypot; Thursday
Davidson, Emma 6–7, 61
deal flow 131
Decoded 26
delegation
  pitching to investors 114–15
  social media 199–200
Deliveroo 35

DesignMyNight 76
Diaz, Nick 143
digital marketing 234, 235, 243
  *see also* influencer marketing; social media
Digital Oracles 84, 234, 240
Digital Voices 191
domain names 56
Dots 77
Dr Will's ketchup 189
*Dragons' Den* 51, 63
Draper Esprit 75
Dunsdon, Alex 5, 6, 14, 81, 82, 129
Duolingo 192

Einstein, Albert 108, 154
elevator pitches 48, 121
Elliott, Ben 46, 47
email pitching 28, 134, 135–40
  follow-ups 139
  frequently asked questions (FAQs) 139–40
  personalising 137
  points to cover 135–6
  response rates 139
  sending 137–8
  style 136–7
  subject line 138
  when to send 138
employees *see* staff
entrepreneurs 5–6
  *see also* founders
ERIC careers festival 24, 29–30, 31, 33, 36, 169
Eventbrite 29, 30, 169
exiting your startup 70, 266
experience, valuing 62
eye on the ball, keeping 113, 255, 268, 269

Facebook 77, 98–9, 171, 174, 197, 237, 241
failed products 38–40, 264–5
failed startups 10, 66, 175–6, 258–9
  bankruptcy 258–9, 265
failure, fear of 26, 265
Fast 175–6
fear of missing out (FOMO) 145, 177, 218
feedback
  customer 229
  ideas and 45
  openness to 160
  product building and 91
  product validation and 43
Fitzpatrick, Rob 42
Flexa 48–50
founders
  benefits and downsides of being a sole founder 72, 73, 75
  co-founders *see* co-founders
  complacency, avoiding 254–5
  equity ownership 66
  experience, valuing 62
  eye on the ball, keeping 113, 255, 268, 269
  full commitment 65
  giving up 10
  luck, making your own 30
  mental and physical health, taking care of 11–12, 14, 15
  mindset 5–7, 236
  mistakes, learning from 33, 230–1, 264–6
  naivety 63–8
  passion for what you're doing 20, 68
  self-awareness 5, 14, 34, 143, 235, 236
  self-presentation 95–6, 118
  setbacks, coping with 13–14
  side hustles 65, 67
  strengths and weaknesses, recognising 9, 34, 143
  support structure 58, 59
  winner, knowing you're a 3, 9, 13, 254, 267, 268–9
friends as co-founders 24, 75, 76–9, 80
  disagreements 78
  transition from friends to family 78–9
funding
  bank loans 106
  bootstrapping 69, 70, 83, 104
  cost calculations 94–105
  time management 113–14
  *see also* investors

Gates, Bill 2, 44, 160
GDXdata 87

General Data Protection Regulation (GDPR) 133
Giphy 77
Google AdWords 241
Google algorithms 171
Gossage, Howard Luck 245
growth, going for 98–9, 117, 146, 259–60

healthy lifestyle 12, 15, 59
Heights 11, 97
Hill, Warwick 9, 10, 22–4, 36, 43, 84, 103, 118, 147
hiring 149–60, 263
  characteristics to look for 156
  CVs and resumés 156–7
  education and experience 157–8
  feedback test 160
  FOMO incentive 155
  hiring the best 149–50, 151
  interviews 158–60
  outsource people 88
  research test 159–60
  selling the vision 152–3, 154–6
  teacher test 158–9
  toxic people, avoiding 156–7
hive mind 76, 158, 188
Hoffman, Reid 152
Holland, Domm 176
Honeypot 176, 177–9
  *see also* Thursday
Hornsby, Samantha 24–6, 27–31, 32–3, 36, 75, 76, 78–9, 169
Horseplay Ventures 32
HubSpot 250
Hughes, Hector 46, 47
Hummus Bros 27

i.Beat blaxx MP3 player 53–5
ideation 16–36
  brainstorming 33
  copying ideas 23, 24, 28, 31, 36, 51
  creativity 19–20
  execution of ideas 35, 36
  feedback 43
  gaps in the market 31–2, 45
  improving an existing product 20–1, 63
  lightbulb moment 17–18, 29, 33, 188
  napkin moment 19, 106, 155
  stealing ideas 51–2
  turning problems into opportunities 19, 22, 23, 32, 33, 35, 36, 43
  uniqueness 45
  validation process 40, 41, 42–3, 45, 57
IMuffs 52, 53
influencer marketing 191–9
  B2B (business to business) marketing 197–8
  becoming an influencer 198
  costs 195, 196
  D2C (direct to consumer) marketing 197
  data 194–5
  failure 194
  followers 198
  matching product to influencer 193–4
  nano influencers 198
  non-scripted 196–7
  reaching out to influencers 195–6
Information Commissioner's Office 133
Instagram 171, 172, 194, 198
intellectual property (IP) 51, 69
  IP theft 85–6
investors 64–6, 106–47
  accelerator programmes 34, 119, 131
  actively approaching 132–4
  angel investing 66, 70, 75, 131, 132
  angel syndicates 131
  criteria for potential investors 133
  equity ownership 66, 142, 243
  expectation of returns 65–6, 117, 142
  fear of missing out (FOMO) 145
  interest in growth 117, 146
  investment rounds 66, 75, 100, 112
  lead generation (list building) 133–4
  pitching to *see* email pitching; pitch deck; pitch meetings; pitching to investors
  preference for co-founders over sole founders 11, 34, 75–6
  referrals to 42, 130, 132
  rejection by 60, 108
  researching background of 134, 142, 144–5
  social media checks by 128, 129

venture capital (VC) investing 66, 70 75
your value to 61–2, 63

James Bond film franchise 212
Jobs, Steve 166
John, Elton 153
Johnson-Jones, Molly 47–8, 49, 50

Kamen, Nick 21
Kardashian, Kim 191
Kelly, Max 11, 41–2, 65, 66, 69, 70, 80
key performance indicators (KPIs) 260, 261
King, Stephen 159
Kniaz, Rob 99, 117

Lapinski, Jens 80–1
lead generation 133–4
legal issues 133, 262
Lego 208, 210
Leppard, Tim 48
Levi 501 commercial 21
lightbulb moments 17–18, 29, 33, 188
LinkedIn 129, 132, 133, 177, 178, 192, 197, 236, 249, 250, 251
Little Moons Mochi Ice Cream 189
Love, Matt McNeill 176–8, 179, 190
luck, making your own 30

market
creating new markets 116–17
gaps in the market 31–2, 45
product–market fit 44–5, 69
size 116–17, 118, 123
understanding your market 27, 116–17, 118
marketing 167–200
community building 179–86, 193, 233, 235, 239–40
copycat marketing 187–9
costs 103–4, 168–9, 176
customer retention 173
fails 175–6
influencer marketing *see* influencer marketing
product marketing *see* product marketing
social media campaigns 174–5
websites *see* websites
Marmite effect 129, 178, 179, 190, 232
Martin, Tom 22, 32, 36, 169–74, 190, 233
Meetup 130
Mensa 55
mentors and coaches 59, 108
Meta 197–8
Microsoft 44, 77
minimum viable product (MVP) 57, 70, 83, 90–2, 93, 182
fake set-ups 93
feedback 91
iterations 91–2
mistakes, learning from 33, 230–1, 264–6
Moberg, Patrick 77
Monzo 188, 223–5, 226, 227, 228, 229, 230
Moss, Sir Stirling 39
Murphy, Paul 69, 76–7, 81
Murray, Dan 11, 97
Myprotein 70

naivety 63–8
names 45, 52–7
domain names 56
name-fails 52–5
in other languages 55
rebranding 176
trademarks 55
in use elsewhere 55–6
validation 56–7
napkin moment 19, 106, 155
networking 41–2, 82, 129–31
expenses 102
feedback and 43
online platforms 130
with other founders 130
Nike 212
non-disclosure agreements (NDAs) 52, 85–6
Notonthehighstreet 45

O'Brien, Maurice 48
Odin 264–5
office space and location 97–8
Ogilvy, David 241, 242

OLIO 180–6, 190
O'Reilly, Philip 75, 79
outsourcing 74, 81, 84, 85–9
  clarity in communication 86–7, 89
  data breaches 86–8
  due diligence in hiring process 88
  issues 85–9
  reviewing work 88, 89
  to another country 85–6

Packfleet 223, 224, 225, 226, 229, 230
Page, Michael 152
pain points 6, 19, 30, 35, 59, 173
partners *see* co-founders
patents 51
Paul, Logan 191
Peloton 117
perfectionism 199
personal profile
  authentic self 237–9
  raising 127, 129, 240
  social media 127–31, 237–9
personal value propositions 214
Pet Sweat 52, 53
PhantomBuster 249
pitch deck 107, 114, 115, 116–26, 136
  accessible to mobile devices 120, 136
  checking for mistakes 125
  colours and fonts 120–1, 123
  content 123–4
  cover pages 122–3
  demonstrating unfair advantage 118, 124
  icons and photos 121, 123, 124
  key takeaways 124
  presenting in person 124, 125
  professional format and design 118–20
  professional help 119
  team slides 123–4
  testing and polishing 124–5
  visuals 120–1
pitch meetings 140, 141–7
  common errors 145–6
  going off-script 144
  invitations to 140
  nerves 143
  practising delivery 142
  readiness to talk about yourself 143
  reading the room 144
  team preparation 141
  two-way street 144–5
  using FOMO as leverage 145
  who's going 114, 141
Pitchdeck podcast 32
pitching to investors 106–15
  angel round at ideation stage (pre-seed process) 107–8, 112
  elevator pitches 48, 121
  listing your pitch online 131
  managing expectations 113
  personal profile 127–30
  pitching the company, not the product 111–12, 116, 135, 145
  rejection 146–7
  roadmap 112
  slow pace of progress 112–13
  teamwork 114–15
  tweaking the pitch 109, 110–11, 125
  *see also* email pitching; pitch deck; pitch meetings
Playdots 77
Playfair Capital 7
Prince's Youth Business Trust 23
procrastination 14, 169
product 37–57, 83–93
  building your product 83–94, 100, 101
  demand for 40–1, 51, 93
  improving on existing products 20–1, 63
  minimum viable product (MVP) 57, 70, 83, 90–2, 93, 182
  names 52–7
  no-frills, bare essentials packages 28, 32, 36
  product-fails 38–40
  product–market fit 44–5, 69
  proof of concept (POC) 41, 70, 90, 92
  validation 40, 41, 69
  you as the product 64, 67
product marketing 221–31
  baby steps 230
  being memorable for the right reasons 230
  branding *see* branding
  building products that sell themselves 226
  fine-tuning the product 229

green credentials 225
mistakes, learning from 230–1, 235
stand-out product, creating 223–4, 229–30
substance, backing your brand with 224–5
talking and listening to customers 226–8
proof of concept (POC) 41, 70, 90, 92
PROPERCORN 188
public relations (PR) 211–20
angles 214
building trust and credibility 216
consultants and agencies 219–20
personal value propositions 214
relations with journalists 213, 214–15, 217–18
'so what' questions 218–19
strategy 217
two-way street 214–15
uses for 216–17
Pugachevsky, Julia 207

Quigley-Jones, Jennifer 191, 192, 193, 194–5, 196, 197, 198, 199–200

Ratner, Gerald 201–2, 212
Rawlings, George 176–8, 179, 190
Read, Brie 20–2, 32, 36, 43, 169–74, 175, 190, 233
recruitment strategies *see* hiring
Redgewell, Hannah 243, 244
release cycles 101
Renee, Arianna 194
Reynolds, Megan 34–5, 36, 74
risk-taking 26, 66
Roberts, Ed 44
Ronaldo, Cristiano 191
Rose, Anthony 40, 41, 42, 55, 56–7, 92–3, 97, 100, 101
Ryan, Paddy 264–5

sales automation 234, 245–53
calls to action 252
credibility 252
data 251
Dos and Don'ts 247–8
email, styling 251–2
fine-tuning 251
natural-sounding copy 250
responding to enquiries 250
setting up a side domain 249
software 249, 250
starting small 249
targeting 247, 248, 249, 250
scalability 64, 117, 244
SeedLegals 56–7
Sega 55
Sega Game Gear 40
self-awareness 5, 14, 34, 143, 235, 236
self-presentation 95–6, 118
serendipity 29, 81, 82, 129, 130
Sergei 17–19, 35
SIM cards 44–5
Simeone, Sara 83, 84, 90, 234, 235, 236, 238, 239, 240
Sinclair, Sir Clive 37, 38, 39–40
Sinclair C5 37, 38–9, 40
Sinclair Research 37–8
Sinek, Simon 163
Slack 35
Smith, Chris 7–9, 15, 44–5, 125
Snag Tights 21–2, 36, 43, 169–74, 190, 233
social conscience 64–5, 179–86, 245–6
social media
business development 235–40
choosing your platforms 236–7
community building 235–40
influencer marketing 191–9
marketing campaigns 174–5
personal profile 127–31, 237–9
power of authenticity 237–9
top tips 199–200
*see also specific platforms*
SolidWorks 85–6
staff 149–66
company culture 161–6, 262–3, 264
empathic approach to managing 49, 225–6
employee value proposition 152
empowering 164, 165–6, 261
firing people 255–8, 263–4
flexible working 48–50
hiring *see* hiring
hybrid working 261
mental health, equality, diversity and inclusion 261, 263

morale 261, 263
motivation 152, 153, 154, 163
payroll commitment 99, 255
retention 150–1, 260
toxic people 151, 156–7, 161, 255
working from home 261
Stakester 1, 2–3, 13, 20, 32, 36, 60–1, 68, 75, 88, 106–9, 120, 122, 123, 124, 130, 261
Stallone, Sylvester 196–7
Stasher 245
Staude Capital 7
strengths, playing to 9, 34, 135
Supercapital Partners LLP 9
SurveyMonkey 181

tech startups 83–93
access to code 89
data breaches 86–8
IP theft 85–6
non-disclosure agreements (NDAs) 85–6
outsourcing issues 85–9
selling to large institutions 103–4
Techstars 80, 143
Telegram 239
Telson, Nick 31–2, 76
Thursday 176–7, 179, 188, 190
TikTok 189, 192, 198, 236
trademarks 55
Treepoints 245–6
Trekstor 53–5
Tulipán 207, 210
Turing, Alan 37
Twitter 98, 236

Uber 99, 122
Umbro 212
underestimating yourself 61–2
Unplugged 46–7
Unwin, Lottie 179, 187–9, 190
Urinal 52, 53

validation 40, 41, 42–3, 45, 68, 69, 216, 226–7
asking the right questions 42
feedback 43
product names 56–7
video production 28, 29, 31
Vimeo 236

websites
attracting traffic to 171
message 172–3
monitoring the metrics 174
one page websites 168–71, 233
Webster, Andrew 31–2, 76
Wedderburn-Day, Jacob 246
working from home 97, 260, 261
Wozniak, Steve 158

Yip, Mae 20, 24, 26–31, 32–3, 36, 75, 76, 78–9, 169
YouTube 191, 192, 236

ZoomInfo 251
ZX Spectrum computer 38
ZX-80 computer 37–8